BRIT GUIDE

# ĐISNEYLAND®

# RESORT
## PARIS

AND PARIS ATTRACTIONS

# 2008/9

Simon & Susan Veness

## foulsham
LONDON • NEW YORK • TORONTO • SYDNEY

# foulsham

## The Publishing House, Bennetts Close, Cippenham, Berkshire, SL1 5AP, England

Foulsham books can be found in all good bookshops and direct from
www.foulsham.com

ISBN: 978-0-572-03405-4

Text copyright © 2008 Simon and Susan Veness

Series, format, logo and layout design copyright © 2008 W. Foulsham & Co. Ltd

Dedication
To Anthony, Mark and Ben – the perfect research team!

Look out for the latest editions in this series:
*Brit Guide to Orlando and Walt Disney World*, Simon and Susan Veness
*Brit Guide to New York*, Amanda Statham
*Brit Guide to Las Vegas*, Karen Marchbank with Richard Evans

Printed in Dubai

# CONTENTS

## Brit Tips

Got a red-hot Brit Tip to pass on? The latest info on how to beat the queues or the best new restaurant? We want to hear from YOU to keep improving the guide each year. Drop us a line at: Brit Guides (Disneyland Resort Paris), W. Foulsham & Co. Ltd, The Publishing House, Bennetts Close, Cippenham, Slough, Berkshire SL1 5AP. Or email us at britsguide@yahoo.com.

*Main Street USA*

© Disney

# FOREWORD

**Simon says...** Welcome to the fourth edition of the brightest guidebook on Europe's No. 1 tourist attraction, as compiled by Britain's leading Disney experts (even if we say so ourselves!). Susan and I have been visiting the theme parks since 1971 and 1987 respectively and have clocked up hundreds of visits to California, Orlando and *Disneyland Resort Paris* in that time. We are still as excited as ever about each one, especially with all the new developments and additions – both recent and imminent – for the Paris version, notably at the *Walt Disney Studios Park*.

Since the opening of the *Studios* in 2002, *Disneyland Resort Paris* has become a much more rounded – and time-consuming! – place to visit, hence your choice for things to do in this corner of the world is now hugely varied and great fun. It remains a world of fantasy and adventure, but it is also complicated, detailed and demanding – especially in the summer – so it is vital you are armed with all the necessary *Brit Guide* insider information to tackle it. This book aims to be your Good Companion throughout the experience – from the moment you start planning, to your journey there, how to enjoy it all while you're on site and all the extra things to appreciate in the vicinity, especially in Paris itself. It is a remarkable and astounding place – just remember to take us with you!

**Susan says...** Having chalked up several more visits to *Disneyland Resort Paris* since the 2006–2007 edition went to print, the parks feel very much like home now, with every visit preceded by a giddy sense of anticipation and an eagerness to see what's new, along with revisiting well-loved favourites. This past year we had the great pleasure of taking our 14-year-old, Ben, for his first ever overseas holiday, including visits to Paris and the *Disneyland Resort* as part of our itinerary. In true teenager-style, Ben was unfailingly candid about each experience. Watching him take it all in – the cultural differences, food, attractions and the impact of walking around one of the world's greatest cities – reminded me how precious and magical it is to travel, whether the destination is new or a comfortable old friend. The reaction Ben had when he saw a familiar-yet-different Main Street, the delight he took in dining at Blue Lagoon, the wide-eyed expression that carried him through Paris and his subsequent comment, 'I love this city!' – those are the moments and emotions we hope you experience as well. And now... relax, settle in, turn the pages and create, with us as your guides, your own magical adventure!

*Simon and Susan in Adventureland*

# Introduction

## *or* An open invitation to the House of Mouse

**T**here is one simple reason why Disney's theme parks are the world's most-visited attractions, be they in America, Japan or, in this case, France. They are simply the best family entertainment you will find anywhere.

And the guaranteed fun is not restricted to families either. For, while children find the allure of Mickey and Co almost irresistible, there is something for everyone in a Disney park – young or old, single, a couple or with the whole family in tow. In fact, we reckon there is more all-round entertainment value here than anywhere else we've seen.

It is a great short-break destination, a perfect location for a week (or even longer, given the additional attractions of the Paris region) and it is easy to reach; it is ideally suited to families (especially those with young children), yet it also attracts honeymooners and other couples; and its appeal is timeless, harking back to a nostalgic yesteryear but remaining contemporary in so many ways.

### Pixie dust

A holiday at *Disneyland Resort Paris* is a beguiling prospect, and it is also one that is sure to bring out the child in (nearly) everyone. If you can envisage grown-ups rushing to hug Mickey or Minnie, then you can imagine the effect Disney's 'Pixie dust' has on just about every person who walks through the gates.

Indeed, Roy Disney, nephew of the great Walt himself, opened the Paris park with words his uncle first used for *Disneyland California* in 1955. He said: 'To all who come to this happy place, welcome! This is your land. Here age relives fond memories of the past and here youth may savour the challenge and promise of the future. We hope it will be a source of joy and

*St Patrick's Day parade*

© Disney

inspiration to the world.' It certainly shapes up that way.

But if that's the broad outline, let us fill in the detail and provide you with a good understanding of how it all works – because this is a complicated business and you must keep your wits about you at all times. Holidaying the Disney way is immense fun but it can also be demanding, confusing and tiring. When the crowds start to flock into the parks it is a challenge to keep up with the ebb and flow of it all. When the queues for many rides top an hour, you need a strategy and the essential tool of all parkgoers: a plan!

In fact, planning is an essential component of your holiday. At quieter times you might just get away with a free-wheeling, make-it-up-as-you-go-along approach. But, even during moderately busy periods, there are plenty of pitfalls that await the unwary and unprepared. This is definitely not like a trip to Alton Towers or Thorpe Park, where a day is usually enough to see everything.

With two fully fledged parks in the Disney experience, there is a significant element of choice. Behind that lies a matter of scale that is hard to convey in advance and that includes an attention to detail both breathtaking and a little bewildering.

*Shopping at Constellations*

*Once Upon A Dream Parade*

It is easy to get side-tracked by some of the clever scenery, shops and other frippery, so that's why planning is important.

Not for nothing did they change the name to *Disneyland Resort Paris* in 2002, for truly this is a resort experience par excellence, and that means a multi-dimensional approach in all things: from the attractions to the hotels, the restaurants and even the shops. There is fun almost everywhere you turn and a host of options at any one time. Therefore, you need to do your homework in advance, so you can be aware of all that lies in store.

## Chequered history

The *Disneyland Resort Paris* story began in the mid-1980s when Michael Eisner, then the new Chief Executive Officer of the Walt Disney Company, came to Europe in search of a new outlet for their theme park creativity. Both France and Spain were firmly in the frame, and the former was chosen for a variety of reasons, not least the strong French connection in many Disney films (*Cinderella, Sleeping Beauty, Hunchback of Notre Dame*) and the wonderful central location offered by the Paris region.

## Who owns the Disneyland Resort Paris?

The Walt Disney Company actually owns only 39.8% of the *Disneyland Resort Paris*, but runs 100% of the management. The other 60.2% is owned by private investors, including 10% by Prince Al-Waleed of Saudi Arabia.

As far back as December 1985, Mr Eisner signed a letter of intent with France to build a park in Marne-la-Vallée, some 32km/20mls east of Paris. That agreement was formalised with Jacques Chirac in March 1987 and what was then about 1,900 hectares/4,700 acres of beet fields became the planning ground for a great adventure in architecture and engineering, or Imagineering, as the Walt Disney Company likes to call it.

The first earth-moving equipment moved in on 2 August 1988, and a 4-year construction period began. Despite some challenges from Mother Nature, the *Euro Disney Park* (as it was then known – the name soon changed to *Euro Disneyland*) opened on time on 12 April 1992, to a massive blaze of publicity.

However, despite the glittering launch, a sceptical press, some French hostility (going back to the project's announcement) – aimed at the supposed 'Americanisation' of their culture – and over-optimistic attendance forecasts all contributed to a painful initiation for the new park.

The media focused on anything negative – long lines for meals and longer queues for some rides, high prices, rumours of empty hotels and staff unhappiness – and the combination of problems, both real and perceived, almost brought the resort to its knees. The whole development – parks, hotels, shops and restaurants, all grouped around a 'village' core, then called *Festival Disney* – had gone way over budget. The lack of immediate profits to pay

off the short-term debt, coupled with a Europe-wide recession, meant there was a real possibility that it might close down, despite 10.8 million visitors in the first 12 months.

Major financial restructuring was necessary in 1994, at which time it became *Disneyland Paris*, and, from there, the story has been one of recovery, although battles with that initial debt continue. Attendance grew through the late 1990s and more development began to spring up around Marne-la-Vallée, both commercial and residential.

**BRITTIP**

*Disneyland Resort Paris* is just 2 hours from Ashford in Kent on the direct Eurostar service and only 2 hours 35 minutes from the new London St Pancras terminal. For the great convenience the train provides, it's definitely worth considering.

The success of Disney's on-site hotels (six of them, plus the camping ground of *Disney's Davy Crockett Ranch* a short drive away) encouraged a mini proliferation of hotels in the vicinity, while the development extended to a new town centre at neighbouring **Val d'Europe**, a combination of businesses, shopping and housing, which adds even more to the picture locally. Here, the immaculate shopping mall is part of an excellent centre that includes the outlet shopping of **La Vallée**, the **Sea Life Centre** and some enticing restaurants.

*La Vallée*

At the same time, a Disney-run **golf complex**, with three nine-hole courses, was developed just 10 minutes' drive from the resort itself, offering yet another diversion for people wanting to enhance their theme park experience.

## The new park

The original plans for the resort included a sister park, along the lines of *Disney's Hollywood Studios* in *Walt Disney World Resort* in Florida. This was scheduled to open 3 years after the first park, but the financial woes of 1994 meant the concept went into storage until 1998. Construction began in earnest shortly afterwards. The eagerly awaited *Walt Disney Studios Park* opened on 16 March 2002, with another burst of publicity – and a new name, *Disneyland Resort Paris*.

Here, finally, was the true resort expansion as originally envisaged by Eisner and his Imagineers, completing a well-rounded picture of accommodation, shopping, restaurants and theme parks, and providing a multi-day experience, even out of busy periods. *Festival Disney*, now known more appropriately as *Disney Village*, has grown to encompass nine restaurants, three bars, a multi-screen cinema and leisure complex (including a new IMAX screen theatre and bowling alley), an adjoining dinner show (the family-friendly Buffalo Bill's Wild West

*There are plenty of golfing opportunities*

Show), a big nightclub and a choice of nine shops. There is also the wonderful Panoramagique tethered balloon ride and a host of other games and activities (see Chapter 8).

With the Marne-la-Vallée railway station at the heart of the whole development linking the resort with central Paris, Charles de Gaulle Airport and, more importantly, London via Eurostar, it is a wonderfully convenient location. It is easy for arrival and well organised to allow access either straight to the theme parks, the hotels (using an efficient bus service) or directly to *Disney Village*.

Anyone familiar with the Orlando resort set-up – 12,173 hectares/30,080 acres of four parks, two water parks, 20 hotels and a mini-town area called *Downtown Disney* – will almost certainly be impressed by the ease with which you can move around this resort in comparison. Everything is within a 20-minute walk at most and the scale is big enough to be exciting, yet manageable enough not to be daunting. Indeed, it is a triumph of the designers' art in making this hugely complex development one of very human dimensions, a riot of visual stimulation and yet easy to negotiate. Yes, there is a lot going on here, but it is not difficult to get around and enjoy.

*Disney Village*

## Facts and figures

- The whole site of *Disneyland Resort Paris* covers 1,943 hectares/4,800 acres, or one-fifth the area of Paris.
- Groundbreaking took place in August 1988.
- 51km/32mls of roads were built and 120,000,000m³/157,000,000yd³ of earth moved.
- Around 450,000 trees and shrubs were planted.
- It employs 12,200 people every year (on average).
- All Disney employees are known as Cast Members, to signify they are part of 'the show'.
- The *Disneyland Park* covers 57 hectares/140 acres.
- The *Walt Disney Studios Park* stands on 25 hectares/62 acres.
- The seven themed hotels have a total of 5,800 rooms.
- There are 68 counter and full-service restaurants throughout the resort.
- In all, there are 54 different shops and boutiques.
- More than 160 million people have visited since it opened.
- Around 40% of visitors are French, 23% British, 8% German, 8% Belgian, 8% Dutch, 8% Spanish and Italian, with 5% from other nations.

## Disney Village

Offering a positive riot of sights and sounds, both by day and night (when the contrast is quite startling, from the peaceful Lake Disney in early morning to the near-disco proportions of the late-evening hubbub), *Disney Village* acts as a conduit between the parks and hotels. It is an exit for weary park-goers (and you can be pretty tired by park closing!) and offers a new source of fun for all those who enjoy their nightlife. It is a heady cocktail but it also requires a good deal of forethought, especially if you have the family in tow, to ensure you get the most out of it (whether for a meal, shopping or the games and other activities) before heading back to your hotel.

Of course, *Disney Village* is not reserved purely for Disney's on-site guests; it attracts a good number of locals (especially on Fridays and Saturdays) too. Its large car park makes it easily accessible for guests at nearby hotels, while the RER service (the main local commuter train) runs until after midnight for those who have chosen not to drive.

## The European touch

*Disneyland Resort Paris* is a wonderfully impressive set-up and is easily the equal of any of Disney's other parks and resorts around the world. In fact, we believe the clever 'Europeanisation' of the traditional Disney style gives it extra appeal. There is more than a hint of French

*The Enchanted Fairytale*

© Disney

flair, Italian chic, Spanish partying, German organisation and Dutch friendliness about the resort, which come together best in the Village. Yes, there are some drawbacks – especially for non-smokers, as avoiding cigarette smoke can be difficult at times – and the mixture of cultures occasionally causes some awkwardness. The toilets could be kept cleaner in many instances (for some reason, this seems a bit of a blind spot in all public areas) and there is occasionally a bit of push and shove (which you don't usually find at the American parks), notably in the scrimmage for character autographs, getting in position for the parades or trying to board a hotel bus at the end of the evening.

It won't be a restful holiday, unless you go out of season in winter and are lucky enough to be blessed by mild, dry weather, and it can make a serious dent in your bank balance. But, all in all, it offers great value and richly rewards those who go with an open mind and the willingness to try those few words of school French they can dredge from memory.

More importantly, it is guaranteed to put a smile on the faces of young and old alike, and reaffirm simple family values. When Walt built Disneyland in California back in 1955, his most famous statement (now etched on the bronze Walt 'n' Mickey statue in front of the Sleeping Beauty Castle) was: 'I think most of all what I want Disneyland to be is a happy place… where parents and children can have fun together.'

*Fantasyland*

© Disney

## Our top 10 family attractions

| | |
|---|---|
| 1 | Pirates of the Caribbean |
| 2 | Cinémagique |
| 3 | 'it's a small world' |
| 4 | Disney's Once Upon A Dream Parade |
| 5 | Legend of the Lion King |
| 6 | Peter Pan's Flight |
| 7 | Art of Disney Animation |
| 8 | Buzz Lightyear's Laser Blast |
| 9 | Phantom Manor |
| 10 | Animagique |

So, don't forget to take time out to enjoy that aspect during your visit; watch your children's faces at the parades, on the Dumbo ride or as they meet the characters (or just look at the reaction of other children); and ensure you do things together, however silly they may be! There is artistry all around you, in the rides, the architecture and the Cast Members, but the most meaningful feeling you can invoke is the bond with your loved ones – and nowhere brings that to the fore quite like a Disney park, whether it be for kids of 6 or 60.

However, perhaps the question most seasoned Disney-goers will want to ask is: 'If I have already been to *Walt Disney World in Florida*, do I need to go to *Disneyland Resort Paris*? We would say unequivocally 'Yes'. Apart from the obvious advantage of this being a closer and more convenient short-visit destination (no 9-hour flights and long queues at Immigration to deal with), we believe the more luxurious theming of the *Disneyland Park*, the updated versions of classic rides like Space Mountain, Haunted Mansion and Big Thunder Mountain, and the all-new thrills of most of the *Walt Disney Studios* make it an absolute must to visit. For some, it is also a handy

## Our top 10 thrill attractions

1   Rock 'n' Roller Coaster starring Aerosmith
2   Twilight Zone Tower of Terror
3   Space Mountain: Mission 2
4   Indiana Jones and the Temple of Peril
5   Big Thunder Mountain Railroad
6   Star Tours
7   Armageddon
8   Panoramagique
9   Crush's Coaster
10  Driving in central Paris!

**BRITTIP**

Need to find your way around Paris public transport? Options are the Métro (the underground), RER train service (regional rail, part underground), Transilien SNCF (suburban rail – not strictly relevant to *Disneyland Resort Paris*), bus and tram. Visit **www.ratp.fr** for more info.

'refresher' of Disney Magic in between visits to Orlando (and of course it is cheaper to spend a few days in Paris than 2 weeks in America). Anyone familiar with the vast Florida resort will also appreciate the convenience of being able to walk everywhere!

## See the city

Another big bonus of the location is the lure of nearby Paris. You certainly do not need to have a car to get to the city (in fact, driving into the city is not advisable). The reliability of the RER service (see Brit Tip) and local buses means you can easily enjoy an evening along the Champs-Elysées or the Bastille district and still get the train back to the resort.

A highly recommended night out for couples is the **Lido de Paris** show in the Champs-Elysées, while another recent development is the **Cityrama** bus tours of the city, picking up at *Disney's Hotel New York* every day. The latter provides an excellent whistle-stop tour of all the main features of this fabulous city, with the great convenience of staying outside the crowds and hubbub. It is also only about 40 minutes on the RER train into central Paris, which is then easy to negotiate either on foot or by the Métro or bus. It is a truly magnificent city with a wealth of history, architecture, art and amazing monuments, plus a dazzling array of fine restaurants and shops. If you are

Bonheur Revue *at the Lido de Paris*

planning a 4-day Disney visit, you should definitely think about spending at least half a day and an evening in Paris itself, especially as there are plenty of attractions geared to the family audience (see Chapter 9).

Those who bring the car can benefit from exploring further afield – and there are some wonderful towns and villages in this region of France, notably the medieval walled town of Provins to the south-east. The road links are good (France also has a system of toll roads, which are superb) and rarely subjected to the kind of congestion we experience in the UK – apart from in central Paris, of course.

### BRITTIP

In keeping with their seasonal approach, the New Year period from January to Easter has become the great Family Value time to visit, with plenty of Kids Go Free (with each adult) deals.

You can also stock up on some wonderful food and wine along the way, as well as in Val d'Europe, where the **Auchan hypermarket** is a highly civilised alternative to the rather tired supermarkets of Calais.

The main focus, however, should be the theme parks themselves. The

*All Cast Members speak at least two languages*

© Disney

## Speaking French

The resort has been a multi-lingual operation since day one and all Disney employees (or Cast Members) should be able to speak at least two languages (many speak four or five). This means you shouldn't have any trouble being understood. However, it is still good practice (and simple good manners) to try to remember a few words of French from time to time. All Cast Members wear a badge with their name and home country, so you can easily spot the occasional Brit working here but, for those who can't remember their basic school French, here is a quick guide to those handy vital words:

| ENGLISH | FRENCH |
| --- | --- |
| Do you speak English? | Parlez-vous Anglais? |
| Good morning/Hello | Bonjour |
| Good evening | Bonsoir |
| Please | S'il vous plaît |
| Thank you | Merci |
| I would like… | Je voudrais… |
| Do you have…? | Avez-vous…? |
| How much is…? | Quel est le prix de…? |
| How much? | C'est combien? |
| A receipt | Un reçu |
| The bill, please | L'addition, s'il vous plaît |
| Coffee | Café |
| White coffee | Café au lait |
| Where are the toilets? | Où sont les toilettes? |
| Toll booths | Les péages |
| Motorway service areas | Aires |
| Autoroutes (toll roads) | Autoroutes des péages |
| Hypermarket | Hypermarché |

original *Disneyland Park* remains the heart and soul of the Magic, especially for families with children under 10, while the *Walt Disney Studios Park* adds an element of excitement and thrills for the older age group. The two provide a complementary experience, but the

© Disney

*Sleeping Beauty Castle's 15th anniversary decorations*

time requirements of each are slightly different. Don't be fooled into thinking you can spend 2 days here and do it all, even during off-peak times. The original park will require at least 2 days to ensure you've seen and done most of what is on offer, while the Studios will need at least a full day when all its new attractions are fully up and running in 2008.

## Seasonal fun

*Disneyland Resort Paris* is unique in the Disney empire of theme parks in providing a huge range of seasonal celebrations. While all their other resorts lay on a brilliantly themed backdrop for Christmas and Halloween, only here will you find a real in-depth and broadly arranged series of attractions throughout the year. There are special winter festivities, a St Patrick's Day event, extra entertainment during summer months, a Bastille Day extravaganza, the amazing transformation of Frontierland to Halloweenland in October, a bonfire spectacular in November and the magic of Christmas in full *Disneyland Resort Paris* style.

## Rain and shine

This is still Western Europe and the climate can be depressingly like our own at times – wet, grey and cold. However, much of both parks has been built with rain and wind in mind, which means there is nearly always somewhere you can escape to if the weather turns nasty. Indeed, almost 80% of the *Walt Disney Studios Park* is under cover, so you don't have to worry too much about the vagaries of Mother Nature. Providing you pack a light raincoat you will be well prepared to carry on enjoying the fun. In fact, spring and autumn can offer some of the best times for visiting *Disneyland Resort Paris* as they rarely

*A magical day at Disneyland*

© Disney

## Top 10 campaign tips

1 Decide what you want to do and try to plan a rough daily schedule (especially in summer).

2 Work out if you want to Do It All (opening hours are longest in summer, everything is available but queues are longer too) or have a quieter time (in spring or autumn with shorter hours and more unpredictable weather).

3 Stay in the resort or outside? The former offers unequalled convenience and essential 'Magic', but the latter is usually cheaper.

4 Choose your mode of transport – Eurostar, car, coach or air. Where you stay will determine which one is the most convenient (see Chapter 3).

5 Long weekend or holiday? The temptation is to pack it all into a weekend, and the ease of the Eurostar makes this appealing. But the weekends are busier and going for 4–5 days instead allows you more variety (see page 19).

6 Take a break. Whether you have a day in Paris, an outing to Provins or Versailles or just a shopping expedition to Val d'Europe, you'll benefit from a Disney break at some stage.

7 Stop and admire the scenery. Often.

8 Enjoy the fact you can have a glass of wine or a beer in the *Disneyland Park*. Alcohol is not served in *Walt Disney World's Magic Kingdom Park* in Florida.

9 Try a little French. The locals are usually more hospitable and forthcoming if you make a token effort to speak their language.

10 Get everyone in your party to read this book!

come up with any seriously anti-social weather, the crowds are more manageable and the queues shorter. And, while the delight of Paris in the springtime is a wonderful cliché, that doesn't mean it isn't true – in fact the months of April (after Easter) and May are just about the best time to visit, with a heavenly combination of pleasant weather, convivial atmosphere and generally lower-than-average attendances.

Yes, this is the biggest tourist attraction in Europe – with around 12 million visitors a year, some 2.5 million from the UK alone – but it can easily be a breeze of a place to visit if you get your tactics right.

And so, with that in mind, it's time to move on to the subject of Planning…

*Do try out your French when you are dining out*

© Disney

# 2 Planning

## or How to do Disney and stay sane!

**I**t used to be the case just a few years ago that you could pop across the Channel to Marne-la-Vallée, have a fun day out and be back home again for tea the next day, safe in the knowledge you had 'done' Disney. Not any more.

The addition of the *Walt Disney Studios Park* in March 2002, the expansion of the surrounding area and continuing influx of visitors mean this is now somewhere you need to consider carefully before you set out for that 'perfect' holiday. It is not quite the same as *Walt Disney World Resort* in Florida, where any visit has to be planned with the precision and accuracy of a military campaign, but you must have a good idea of what you are letting yourself in for and it is still advisable to plan around some of the pitfalls that await the unwary.

First of all, the two parks – the original *Disneyland Park* and the newer *Walt Disney Studios Park* – are a complete contrast from each other. They are different sizes, with different time requirements and appeal to different people. They provide a complementary experience for all but the youngest children (the Studios has fewer attractions for under 5s), but, while you will probably need 2 full days to explore all of the *Disneyland Park*, a day is usually sufficient at the *Walt Disney Studios Park*.

### BRITTIP

Can't find the characters? Check out Main Street USA in the *Disneyland Park* in the morning and the Animation Courtyard area of the *Walt Disney Studios Park* throughout the day. Better still, book one of the character meals at a restaurant like Café Mickey or the Lucky Nugget Saloon.

*On the way to Disney on Eurostar*

# Disneyland Park

The *Disneyland Park* follows the rough formula of the *Magic Kingdom Park* in Orlando, and *Disneyland California* in Anaheim, Los Angeles. It is subdivided into five 'lands' around a central hub and features almost 50 attractions in the form of rides, shows, parades and other live entertainment. There is an impressive choice of accompanying shops and restaurants, all themed to the various lands and offering useful browsing opportunities. At 57 hectares/140 acres, it requires some serious legwork to see it all. You'll be amazed at how time-consuming it can be to get from one land to another with the number of diversions you encounter on the way.

This is the park that families with younger children tend to focus on (although there are terrific thrill rides, like Space Mountain: Mission 2 and Indiana Jones and The Temple of Peril). There is a huge choice of dining and some wonderful character meal opportunities (that kids adore), but you need to pace yourself here as it's easy to get worn to a frazzle – and end up with fractious children – with too much to-ing and fro-ing.

*Space Mountain: Mission 2*

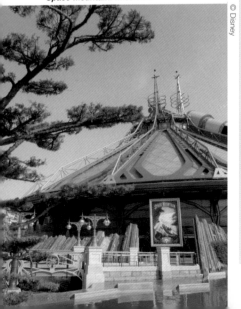

© Disney

*Narnia Meet ' n' Greet at Walt Disney Studios*

# Walt Disney Studios Park

This park is subdivided into four areas and, at slightly less than half the size of its sister park, it is easier to negotiate. As the name suggests, it is themed around the magic of the film world, but it is a different proposition to *Disney's Hollywood Studios* in Orlando (although three of the rides are similar and another is a transplant from Orlando's *Magic Kingdom Park*). It is more show-based, hence its attractions take place at specific times of the day (like the amazing Stunt Show), and more of it is indoors, which is handy when the weather is too cold, hot or wet! There are fewer things for younger children here and the dining options are ordinary, but you still have the all-important Disney characters and some wonderful live entertainment as well.

# Beyond the theme parks

Once you have visited the parks, the delights of *Disney Village* await you. You can dine, dance, shop, go to the cinema or catch a show in this lively, bustling hub, which is a pure delight at night. The choice of dining is terrific, with the superb theming of international duo Planet Hollywood (one of our favourites) and Rainforest Café, the unique Steakhouse and the fun Bavarian-style of King Ludwig's Castle the pick of the bunch. Then there is the 1950s' Americana of Annette's Diner, the country and

© Disney

*The breathtaking Panoramagique*

western style of Billy Bob's Saloon, an all-day character-fest at Café Mickey (with excellent food, too), a Sports Bar and a New York Sandwiches deli, not forgetting a large McDonald's.

Live bands are an outstanding feature of Billy Bob's, while Hurricanes disco (free entry to Disney resort guests) starts bopping around midnight (although it can be quiet Sun–Thur out of season).

### BRITTIP

Too crowded for lunch in the theme parks? Step outside and enjoy a more relaxed meal in *Disney Village*, with none of the long queues, at restaurants like Planet Hollywood, Café Mickey and Annette's Diner.

Nine fully fledged boutique stores stay open usually until midnight and there is periodic live entertainment, notably in the busier seasons. The **Gaumont Cinema** is a 12-screen complex showing the latest movies but there is only one English-language presentation – every Monday night, the rest are in French. The large-screen IMAX theatre adds an extra dimension here as they should now be able to provide multi-lingual headphones for all performances (but check before you book). There is also the inevitable video arcade (with many new high-tech games) and a smart Fun Bowling alley, with a condensed version of 10-pin bowling.

For live entertainment, **Buffalo Bill's Wild West Show** is a *Disney Village* institution, a corny but fun dinner show that is usually a huge hit with kids (even grown-up ones!). It offers the chance to shout, cheer and wave your (free) cowboy hat in support of the various acts, who perform in the indoor auditorium during a typical cowboy dinner. In the summer there is a daily Wild West parade outside before the first of the two shows (around 6pm).

A new element in 2005 was **Panoramagique**, a breathtaking tethered balloon ride over the Village that soars to some 180m/600ft and provides an awesome view of the surrounding area. Add in pedal boats, bungee trampolines and other hands-on activities (including cycling and, in winter, ice-skating) and you have a veritable interactive playground that will keep everyone amused for up to half a day. For the full details on *Disney Village*, see Chapter 8.

As if all that were not enough, you will find the additional lure of **Val d'Europe** quite strong (it continues to develop as a major business centre) as there is some excellent shopping here and at the adjoining **La Vallée** outlet village. This is just 5 minutes away on the RER train (free buses run between the Disney resorts and La Vallée at various times) and can provide a refreshing break from the world of the Mouse after a few days. Here you will find a huge indoor

*The Gaumont Cinema*

© Disney

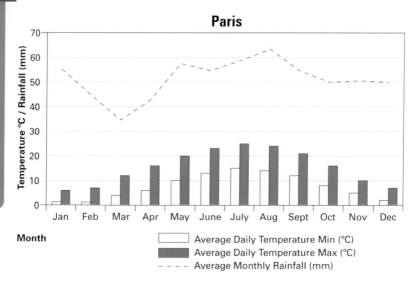

## Paris

Month

Average Daily Temperature Min (°C)
Average Daily Temperature Max (°C)
- - - Average Monthly Rainfall (mm)

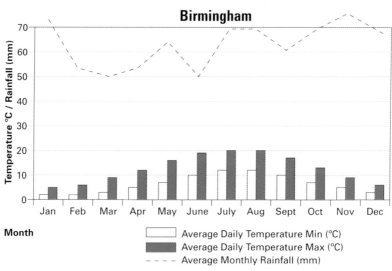

## Birmingham

Month

Average Daily Temperature Min (°C)
Average Daily Temperature Max (°C)
- - - Average Monthly Rainfall (mm)

*Disney Village*

© Disney

shopping mall, some excellent restaurants in an upmarket food court and the exceedingly child-friendly **Sea Life Centre**, a major aquarium run by the chain that owns 13 similar attractions throughout Europe. It is a great diversion for kids aged 2–12 especially and provides a good 2-hour lure if mum or dad want to go shopping!

## The 4-night test

Leger Holidays are the UK's largest tour operator to *Disneyland Resort Paris*, with the biggest variety of packages and travel options. Their stock-in-trade is a 4-night holiday using coach transport to and from the resort, with Disney accommodation. Here is a typical example, using a family of four (with children of 4 and 6) and leaving from the south-east:

DAY ONE: Arrive at *Disney's Hotel Santa Fe* at 9.30pm after 8½-hour journey, including P&O Ferry crossing. Everyone straight to bed!

DAY TWO: Up at 8am for hotel breakfast and off to the *Disneyland Park* soon after. Full day in the theme park, with lunch (pre-booked) at The Lucky Nugget Saloon. Take a break after the 3pm parade back at the hotel (nap time for youngest child!). Dinner at Planet Hollywood at 6.30pm, followed by a slow wander back to the hotel through *Disney Village* (with much to sidetrack two children).

DAY THREE: A later start, with hotel breakfast at 10am, then off to the *Walt Disney Studios*, just in time to catch the 11am Stunt Show. Take in two more shows before lunch at Backlot Express (self-service), then complete the full range of attractions by 5.30pm. Switch to *Disneyland Park* for dinner at Silver Spur Steakhouse at 6.30pm (pre-booked), then one last ride before catching bus back to hotel.

DAY FOUR: An 8am hotel breakfast followed by a return visit to the *Disneyland Park*. Spend 2 hours doing many of the rides in Fantasyland, then leave park to take RER one stop to Val d'Europe and visit the Sea Life Centre*. Have lunch and shop, and let children loose in La Vallée play area, before catching the train back. Revisit the Studios for another chance to see the Stunt Show and Animagique before heading back to the other park for a planned late night. Dinner at 8pm watching a show at Videopolis, and then keep going on various rides until the 10.30 evening parade and fireworks.

DAY FIVE: An 8am breakfast, then time to pack and load luggage back on the coach. Visit the petrol station (next to *Disney's Hotel Santa Fe*) to grab a few snacks for the journey back to Calais. Coach departs at 10am, non-stop to Calais hypermarket. Home again – very tired but with very happy children! – at 4.30pm UK time.

*With older children you might consider the full-day Paris sightseeing tour with Cityrama (see Chapter 9) for a break from the theme parks.

## When to go

The majority of people who visit do so in full family mode, so they are usually here in the school holidays. This is unfortunate because both the cost and the crowds increase during these times, while the summer can also be uncomfortably hot – in excess of 30ºC/86ºF (and two of the resort hotels, *Disney's Hotel Cheyenne* and *Disney's Hotel Santa Fe*, plus the Explorers Hotel, do not have air-conditioning). So you will need to consider your options carefully.

If you are confined to the school holidays, try to opt for late Easter or late summer. The spring and autumn half-term holidays are also prime opportunities, although, once again, the cost increases at these times. The big pay-off with a summer visit is the bonus of **extended opening hours** (usually to 11pm) and a full show and parade schedule. If you can avoid 'Le Weekend' crowds, you still benefit from the pure magic of long nights in the *Disneyland Park* with the evening

*Pony riding at Disney's Hotel Cheyenne*

© Disney

finale fireworks. As ever, it is a case of swings and roundabouts, and you really need to consider what might work best for you.

## Busy times

If you are able to visit in the non-peak periods, you will really feel the benefit. And, by non-peak periods, we also mean weekdays rather than weekends. While the local populace didn't embrace Disney at the beginning, the theme parks (and *Disney Village*) have since developed into a major source of local recreation. So much so that the French attendance on a Saturday and Sunday can be 50% or more. Put simply, this is where much of suburban Paris comes to play at the weekend, and Saturdays can be especially hectic.

Both parks cope pretty well with the thousands who pour in during the first few hours of the day, but the queues build up quickly at the main rides (and just about everywhere in Fantasyland in the *Disneyland Park*). The wait time for rides like Peter Pan's Flight and Dumbo can easily top an hour, which means an uncomfortable period in a queue, especially when it's hot. However, Disney has developed a nifty virtual queuing system called **FastPass** (see page 119), which takes a lot of the

*Character Meet 'n' Greet in Adventureland*

© Disney

### France on holiday

France has 11 public holidays when government departments, banks and shops are usually closed: 1 January, Easter Monday, 1 May, 8 May, Ascension Day, Whit Monday, 14 July, 15 August, 1 November, 11 November and Christmas Day. French schoolchildren also have FIVE holidays a year: a week at the end of October, 2 weeks at Christmas, 2 in February, 2 in spring and the whole of July and August. Consequently, *Disneyland Resort Paris* is noticeably busier during those periods. More details on French school holidays at **www.education.gouv.fr/pid184/le-calendrier-scolaire.html**. You may also want to negotiate around some of the other main European school holidays; see **www.eurydice.org**.

sting out of the waits for many attractions. But even that has its limitations, and so during Easter, summer and Christmas (and any weekend when the weather is fair), you will spend a lot of time on your feet.

### BRITTIP

Disney's FastPass system is an invaluable aid to your park visit, but many people overlook it because they don't understand it. It is FREE to use and simply gives you a time to return to the ride and bypass the main queue with only a short wait. It is fully explained in Chapter 5.

If you prefer to avoid school holidays, most of the summer and the weekends, when should you go? Well, the spring usually sees Paris at its best, and this tends to rub off on *Disneyland Resort Paris* too. Of all Disney's parks around the world, this one is designed and landscaped with distinctly European tastes in mind. There is a much greater emphasis on plants and greenery, providing a naturalistic element to the *Disneyland Park* in particular, which is a joy to behold in the spring and early summer.

*Easter egg painting*

That is not to say that both parks don't have year-round charm or that you can't have as much fun on the rides in November as you can in April. But, there is something genuinely special about a bright spring day that perfectly sets off the Magic provided by Disney's Imagineers. The Adventureland section of the *Disneyland Park* is a particular example of this, as it is an area that envelops you with its sense of grand design and wonderful creativity.

## Visiting off-peak

The weather in Paris in the springtime tends to be more consistent than back across the Channel. Here you can compare the two typical temperature and rainfall charts for Paris and Birmingham on page 20. However, the winters can be as unpleasant as our own in terms of the wet and the cold, so there are several factors you must bear in mind if you opt to visit from November to February. The most obvious is the downturn in business in the winter, with not only the crowds dropping off appreciably, but some of the restaurants and attractions closing too. All Disney's rides, shows and attractions go through a regular process of refurbishment and much of this is carried out in winter, so you may find one or two things shut down at this time. For example, if you enjoyed the Lion King-style dining at Hakuna Matata (in the *Disneyland Park*) during a summer visit, be aware it is frequently closed at off-peak times.

**BRIT TIP**

The excellent German-English website **www.dlp.info/Guide/** includes a section on Closed Attractions, which lists rides due for a revamp more than 6 months in advance (go to Tips & Info, then Planning Your Holiday and click on Closed Attractions).

Some entertainment takes place only during peak periods, when the theme parks are open longer. A nightly fireworks show, Wishes, and a special evening parade extravaganza in the *Disneyland Park* are real highlights in summer and at Christmas, while the Winnie The Pooh & Friends show is high season only. Bad weather (notably heavy rain) can scupper some of the outdoor entertainment at any time, but this is more likely in the winter. However, the Disney team is adept at creating extra Magic in the form of shows and theming at various times of the year, which make **Halloween** and **Christmas** especially appealing and provides an extra reason for visiting at these times (see opposite).

The obvious advantage of visiting out of season is that there are shorter queues. We have been in the parks at a variety of different times and nothing beats being able to wander around Fantasyland and

*Sleeping Beauty Castle decorated for the 15th anniversary*

Discoveryland with the choice of any ride without queuing (and without running into hordes of pushchairs!). The Cast Members have more time for you and the atmosphere is less frenetic, which adds to the enjoyment.

The other big bonus is the regular **'Kids Go Free'** season (another unique Disney feature here) whereby, with any Disney hotel package, every child stays free with a full fare-paying adult, including free continental breakfast and park entry. Park hours are shorter at this time of year (usually 10am–8pm at the *Disneyland Park* and 10am–6pm at the *Walt Disney Studios Park*), but it is easier to get around, so you shouldn't feel short-changed (8pm is often late enough for many children anyway).

## A weather eye

'Ah, but what about the weather?' you might well be asking. *Disneyland Resort Paris* can organise many things, but they have yet to discover how to keep the rain at bay. That means your day in the parks might fall foul of unwelcome precipitation that could literally rain on your parade. But the park designers firmly took the weather into consideration when they were busy Imagineering and you will find more attractions protected from the elements than at any other theme park in the world. It

© Disney

*'Kids Go Free' is a great Disney bonus*

is even possible to walk deep into the *Disneyland Park* mainly under cover (follow the route in Chapter 6).

The provision of arcades down both sides of Main Street USA (the entrance to the main park), some capacious indoor restaurants and very few real 'outdoor' rides (not to mention all the shops, which can provide welcome shelter) means much of your enjoyment should be unspoilt by the vagaries of the weather. In addition, if you bring a waterproof (or buy one of the cheap plastic ponchos on sale throughout the resort) you will be able to continue enjoying the rides with fewer people around.

*Disneyland Railroad station at Main Street USA*

© Disney

*Meeting the Cast Members*

# Christmas events

You may want to take the resort's seasonal events into consideration when planning your visit. Foremost is the Christmas programme, which features special shows, parades, fireworks, characters, decorations and other events in the theme parks, hotels and *Disney Village* from early November to early January.

Main Street USA in the *Disneyland Park* becomes the focus of all this festive fun as it is transformed into a genuine winter wonderland. There is a Yule overtone to the daily **Once Upon A Dream Parade** (with Father Christmas, 'Santa' Goofy and their reindeer, plus a host of other Disney characters in seasonal costume), along with a guaranteed **snowfall** up to five times a day. Main Street is also illuminated in sparkling fashion with a series of glittering street lamps representing the Disney Princesses.

Other highlights are **Belle's Christmas Village** – a charming medieval village themed on *Beauty and the Beast*, with a chance to meet favourite characters from Disney's animated classic (and sample some Yuletide fare!) and **Mickey's Winter Wonderland** – a 20-minute song-and-dance ice-skating frolic with Mickey and the gang at the Chaparral Theatre in Frontierland (which is the one Christmas element that usually continues until the beginning of March). In Fantasyland, look out for **Winnie The Pooh and**

**Christmas, Too**, as the Hundred Acre Wood gang add a seasonal twist to their indoor show. An extra new element in 2005 was the **Enchanted Fairytale Ceremony**, a truly magical finale to each festive evening, with Aurora, Snow White, Belle and Cinderella (and their Princes) in a musical extravaganza culminating with an appearance by Tinker Bell, who waves her magic wand to light up the Main Street USA illuminations and bring the Castle to colourful life. A nightly performance of the grand **Disney's Fantillusion** parade rounds out the park's festive events.

## BRITTIP

Some of the Disney characters have different names in France and will occasionally give their autograph in French fashion. Chip 'n' Dale translate into Tic and Tac, Goofy can become Dingo and Winnie The Pooh is Winnie l'Ourson.

At the *Walt Disney Studios Park*, the theme is a glamorous Hollywood Christmas, with a seasonal celebration centred on the entrance courtyard. Inside **Disney Studio 1**, the Ciné Folies invite parkgoers to be the 'stars' of their seasonally themed movie productions, while the whole of this indoor 'movie set' is decked out in suitably tinsel-clad style to make it 'Lights! Camera! Christmas!'

*Mickey's Winter Wonderland*

© Disney

*Geysers in the snow at Frontierland*

The travelling show **Merry Christmas Walt Disney Studios** departs Toon Studio daily at 10.30am for Production Courtyard, where Santa Goofy, Minnie Mouse and Daisy Duck leave their limousines for a rousing festive singalong. Finally, at the Umbrellas of Cherbourg in the Backlot area, the normal sprinkling of rain turns to snow for the holiday season (beware lurking Disney characters who may have a few snowballs in hand!).

The highly decorated theme is recurrent through all areas of the resort, including a special **Christmas market** in *Disney Village* and a chance to sample a host of traditional culinary specialities, including mulled wine. If you have seen how

*Christmas market in Disney Village*

© Disney

brilliantly Disney prepares its Orlando theme parks for the festive season, we can assure you they take it to new heights in *Disneyland Resort Paris* and it is definitely worth braving the wintry elements for the experience.

**BRITTIP**

If you can visit in late November or the first 2 weeks of December, you will benefit from the full Christmas festivities but without the heavy crowds that they attract later in the month.

You can enjoy another great winter touch at *Disney's Hotel New York*, with a clever **ice-skating rink** outside, while all the Disney resorts feature a spectacular **Christmas Tree** in the lobby area with more decorations than you can shake a Mickey wand at. From 21–31 December, *Disney's Newport Bay Club* hotel also features a special musical gala dinner, **Mickey's Holiday Dinner Show** aboard HMS *Newport*, with Mickey, Minnie and Co setting off on a journey of song and dance around the globe. To enjoy it, you should book from the UK on 00 33 1 60 30 40 50, but be aware prices range from £79–£122 for adults and £29–£40 for children (3–11). There is even a **Merry Christmas Lunch** with characters on Christmas Day at the *Disney's Hotel New York* (£79 and £29) and Festive Dinner Buffets at *Disney's Hotel New York* and Hollywood Boulevard in the

## Party time

Disney knows how to throw a good party, and you should keep an eye out for several notable one-off events. 17 March sees the high jinks of the annual **St Patrick's Day** celebration in *Disney Village*, while 14 July is **Bastille Day**, mixing spectacular fireworks and music in the *Disneyland Park*. Both parks celebrate their 'birthdays' in enchanting fashion too – the *Disneyland Park* on 12 April and the Walt *Disney Studios Park* on 16 March. The resort's 15th anniversary was also highlighted in wonderful fashion in 2007, and was so successful Disney extended it through to the end of 2008 (see Chapter 6).

*Halloween in Frontierland*

*Walt Disney Studios Park* (from £77–£108 and £27–£33).

NB: the *Disneyland Park* stays open until 10pm from 22 December to the New Year and until 1am on New Year's Eve, when there are party festivities throughout the park and *Disney Village*.

## Summer season

From mid-July to the end of August, the full range of park entertainment is up and running. The *Disneyland Park* is open until 11pm and crowds are at their highest. At this time of year the **Fantillusion** parade is one of the main highlights, followed by the fabulous **Wishes** fireworks, which bring down the curtain each evening. The Studios also features the **Good**

**Morning Walt Disney Studios** event, a mini-parade with a big character meet 'n' greet.

## Halloween

The next great festive period is Halloween, and Disney makes a big feature of this. While the idea is certainly more American than European, the style with which *Disneyland Resort Paris* has adopted this tradition is quite breathtaking. Not only is there a daily **Halloween Happening** parade but the whole of Frontierland becomes Halloweenland for all of October, with a wonderfully imaginative series of tableaux (and it is amusing rather than scary for young children). The extra parade follows the same route as the usual daily one, but it is a showcase for the Disney Villains (and is actually more fun!). Kids automatically gravitate towards the Halloween **face-painting**

*Good Morning Walt Disney Studios parade*

stalls, and two late-evening **Halloween Parties** mean the theme park opens from 9pm–2am for more ghostly goings-on (see page 126), plus a late-night party in *Disney Village*.

Finally, the **Bonfire Night specials** run for 3–4 nights each year around 5 November in best Guy Fawkes tradition. This magnificent fireworks spectacular takes place above Lake Disney, adjacent to *Disney Village*.

## How long do you need?

So, once you have worked out WHEN is the right time to visit, you need to work out HOW LONG you'd like to go for. First-time visitors should opt for the maximum time they can afford, especially at busy periods. The standard packages now offer 2-, 3- and 4-night stays and, as indicated on page 19, the 4-night duration is only just enough these days, especially if you have young children to consider. If you can afford a week in summer, you will have the ideal amount of time to fully explore *Disneyland Resort Paris* and see some of the surrounding area and Paris as well (and not return home too frazzled!). However, because we know that the majority of people book one of the standard packages, we have drawn up an example of how to plan for each length of stay in **Your Holiday Planner** in Chapter 10.

*Halloween make-up workshop*

© Disney

© Disney

*Bonfire spectacular over Lake Disney*

If you're already familiar with the *Disneyland Park* and have yet to see the *Walt Disney Studios Park*, you will probably be comfortable with a 2-night stay, concentrating on the newer park during your full day on site. Couples without children or with older kids who can safely survive the demands of a bit of hectic park-hopping can probably negotiate both parks and, perhaps, Val d'Europe, on a 3-night package. But let us stress – you simply will not be able to 'do it all' in one of the peak periods!

Ideally, you should plan your trip to avoid weekends if possible. The perfect 4-night visit would run Monday to Thursday, returning on Friday before the place starts to get seriously busy. However, if you can't go for this long or if you have to include a weekend, let us reassure you that you can still have a great time. There are a number of dodges, tips and short cuts that will give you a head start over the rest of the crowds. These will become obvious in the three chapters on the theme parks themselves.

## Clothing and comfort

The most important part of your holiday wardrobe is footwear – you will spend a lot of time on your feet, even during off-peak periods. The two parks may not be gigantic but that is irrelevant to the amount of time you'll spend walking and standing in queues. This is not the time to break

## Disneyland Resort Paris calendar

**January–March:** Kids Go Free Season

**16 March:** Birthday of *Walt Disney Studios Park*

**17 March:** St Patrick's Day

**12 April:** Birthday of *Disneyland Resort Paris*

**14 July:** French National Day fireworks

**Mid-July–end August:** Summer Season

**October:** Disney's Halloween Festival

**3–9 November:** Bonfire Night Specials

**December:** Christmas Season

**31 December:** New Year's Eve festivities in *Disneyland Park* and *Disney Village*

*Disney Village*! Some love the Disney characters at first sight, while others find their size frightening. There is simply no predicting how they will react, but Simon's eldest boy (then 4½) loved just about every second of his first experience (apart from the fireworks). A 3-year-old may not remember much, but you can be sure they WILL have fun and provide YOU with great memories and photos.

Here are a few tips, put together from personal experience and with advice from other parents.

**The journey:** Try to look calm (even if you don't feel it) and relaxed. Small children soon pick up on any anxieties, which makes them worse! Pack a bag with plenty of little bits for them (comics, sweets, colouring books, small surprise toys, etc.) and keep vital 'extras' like Calpol® (in sachets, if possible), change of clothes, small first-aid kit (plasters, antiseptic cream, baby wipes), sunglasses, hat and suncream in your hand luggage – but remember to check on the latest security advice with regard to liquids. If they are fussy with their food, you may want to take a bottle of their favourite squash, etc. Ribena® is unheard of in European supermarkets, for example.

*Goofy in Frontierland*

© Disney

in new sandals or trainers. Comfortable shoes or trainers are essential. Otherwise, you need dress only as the climate dictates. T-shirts and shorts are quite acceptable in both parks when it's warm enough and most restaurants accept informal dress. Shoes and shirts must be worn at all times, though. In summer, bring a mac for those sudden showers. Warm, waterproof footwear is best in winter, along with extra-thick (or thermal) socks.

If you feel you will need a change of clothes after a long day or some extra layers for the evening, you can leave them in a bag at the Luggage Check next to Guest Relations in both parks (€2 per bag) when you arrive. Both parks are well equipped with pushchairs for a small charge and baby-changing areas can be found in most toilets.

## Disney with children

We are often asked what we think is the perfect age to take children to Disney for the first time, but there is no right answer. Some toddlers take to it instantly, while some 6- or even 7-year-olds are left rather bemused. Quite often, the best attractions for young children are the hotel swimming pool or the kiddie rides in

© Disney

*The Lucky Nugget Saloon in Frontierland*

### BRITTIP

Pushchairs are essential, even if your children have been out of them for a year or two. The distances involved around *Disneyland Resort Paris* can still wear kids out quickly and a pushchair can save a lot of discomfort (for dads especially!). You can take your own, hire them at the theme parks or even buy one relatively cheaply at the Auchan supermarket in Val d'Europe.

**Once there:** Take things slowly and let the children dictate the pace to a large extent. Remember to carry your small first-aid kit with you. Things like baby wipes always come in handy and it is a good idea to take spare clothes, which you can leave at the Luggage Check at both parks. Going back to the hotel for an afternoon break is a good idea – the late afternoon and early evening are usually the best times to be at the parks in terms of cooler temperatures (in summer),

*Rendezvous Des Stars*

© Disney

fewer crowds and pure enjoyment. Both parks have a Lost Children meeting place (see page 122).

**In the summer:** Carry suncream and sunblock at all times and use it frequently – in queues, on buses, etc. A children's after-sun cream is also a good idea and don't forget to offer plenty of water or non-fizzy drinks. Tiredness and irritability are often caused by mild dehydration.

### BRITTIP

The summer heat can make children irritable in no time at all, so take breaks for drinks and visit indoor attractions that have air-conditioning.

**Dining out:** Look for the all-you-can-eat buffets as these are a great way to fill the family up (you may get away with two meals a day) and cater for picky eaters. The Lucky Nugget Saloon, Plaza Gardens Restaurant (in the *Disneyland Park*), Rendezvous Des Stars (*Walt Disney Studios Park*) and Billy Bob's (*Disney Village*) all offer some serious buffets. Try to let your children get used to the size of the characters before you eat at a restaurant where they visit.

**Having fun:** Try to involve your children in some of the decision-making and be prepared to go with the flow if they find something unexpected they like (the Pocahontas Indian Village playground in the *Disneyland Park* is a good example).

*Meeting Cinderella in Fantasyland*

With young children you are unlikely to see and do everything, so just take your time and make the most of what you can all do together.

### BRITTIP

Baby Care Centres (for changing, preparing food and feeding, with nappies and baby food for sale) can be found behind the Studio Services, just inside the entrance to the *Walt Disney Studios Park* and next door to the Plaza Gardens Restaurant in the *Disneyland Park*.

## Travellers with disabilities

Disney pays close attention to the needs of guests with disabilities, and there are few rides and attractions that cannot cater for them, while wheelchair availability and access is almost always good. As the *Walt Disney Studios Park* is so recent, much thought and care has gone into the arrangements for people with various disabilities (from the wheelchair-bound to those with autism and epileptic concerns). It is worth taking time to familiarise yourself with all the ways in which you can take advantage of the facilities. The Cast Members should be fully prepared to help and assist, ensuring you get full value from all the thoughtful extra touches. The main car park also has areas closer to the park entrances set aside for guests with reduced mobility and you should ask for one of these on arrival. There are even specially adapted minibuses for transfers from the Disney hotels to the parks (on request at your hotel reception desk and at Guest Relations in the parks).

All Disney hotels (except *Disney's Davy Crockett Ranch*) have rooms accessible for guests with disabilities, while they also publish a free *Guide for Guests with Special Needs* (outlining all the necessary information for an enjoyable visit), which is available at hotel receptions and Guest Services at both parks. The guide can be sent to you in advance from: *Disneyland Resort Paris*, Guest Communication, PO Box 100, 77777 Marne-la-Vallée, Cedex, France.

Guidebooks in Braille are also provided and guide dogs are allowed in (although they are not permitted on certain attractions). Start by going to Guest Services at either park and asking for a copy of the *Guide for Guests with Special Needs*. You can also ask for an **Assisted Access Card** that allows access to special waiting areas for many attractions for a person with disabilities and up to three companions (although this does not provide special access to the rides, as most queue lines have now been made wheelchair-accessible). There are also special areas at the

*Fantasyland façades*

many shows and parades for the disabled. However, not all rides at the *Disneyland Park* are fully accessible to the disabled as some require transfer and therefore the help of a companion is needed.

Visitors with hearing disabilities are not terribly well catered for, apart from a handful of attractions that have subtitles on video screens rather than bilingual commentaries or headphone translators (Animagique and Cinemagique in the *Walt Disney Studios* both have induction loops, for example). The multi-lingual nature of the resort makes it difficult to use a close-captioning system effectively, as in Disney's American parks, and they still seem to be some way off from solving this problem.

# Disney for grown-ups

It may sound daft to include something specifically for adults but it is an often overlooked aspect that you don't need to have kids in tow to enjoy *Disneyland Resort Paris*. In fact, we've often felt the place is actually too good for kids! There is so much clever detail and creativity that the majority of youngsters miss in their eagerness for the next ride, it is usually the grown-ups who get the most out of the experience. In fact, there are just as many couples without children and young adults on

*Auberge de Cendrillon*

their own visiting the theme parks, making it a legitimate holiday for all ages. Certainly, when you look at some of the sophisticated dining on offer and the evening entertainment at places like Billy Bob's and Hurricanes in *Disney Village*, it is easy to see the attraction for those aged over 21.

Paris obviously makes a wonderful honeymoon destination and newly-weds are just as likely to visit one of Disney's parks as the Eiffel Tower. Restaurants like the Blue Lagoon and Auberge de Cendrillon in the *Disneyland Park*, The Steakhouse in *Disney Village*, the Hunter's Grill Restaurant at *Disney's Sequoia Lodge* and the superb California Grill at the *Disneyland Hotel* all offer a genuine romantic touch to dining à la Disney.

*The Blue Lagoon*

## Top 10 things to do in Disneyland Resort Paris

Here is our guide to the ten things you MUST do on any visit to this wonderful resort.

1 Have a character meal.

2 Dine at the Blue Lagoon restaurant.

3 See the daily parades (especially if Fantillusion is running).

4 Take a stroll around Lake Disney.

5 Have dinner at Planet Hollywood and then check out the live music at Billy Bob's Saloon in *Disney Village.*

6 See Buffalo Bill's Wild West Show.

7 Have a drink in the Redwood Bar and Lounge at *Disney's Sequoia Lodge.*

8 Go shopping at La Vallée.

9 Try the Panoramagique balloon ride at *Disney Village.*

10 See the unique Cinémagique show in the *Walt Disney Studios Park.*

## Being practical

When it comes to the practicalities of your holiday, your obvious needs include **passports** for all the family (double-check that the name on your passport matches that on your travel tickets) and remember that all children must have their own passport these days. All British subjects MUST have a full, valid 10-year passport that will not expire for at least 3 months after you enter France. Non-British subjects should check their visa requirements in advance. For UK passport enquiries, call 08705 210410 or look up **www.passport.gov.uk.**

## Travel insurance

You can get free or reduced cost treatment in all European Union countries. However, you must possess the new European Health Insurance Card (EHIC), which replaced the old E111 in 2006. You can apply for the EHIC, which is free, online at **www.dh.gov.uk/travellers**, by phone on 0845 606 2030 or 0845 605 0707, or by post – you can obtain a form at the Post Office. You need to know your NHS/National Insurance number. The EHIC does not cover all medical expenses, however, or the cost of bringing a person back to the UK in the event of illness or death, so it is essential to have adequate travel insurance cover as well.

Having said you should not travel without good insurance, you should also not pay over the odds for it. Tour operators may imply you need to buy their insurance policy, which you don't and their policies can be expensive. Make sure your policy covers you for: **medical treatment** up to £1 million; **personal liability** up to £1million; **cancellation or curtailment** up to £3,000; **personal property** up to £1,500 (but check on expensive items, as most policies limit single articles to £250); **cash and documents**, including your passport and tickets; and finally that the policy gives you a **24-hour emergency helpline**.

Shop around at reputable dealers like **American Express** (0800 028 7573, **www.americanexpress.com/uk**), **AA** (0800 085 7240, **www.theaa.com**), **Direct Travel** (0845 605 2700, **www.direct-travel.co.uk**), **Club Direct** (0800 083 2466, **www.clubdirect.com**), **Columbus** (0870 033 9988, **www.columbusdirect.com**), **Norwich Union** (0808 101 6705, **www.norwich union.com**), **Egg** (08451 222 888,

*Lake Disney*

## Disney for seniors

If Simon's parents are anything to go by, the over-60 age group can also get a huge amount of enjoyment from the Disney experience. The greater ease of getting here (as opposed to the American parks) is high on their list of plus factors, while the convenience of just about everything being within walking distance or a short bus or train ride away scores highly, too. They preferred the *Disney Village* and hotel areas during the day when crowds were few. Within 2 days they were fully *au fait* with the whole resort and extremely comfortable with the set-up. Here is their own top 10 attractions suitable for the over 60s:

1  Cinémagique (*Walt Disney Studios Park*)
2  Star Tours (*Disneyland Park*)
3  Pirates of the Caribbean (*Disneyland Park*)
4  Moteurs … Action! Stunt Show (*Walt Disney Studios Park*)
5  Studio Tram Tour (*Walt Disney Studios Park*)
6  Phantom Manor (*Disneyland Park*)
7  Animagique (*Walt Disney Studios Park*)
8  Tarzan Encounter (*Disneyland Park*)
9  'it's a small world' (*Disneyland Park*)
10  Flying Carpets Over Agrabah (*Walt Disney Studios Park*)

They would even go as far as listing the walk around Lake Disney as an attraction in its own right, while they also felt the more show-based style of the *Walt Disney Studios Park* suited them better than the rather more hectic ride-orientated nature of the original park. However, they still acknowledge that the essential Magic of the latter is totally unmissable.

www.egg.com), **Thomas Cook** (0870 750 5711, **www.thomascook.com**) and **Worldwide Travel Insurance** (0870 112 8100, **www.worldwideinsure.com**). **MoneySupermarket** also compares different travel insurers at **www.moneysupermarket.com/insurance**.

*Tarzan Encounter is a popular show*

© Disney

## Medical matters

When it comes to anything of a medical nature, it is worth knowing that there are two fully English-speaking hospitals in Paris. The **American Hospital in Neuilly** is located at 63 Boulevard Victor Hugo, 92200 Neuilly-sur-Seine (Métro Porte Maillot); tel. (in Paris) 01 46 41 25 25 and the **Hertford British Hospital** can be found at 3 Rue Barbès, 92300 Levallois-Perret (Métro Anatole France); tel. 01 46 39 22 22. For an after-hours chemist, the **Drugstore Champs-Elysées** at 133 Avenue des Champs-Elysées (Métro Charles de Gaulle-Etoile); tel. 01 47 20 39 25, is open until 2am daily, while the **Pharmacie Dhery** at 84 Avenue des Champs-Elysées (by Métro Georges V); tel. 01 45 62 02 41, is open around the clock. There is also a pharmacy at the entrance to the big Val d'Europe shopping mall, closest to the RER

*Mickey and Minnie on Main Street USA*

station entrance, open from 10am–9pm Mon–Sat.

## Emergencies

In the event of an emergency, dial 17 or 112 for the police, 18 or 112 for the fire brigade or 15 or 112 for 24-hour medical emergencies (18 or 112 for less serious incidents). The public ambulance service can be called on 01 45 13 67 89. For a 24-hour doctor's service, call 01 47 07 77 77.

## Safety first

Crime has never been a major issue at *Disneyland Resort Paris*, but you just need to use your common sense as you would in any city (especially in the vicinity of the RER station, where pickpockets sometimes operate). Keep your hotel door locked at all times (even if you are just popping down the corridor) and don't leave things like cameras or camcorders on view in the car when you leave it parked. Both parks have a Lost and Found office and Guest Services can advise you of any additional security requirements (only the *Disneyland Hotel, Disney's Hotel New York* and *Disney's Newport Bay Club* have rooms that are equipped with safety deposit boxes).

The Paris **lost property office** is located at the Préfecture de Police, 36 Rue des Morillons, 75015 Paris (Métro Convention); tel. 08 21 00 25 25. It is open Mon, Wed and Fri 8.30am–5pm, Tue and Thur 8.30am–8pm. If for any reason you need to contact the **British Embassy** in Paris, it can be found at 18 bis rue d'Anjou, 75008, Paris; tel. 01 44 51 31 00.

## Money

As ever on a foreign holiday, it is advisable not to carry too much cash with you. Travellers' cheques are easier to replace if lost or stolen (make a note of the serial numbers), but, generally speaking, cash and credit cards are almost universally

*Snow White on parade*

accepted (although not by many small hotels and cafés in some areas of France). You can also use Switch, Visa and Mastercard at the several cash dispensers around the resort.

The currency, of course, is the euro. At the time of writing, £1 = €1.47, or €1 = 68 pence, so, roughly speaking, £5 would be a touch more than €7. For those who have yet to encounter the euro, there are eight coins – 1 and 2 euros, and 1, 2, 5, 10, 20 and 50 cents – and seven notes in 5, 10, 20, 50, 100 and 200 denominations.

In France, a 15% service charge is sometimes added to restaurant and hotel bills but the usual practice of tipping is simply to leave a few euros at the end of a meal. A taxi driver would expect a 10–15% tip, while a porter would expect €1 a bag.

## Phone calls

If you need to **phone home**, avoid using the hotel phones as they are fiendishly expensive (and Disney hotels are no exception). Your mobile phone will probably also have expensive connection charges for calling from abroad (or even for receiving calls). It is better to use a public payphone and pay via your BT Chargecard or another kind of phone card. To call the UK from France, dial 00 44 and then the UK number (omit the first 0 from the area code).

© Disney

*The iconic Sleeping Beauty Castle*

## Tourist info

If you are out and about in France, look for the local **Offices du Touris** **and Syndicats d'Initiative** for map advice and info on the local sights and attractions. Most tourist attractions are open 10am–5pm, w one late opening day per week, bu surprisingly, many close on public holidays (although not in *Disneyla Resort Paris*).

**BRITTIP**

Look for a character meet-and-greet *without* the crowds – in the lobby of the *Disneyland Hotel* twice a day, usually at 11am and at teatime or the first floor. Ask at the hotel's Guest Relations desk for exact times.

*Disney's Fantillusion Parade*

# Top 10 'hidden secrets' of Disneyland Resort Paris

Look out for the many special 'extras' that may not be so obvious to the busy visitor. Here is our guide to the best.

1   La Tanière Du Dragon – the 'Dragon's Lair' under the Castle at the *Disneyland Park*, which many people miss.

2   Lighting effects – you can change the lights inside Studio 1 at the *Walt Disney Studios Park*, in front of Club Swankadero and in the Liki Tiki Lounge.

3   Take a phone call – pick up the phone next to Walt's bureau inside the Photo Shop on the corner of the *Disneyland Park*'s Town Square and listen for a message!

4   Get breezy – approach the giant fan at the exit to the Armageddon attraction in the *Walt Disney Studios Park*; it works via a motion sensor.

5   Heavy rock – sit on the large stone underneath the suspended bridge in Adventure Isle (*Disneyland Park*) – it rocks from side to side!

6   Puppet parade – be outside 'it's a small world' on the hour for a fun parade of ride characters on the 'clock tower'.

7   Take a ride – sit on the motorcycle outside the Café des Cascadeurs in the *Walt Disney Studios Park* and be startled by the sound effects!

8   Get a haircut – in Dapper Dan's, the period barber's shop on Main Street USA in the *Disneyland Park*.

9   Make it rain – stand under the Umbrellas de Cherbourg next to the Backlot Express restaurant in the *Walt Disney Studios Park*.

10  Make some music – try out the working keyboard in the back of the technician's van outside Rock 'n' Roller Coaster starring Aerosmith, again at the *Walt Disney Studios Park*.

*Parapluies de Cherbourg*

# A question of characters – where are they?

The biggest question on most visitors' lips (especially those with children!) is usually 'Where can we find the characters?' There are invariably some that leave frustrated because they simply miss out on this essential photo and autograph opportunity. Therefore, to give you a head start on your character hunting, here is a quick rundown of where you can usually meet Mickey and Co:

**Disneyland Park:** At the top of Main Street USA for the Main Street Park Opening at 9–9.30am (or 10–10.30am on later opening hours) every day; Meet Mickey just in front of the upper exit of the Liberty Arcade by Casey's Corner and Meet Minnie under the Gazebo on Main Street USA periodically throughout the day; on Disney's Character Express along Main Street four or five times a day; at regular intervals on the Castle Stage (to the right of the Castle at the entrance to Fantasyland), with Winnie the Pooh and Friends (usually in the morning) and other Disney favourites (in the afternoon); periodically outside Colonel Hathi's Pizza Outpost in Adventureland; from time to time outside 'it's a small world' in Fantasyland; at lunch or dinner in the

*Colonel Hathi's Pizza Outpost*

© Disney

Lucky Nugget Saloon in Frontierland or Auberge de Cendrillon (with Cinderella characters) in Fantasyland; or for tea at the Plaza Gardens Restaurant on Main Street USA.

**Walt Disney Studios Park:** In the entrance courtyard in front of Studio 1 for the first hour of the day, and periodically thereafter; at Meet Mickey in Hollywood Boulevard or Toon Studio; periodically throughout Toon Studio; and at the Good Morning Walt Disney Studios Parade shortly after opening in peak season.

**Disney Village:** At one of the character meals that are served throughout the day at Café Mickey (7.30 and 9.30am for breakfast, noon–2.30pm for lunch and 3–11pm for dinner); for breakfast (periodically) at The Steakhouse; and also for Sunday brunch at The Steakhouse (midday–3pm).

**Disneyland Hotel:** At dinner at the Inventions Restaurant.

**All Disney Hotels (including Disney's Davy Crockett Ranch):** In the lobby area at regular intervals throughout the morning.

For all character meals you need to make a reservation either when you book your Disney package, through reception at your Disney hotel or in advance by phoning (from the UK) 00 33 1 60 30 40 50 (just 01 60 30 40 50 in France) up to 2 months in advance.

To check when and where to meet the characters in the parks, always call in at City Hall at the *Disneyland Park* or Guest Relations at the *Walt Disney Studios Park.*

## Know before you go

As hard as we work to keep this guide up to date, there are always things that change after our deadlines or areas we can't cover fully in this relatively small volume. Stay on the ball by using the internet as much as possible and there are a number of websites to help you (as well as our own – **www.askdaisy.net/paris**). First

# Key contacts

Here are the principal contact numbers for all the main agencies at *Disneyland Resort Paris* (from the UK, omit the first 0 and add 00 33 to the number, e.g. to call Seine-et-Marne Tourist Office, dial 00 33 1 60 39 60 39):

**Annual Passport Hotline:** 01 60 30 60 69

**Baby Care Centre:** 01 64 74 26 00

**Billy Bob's Buffet:** 01 60 30 40 50

**Buffalo Bill's Wild West Show:** 01 60 45 71 00

**Café Mickey:** 01 60 30 40 50

**Davy Crockett Ranch:** 01 60 45 69 00

**Davy Crockett's Adventure:** 0825 150 280

**Disneyland Hotel:** 01 60 45 65 00

**Disneyland Paris First Aid Centre:** 01 64 74 23 03

**Disneyland Paris Lost Children:** 01 64 74 24 00

**Disney Village:** 01 60 30 20 20

**Disney Village Tourist Office:** 01 60 43 33 33

**Euro Disney SCA, Shareholders Info & Club:** 01 64 74 56 30 (or e-mail **dlp.actionnaires@disney.com**)

**France Tourist Office, London:** 09068 244 123 (60p/min) or **info.uk@franceguide.com**

**Golf Disneyland:** 01 60 45 68 90

**Hotel Cheyenne:** 01 60 45 62 00

**Hotel New York:** 01 60 45 73 00

**Hotel Santa Fe:** 01 60 45 78 00

**King Ludwig's Castle:** 01 60 42 71 80

**Lost and Found:** 01 64 74 25 00

**Mail Order Service:** 01 64 74 48 48 (or e-mail **dlp.mail.order@disney.com**)

**Newport Bay Club Hotel:** 01 60 45 55 00

**Panoramagique:** 01 60 45 70 52

**Planet Hollywood:** 01 60 43 78 27

**Rainforest Café:** 01 60 43 65 65

**Resort Guest Relations:** 01 60 30 60 53 (or e-mail **dlp.guest.communication.@disney.com**)

**Resort Restaurant Reservations (up to 2 months in advance):** 01 60 30 40 50

**Sea Life Aquarium:** 01 60 42 33 66

**Seine-et-Marne Tourist Office:** 01 60 39 60 39 or **cdt@tourisme77.fr**

**Sequoia Lodge Hotel:** 01 60 45 51 00

**The Steakhouse:** 01 60 45 70 45

**UK bookings (to book a *Disneyland Resort Paris* stay from the UK):** 08705 030 303

**VEA Airport Shuttle Bus:** 01 53 48 39 38

**VIP Guided Tours:** 01 64 74 21 26

Write to *Disneyland Resort Paris* Guest Relations: *Disneyland Resort Paris*, Communication Visiteurs, BP 100, 77777 Marne-la-Vallée, Cedex 4, France.

PLANNING

and foremost is the official Disney website **www.disneyland paris.com**, with the opportunity to book online and save money (although it can be hard to navigate), while by far the most comprehensive of the 'unofficial' sites is **www.dlp.info/ Guide/**, the English translation of a superb German fan site. This includes excellent sections on the resort's history, current shows and parades, hours of operation, rumours, downloads and newsletters, plus the latest practical advice, and a chat and discussion forum. Another sharp site is **www.dlrpmagic.com**, while for some of the best photos and news of the resort, visit the excellent **www.clickmagique.com** and **www.photosmagiques.com**. Log into

**www.dlpfoodguide.com/indexphp** for the ultimate guide to dining Disney-style.

Another website to which we also contribute – **www.disboards.com** – has a special forum on *Disneyland Resort Paris* as part of their busy discussion boards, as does **www.thedibb.co.uk**. Other general tourist information websites are: **http://uk.franceguide.com**, **http://english.pidf.com**, **http://en.parisinfo.com**, **www.paris.org** and **www.tourism77.co.uk**.

Well, that should give you enough food for thought in the planning stage for now. Let's move on to another vital subject in your preparations, that of actually Getting There…

*Fantillusion – the Happy Ending*

© Disney

# 3 Getting There

## or Trains, planes and automobiles, plus coaches and ferries!

In many ways, your choice of **when** to go to *Disneyland Resort Paris* pales into insignificance compared with the issue of how to get there. The options for travel for this relatively short journey are almost as wide-ranging as the resort itself.

Obviously, your location in the UK plays a large part in deciding what is best for you. The Eurostar service may be a wonderful method of transport but it is not ideal if you live in Newcastle or Bangor. Equally, going by coach and letting someone else do all the driving has a lot of appeal but it can seem a long way of doing things if you live in the South East (where Eurostar and Eurotunnel are quicker options). Flying is increasingly popular and affordable with the low-cost airlines, and the advantages are especially noticeable from regional airports like Newcastle, Aberdeen, Bristol and even Southampton. So here is an outline of each of the main possibilities, along with their pros and cons.

## By car

With the opening of the Channel Tunnel in 1994, the dream of quick, reliable transport to the Continent became a reality. A permanent link was established along with a whole new realm of Channel-hopping

possibilities. Some 85 million people used the longest undersea tunnel in the world (50km/31mls in length, 39km/24mls of them under the sea itself) in the first 10 years alone. In 2006, the figures were: 2,021,543 cars, 67,201 coaches and 7,858,337 Eurostar passengers.

### BRITTIP

If you exceed the speed limit by more than 40kph/25mph, the French police have the power to take your driving licence immediately, so you won't be able to drive. For serious offences they can confiscate your car.

While the Channel Tunnel obviously opened in direct competition with cross-Channel ferry businesses, it actually served to quite significantly increase the total traffic between the UK and Europe. Not only did the day-tripping habit pick up (as did the

*The Channel Tunnel*

© www.answers.com

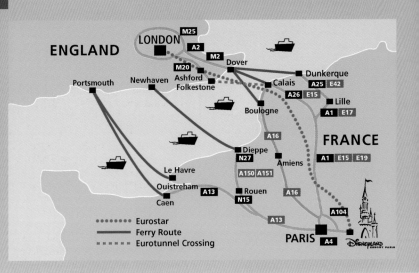

number of British-orientated supermarkets in the Calais vicinity), but driving holidays to France, Belgium, Holland, Spain, Germany and even Italy also received a major boost. So, just two years after the opening of the *Disneyland Resort Paris*, it stands to reason the tunnel would become a prime route in getting people there (in fact, one of the many reasons why Disney eventually settled on the Paris site was because of the forthcoming tunnel link).

*Disneyland Hotel*

© Disney

The combination of the tunnel and the well-established ferry links from Dover, Newhaven and Portsmouth now provide a wealth of opportunity for routes into France by car and coach, and more people travel by car than any other mode of transport. France is also blessed with well-organised and relatively smooth-flowing motorways (certainly compared to our M25), many of which are toll-road autoroutes (*autoroutes des péages*). In summer 2007, the tolls amounted to just €19.20 one way to use this quickest and most convenient of routes (A26 from Calais, then A1, A104 and A4 – see maps below and opposite). Basically, it is 104km/65mls on the A26, 156km/97mls on the A1, 25km/16mls on the A104 and then another 11.5km/7mls on the A4 before the turn-off (Exit 14) for 'Les Parcs Disneyland'.

### BRITTIP

Watch out for the A26 junction with the A1, as the signposting is not terribly clear here and it is easy to miss. The motorway turn-off signs are all in white (and set off to the right-hand side) and you need to follow the big blue overhead destination signs for Paris.

## Autoroutes des péages

Tickets are issued at the beginning of each of the paid motorway networks. Payments are then calculated on the distance you travel and must be paid on leaving the motorway. You pay at the *péages* (toll-gates) with either cash or credit card. For short local journeys it is a good idea to keep some small change handy to avoid the hassle of using your credit card. Payments vary according to the type of vehicle, with different price bands for cars, vans, cars with trailers, lorries and motorbikes.

From Calais ferry port, you are directed straight on to the A26 (via the E15 – follow the clear signs for Paris, Reims), while from the Channel Tunnel, you have a short 6km/3½ml stretch south-west on the A16 (signs for Calais) before picking up the A26.

It is advisable to navigate by the directional signs rather than the route numbers, hence from Calais on the A26, initially follow the signs for Saint-Omer, Arras, Reims, Paris; at the junctions with the A1, follow signs for Paris, Arras Est; immediately after

Charles de Gaulle Airport, follow signs for Bordeaux, Nantes, Lyon, Marne-la-Vallée, Paris Est, Bobigny; once on the A104, look for Lyon, Meaux, Marne-la-Vallée and 'Les Parcs Disneyland'; at the junction with the A4, follow signs for Meaux, Reims.

### BRITTIP

Although *Disneyland Resort Paris* is officially located in Marne-la-Vallée, the whole area along the A4 here is designated Marne-la-Vallée, hence it is easy to get sidetracked. From the A104, follow the signs for 'Les Parcs Disneyland'.

The only other area to watch out for is switching from the A1 to the A104 at Charles de Gaulle Airport, although there is a sign for 'Les Parcs Disneyland' just before and after the airport, directing you on to the A104. Immediately after the airport the autoroute splits and you need to be in the right-hand lanes for Marne-la-Vallée; it then splits again and the two right lanes bring you on to the A104 heading south (see map below).

It should take you a shade under 3 hours to drive from Calais, with the

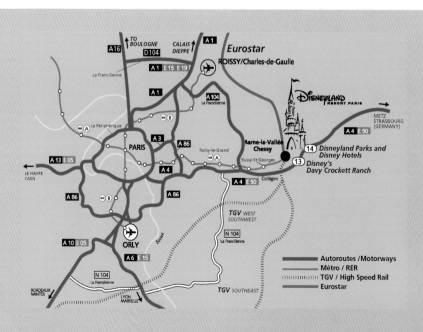

speed limit up to 130kph/80mph on the autoroutes. You can save the toll money by taking the Routes Nationales (or N-roads), but that would add nearly an hour to your journey. The toll-road system in France is split into eight privately owned networks, but the one from Calais to Marne-la-Vallée is all under the control of SANEF (**www.sanef.com/en/**). Check out **www.autoroutes.fr** for more details on your journey and a handy route planner, while the Eurotunnel website **www.euro tunnel.com** has some helpful route advice as well. Other useful travel sites are **www.multi map.com** and **www.mapquest.com**, while the AA website (**www.theaa.com**) also features a good route planner.

### BRITTIP

The autoroute speed limit is 130kph/80mph, but 110kph/68mph when it is wet. It is 110kph/68mph on non-toll motorways and 90kph/56mph on other roads, 80kph/50mph when wet and 50kph/30mph in towns.

The first tollbooths you come to on the A26 are after about 61km/38mls between Exits 4 and 5, and here you simply collect a ticket from the machine, which records the point at which you join the A-route system, and then you pay at the tollbooths just north of Charles de Gaulle Airport (just after Exit 7). These are the only tolls you will pay on the direct Calais–Marne-la-Vallée route.

From the ferry port at Boulogne, follow the 'Toutes Directions' signs and these quickly bring you on to the A16 via a new stretch of dual

*Hakuna Matata in Adventureland*

*Meet Cinderella and Prince Charming*

carriageway. Once on the A16, head south for 200km/125mls until it becomes the N1, then follow N1 around until it hits the junction with D104 (after about 7.5km/4½mls. Take D104 (La Francilienne) for 16km/10mls to the A1 just north of the airport. Go south on the A1 and follow the same directions as above (A104–A4). Tolls will be about €17.30 and the journey will take around 2½ hours.

### BRITTIP

Speed camera detectors are illegal in France, and if found by police will be confiscated and incur a fine of €750 or more.

If you take the Portsmouth–Caen ferry route, your journey will be around 265km/164mls via the A13, the Paris *périphérique* and the A4, and the tolls will be €16.90.

Once in the Marne-la-Vallée area, your main route to and from the theme parks is likely to be the A4, a busy stretch of motorway at peak periods (especially into Paris itself) but otherwise an easy-to-use arterial. There are no tollbooths along this section at all, hence you can use the A4 as frequently as you like at no extra cost. Once you turn off at Exit 14 for the theme parks, everything is well signposted to the hotels and main car parks. A huge, ring road encompassing the whole resort (plus Val d'Europe), called the Boulevard de

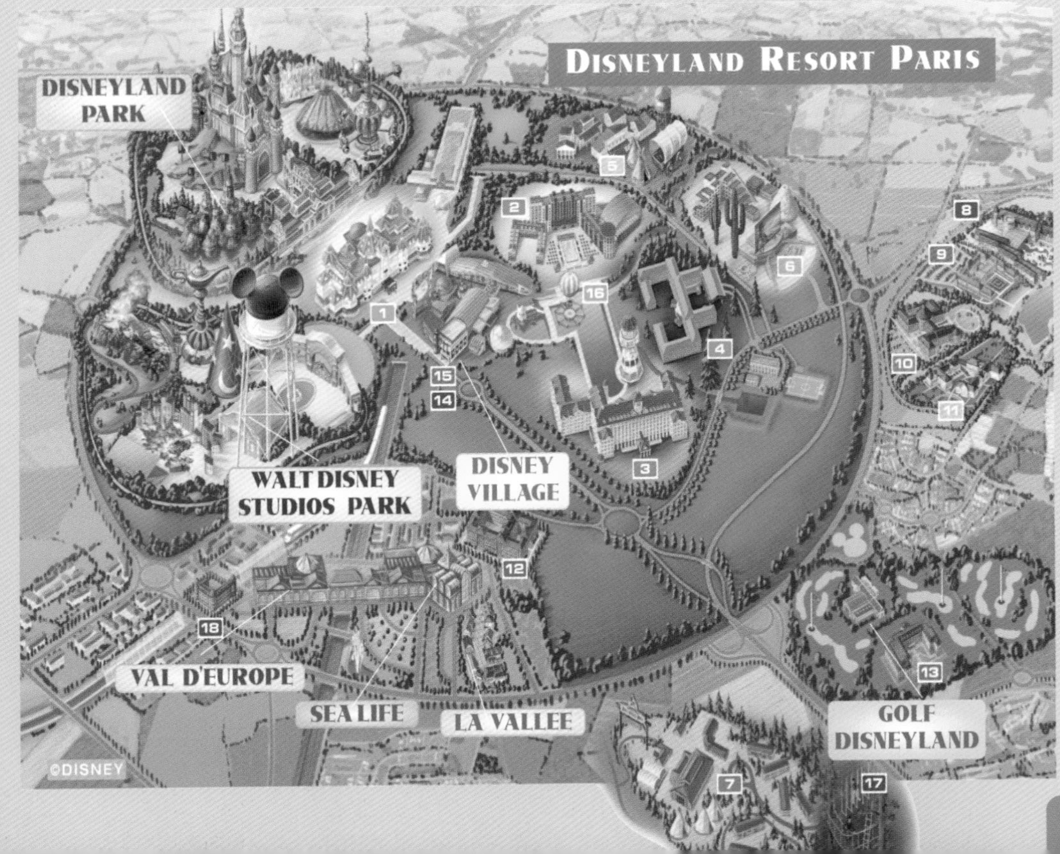

# Disneyland Resort Paris

1  Disneyland Hotel
2  Disney's Hotel New York
3  Disney's Newport Bay Club
4  Disney's Sequoia Lodge
5  Disney's Hotel Cheyenne
6  Disney's Hotel Santa Fe
7  Disney's Davy Crocket Ranch
8  Explorers Hotel
9  Vienna International Dream Castle Hotel
10  Holiday Inn at Disneyland Resort Paris
11  Kyriad at Disneyland Resort Paris
12  Pierre & Vacances
13  Radisson Hotel
14  Vinci multi-storey car park
15  IMAX Cinema
16  Panaramagique
17  Davy Crockett's Adventure
18  Hotel L'Elysée

DISNEYLAND RESORT PARIS

DISNEYLAND PARK

WALT DISNEY STUDIOS PARK

DISNEY VILLAGE

GOLF DISNEYLAND

VAL D'EUROPE

SEA LIFE

LA VALLÉE

©DISNEY

l'Europe, makes an interesting drive as you can get some unusual glimpses of the theme parks from it.

Children under 10 are forbidden to travel in the front seat. On-the-spot fines or deposits (in cash – you should get an official receipt) can be demanded for not wearing seat-belts (compulsory front AND back), drink-driving, driving on a provisional licence and speeding offences (and French police are pretty hot on the latter). The use of mobile phones while driving is strictly prohibited.

**BRITTIP**

If a French driver flashes their lights at you, it means they intend to go first, NOT that they are giving you right of way.

Parking and rest zones are situated every 10–20km/6–12mls on motorways, with 24-hour petrol stations about every 40km/25mls. If you break down, pull up on the right, put on your hazard lights and place a red warning triangle 30m/33yds behind your vehicle (compulsory for vans and cars with trailers). Orange emergency telephones are usually every 2km/1¼mls apart on motorways. If you break down and can't leave your vehicle, there are regular road patrols on all autoroutes. In addition, you must not park on yellow kerbs.

*Carnival time at Disneyland Resort Paris*

© Disney

© Disney

*Disney characters in Frontierland*

French motorway service areas (or *aires*) are generally open 24 hours and offer a combination of facilities way beyond anything in the UK in terms of quality. There are two types of *aire*: one has full fuel, catering and shopping facilities, while the other is a picnic area with toilets. The latter are often pretty places to stop, but bring your own toilet paper (for some reason it is not a standard French provision!). Both AA and RAC members can take advantage of their organisation's European Breakdown Assistance service, which is highly valuable when travelling on the Continent. Look up **www.theaa.com** (tel. 0870 600 0371) or **www.rac.co.uk** (tel. 08705 722 722).

**BRITTIP**

Buying petrol in motorway service stations in France is as exorbitant as it is in the UK. You can save 12–15% by filling up at the nearest hypermarket (*hypermarché*) in Calais or Le Havre. Savings on diesel can be even greater.

For **maps**, the AA's *Touring Map France* series (£4.99 each) are among the best available. Look for *Paris & The North* for the full route from Calais to Marne-la-Vallée, while you would need *Normandy* and *Paris & The North* to cover the journey from Caen. Online, the website **www.viamichelin. co.uk** also offers some valuable maps and info. All autoroutes have an information radio station. In northern France, English-

## Driving in France

There are no major differences in the traffic rules in France (other than driving on the right-hand side!), but driving with dipped headlights is compulsory in poor visibility – so don't leave home without a pair of headlight beam adjusters. It is also advisable to take a set of spare bulbs, while a red hazard warning triangle is compulsory (for vans and cars with trailers) in case of a breakdown. You should take your vehicle registration document and insurance certificate, as well as your driving licence (it is a legal requirement to have it with you whenever you are behind the wheel). Check with your insurance company to ensure you have full cover while driving in France. Green cards are no longer required, but some insurance companies issue them anyway as they are a sure way of convincing local police you are properly insured. Road signs are pretty much universal, but additional signs or warnings to watch for are:

| | | | |
|---|---|---|---|
| Allumez vos phares/feux | Switch on your lights | Interdit aux piétons | Forbidden to pedestrians |
| Attention au feu | Fire hazard | Rappel | Remember (often on speed limit signs) |
| Attention travaux | Beware roadworks | | |
| Cedée le passage | Give way | Route barrée | Road closed |
| Chaussée déformée | Uneven road surface | Sens unique | One way |
| | | Sens interdit | No entry |
| Essence sans plomb | Unleaded petrol | Supercarburant | Lead replacement petrol |
| Fin d'interdiction de stationner | End of prohibited parking | | |
| Gazole | Diesel | Verglas | Black ice |

language bulletins are on 107.7FM on the hour and half-hour.

## By ferry

Of course, if you are taking the car, you need to decide which method of cross-Channel travel you prefer – the various ferry services from one of three south coast ports or the Eurotunnel service from Folkestone. If you opt for the more traditional ferry route, you can go from Dover, Portsmouth and Newhaven. Here's how they break down.

## Dover

To start with, Dover is an easy port to get to by road – either straight down the M2/A2 in north Kent or (our preferred route) via the M20/A20, both of which come off the M25 London orbital. It is about 1¾ hours from central London (given a relatively traffic-free run) and you need to head to the Eastern Docks for

the main ferry operators. Dover is a thoroughly modern, well-organised port and should get you aboard your ferry with the minimum of fuss.

The main passenger terminal includes a bureau de change, a bank and cashpoint, an AA shop, a café and newsagent, information desks, phones, toilets and baby-changing facilities. Also, once you have driven into the terminal area itself, there are

*View across Paris from the Eiffel Tower*

two mini food villages offering another café, a Burger King, a bar, bureau de change and cashpoint, a shop, plus toilets, baby-changing facilities and telephones. You should arrive at least 30 minutes before your sailing time and have passports ready as you drive in.

If you have booked in advance (which is highly advisable), you proceed straight through to your ferry operator's check-in. If you haven't got a ticket, you can park up in the short-stay parking area at the main entrance to the passenger terminal and buy one from the Travel Centre (6am–9pm). Alternatively, you can now pass straight to check-in and purchase a ticket there. There are NO services by any operator on Christmas Day.

Once through the Eastern Docks' main reception area, follow the 'Ferry' signs to Border Control, where you will need to show your passports. Remember, all British subjects MUST have a full, valid 10-year passport that will not expire for at least 3 months after you return. Non-British subjects should check their visa requirements in advance. Then follow the ferry operator signs to check-in, where you will be allocated a numbered embarkation lane to proceed to, from where you will be directed on to the ferry when it is ready to board. While waiting here, you can take advantage of the food villages and facilities.

*Les Deux Magots café in Paris*

*P&O* **Pride of Dover**

Four main companies operate from this busy cross-Channel hub, three from the Eastern Docks:

**P&O Ferries** is Dover's biggest and most sophisticated operator, with up to 29 crossings to Calais a day, 364 days a year. They operate the most frequent services on this route and, if you haven't travelled on a cross-Channel ferry for a while, you will probably be pleasantly surprised by the comfort and quality on offer these days. The crossing time from Dover is 90 minutes, although you mustn't forget to put your watches forward an hour on arrival in France.

**BRITTIP**

Visit their website **www.poferries.com** to take advantage of their 'Best Fare Search', which offers cheaper fares the earlier you book.

Once settled aboard, you have a good choice of bars, shops, lounges and cafés in which to while away the time. All P&O Ferries' ships now include an International Food Court (usually the busiest area on board, especially just after embarkation), a First Base fast-food counter, the Harbour Coffee Company, Silverstones Sports Bar and a shop selling sweets and other snacks. Langan's Brasserie offers a more upmarket choice for a meal in mid-Channel and, if you have opted for Club Plus when you booked, you also get the benefit of the Club

## Join the club

P&O Ferries offers three distinct extra services, which can be pre-booked or, in the case of the Club Lounge, booked onboard (although it then costs more). The **Club Lounge** is an exclusive quiet lounge, complete with comfy leather armchairs, where you are greeted with a complimentary glass of champagne and offered tea and coffee, biscuits, fruit and newspapers by its own waiter/waitress service. There is also a business area where laptops can be used.

The **Priorité** service is a pre-booked priority loading system, which allows you to embark early and unload first, which is highly worthwhile when time is of the essence. The two can then be combined in a **Club Plus** service, which provides use of the Club Lounge and the priority loading/unloading as well. At the time of writing, the prices were: £12/person each way for the Club Lounge, if booked in advance (£14 if booked onboard); £12/vehicle each way for Priorité; if opting for Club Plus, £12/person each way plus £6/vehicle. For two people, Club Plus would be £60 return.

Lounge and its personalised service, as well as priority embarkation and unloading at the other end. For the young ones, there are new children's entertainers onboard the five Dover–Calais ferries for the school holidays, along with soft play areas. Provisions for the youngest members of the family now extend to free Heinz baby food. There is also a good video games centre, the Megadrome, to keep older children amused.

For shoppers, some of the biggest savings available are on fragrances, at up to 50% off UK high-street prices.

### BRITTIP

You can save money on P&O Ferries by booking a night crossing. Some onboard services are closed (Club Lounge and Langan's Brasserie, for example) but prices are reduced for these 'Nite Lites' crossings.

Top brand designer sunglasses at up to 20% cheaper include Gucci, Prada, Ray Ban and Police. Wines start from just £12 for six bottles and an extensive range of spirits is available at 2 litres for £22.

For more info, visit their website **www.poferries.com** or call 08705 980333.

**SeaFrance** is the only French ferry operator on the Dover-Calais route, offering 30 daily crossings, 364 days of the year (not Christmas Day). In early 2005, it launched its latest superferry, the *SeaFrance Berlioz*, sister ship to the award-winning *SeaFrance Rodin*. Both offer crossings in just 75 minutes and provide 20 of the daily crossings, while the others are handled by the smaller ships the *SeaFrance Cézanne* and *SeaFrance Renoir*. Across the fleet, SeaFrance provides a decent range of restaurants and onboard activities. Each ship offers a choice of restaurant areas: Le Relais, a self-service restaurant; Le Parisien, a French café; Le Pub, a traditional bar; and La Brasserie, a fine-dining restaurant serving gourmet French cuisine. All ships have a well-stocked shop, with major discounts on High Street prices and at least one major lounge area. The two superferries add extra-smart lounge facilities, a good children's play area and video arcade.

Prices fluctuate depending on the month of travel and, again, early booking is strongly advised, with

*P&O Ferries Club Lounge*

discounts often available. SeaFrance's website displays prices next to each crossing and alternative crossing times, so passengers can see which will suit them best. They also offer three types of ticket: *Saver*, their lowest-rate non-refundable fare (with a £10 booking modification fee); *Amendable*, with a lower modification fee (£5) and a flat-rate fee (£30) if you need to cancel more than 24 hours before your travel date; and *Freedom*, with no modification or cancellation fee at least 24 hours before travelling. SeaFrance's web-based travel operator arm, **www.seafrance holidays.com**, also offers good value packages to *Disneyland Resort Paris* for a variety of budgets. For more info, visit **www.seafrance.com** or call 0871 22 22 500.

**Norfolkline** provides an alternative to the occasionally hectic Calais crossings, with up to 12 sailings a day to Dunkerque, just over 40km/25mls further along the French coast from Calais. The crossing time is a slightly long (by Calais standards) 2 hours but the Dunkerque port facilities are well run, usually uncongested and easy to negotiate for the tourist. There is a distinctive Norfolkline travel centre within the Dover Ferry Terminal while, at the Dunkerque Terminal, there is a lounge area with facilities for the disabled and a snack bar, La Véranda, offering non-alcoholic drinks and food from 9.30am to 5.30pm (Sat–Thur).

More importantly, in recent years Norfolkline has introduced a fleet of three new, modern ferries, each of 35,293 tons, which have added significantly to their onboard facilities. They include relaxation areas, gaming areas, a cinema, two playrooms for children (the Games Castle and Little Nippers), a full-service restaurant, fast-food restaurant and bistro. Freight drivers also have a separate restaurant and relaxation area. You can upgrade (for £12/person in advance) to the onboard **Executive Lounge**, which has an exclusive seating area, free internet access and complimentary tea, coffee, soft drinks and pastries. All Norfolkline ferries' interior facilities are smoke-free but there is an outside deck area for smokers.

For the tourist market, Norfolkline continues to focus on the needs of the motorist by carrying only cars, caravans and trailers, motorhomes and motorcycles, not coaches and foot passengers. The gift shop (taking advantage of French duty-paid prices) offers fairly standard fare but is worth a visit, especially on your return, to grab a last-minute bargain in wines, spirits, beers, tobacco and perfumes.

You are advised to check in 1–2 hours before your departure time. From Dunkerque, Marne-la-Vallée is just over 300km/186mls away – follow the signs for the A16, then take the E42 to the A25 all the way to Lille and pick up the A1 to Paris. For more info, visit

*Sea France* Berlioz

their website **www.norfolkline.com** or call 0870 870 1020.

**SpeedFerries** is the new kid on the block in Dover, starting operations in the Eastern Docks before securing exclusive use of the old Hoverport at the Western Docks in 2007 (with few queues), featuring a year-round service to Boulogne rather than Calais. The company established a new style of ferry operation on its debut in 2004, similar to the low-cost airlines, and this has become fairly standard for cross-Channel operators now – the earlier you book, the cheaper the fare. The fare increases as a sailing fills up. Price is also independent of the length of stay. Lead-in price in summer 2007 was an eye-catching £20 one-way for a standard car and up to five passengers. The super-fast catamaran *SpeedOne* makes the journey in just 50 minutes, with up to five return trips a day. It is also designed only for cars (and small vans and motorhomes); there are no foot passengers, coaches or trucks.

Tickets come in a choice of BASIC (non-refundable and changeable, and with a 45-minute check-in period); FLEX (changeable and deferrable, and with a 30-minute check-in time); and PREMIER (adding priority loading, an exclusive lounge, service at your seat and a complimentary drink, newspaper and pastry).

The onboard experience is

surprisingly stylish, with spacious air-conditioned lounges, as well as a cafeteria, coffee and wine bar, sundeck, family lounge, video arcade and a shop. There is even a handy SpeedShop at Boulogne that you can visit for all your duty-free shopping. To book, visit **www.speedferries.com** or call 08702 200570 (there is a £10 phone supplement, so the internet is cheaper). On returning to Boulogne, simply follow the signs to Boulogne Port (not the town itself).

For more info on the port of Dover, look up **www.doverport.co.uk** or call 01304 241427.

## Newhaven

Between Brighton and Eastbourne on the Sussex coast is this small but busy port featuring the French company **Transmanche Ferries**, now the only ferry service on the Newhaven–Dieppe route. It also offers Newhaven–Le Havre once a day in summer (through sister company LD Lines but still using a Transmanche vessel). Newhaven is on the A259 coast road, but is best reached (from London) via the M23, A23, A27 (at Brighton) and A26. Transmanche brought in two smart new ferries in 2006 (*Seven Sisters* and *Côte D'Albâtre*), with all modern onboard amenities, covering the journey in just 4 hours, with up to three crossings per day (in peak periods). You can add a cabin to your booking, for £15–30 depending on whether it is

*The Channel is one of the busiest shipping lanes*

a day or night crossing, or just opt to stay in the lounge, bar or cafeteria. Both ships have an extensive choice of shopping opportunities and a video lounge, while they also boast a full-service restaurant, bar, games arcade and children's playroom. Check-in begins 2 hours before sailing and passengers must arrive at least 45 minutes before departure.

Call Transmanche on 0800 917 1201 or book online at **www.transmanche ferries.com**. From Dieppe, it is 257km/160mls to *Disneyland Resort Paris*; follow the N27, A151, A150 and N15 before picking up the A13 and the route from Caen.

## Portsmouth

For the closest port to Paris, head for Caen with **Brittany Ferries** or Le Havre with French **LD Lines**. The French capital is barely 2 hours from the Normandy ports (see map on page 38) and Portsmouth is more accessible from the Midlands and West Country than Dover or Newhaven. The down side is it is a much longer crossing. Brittany's new high-speed *Normandie Express* can do it in 3¾ hours, but their older classic ferry offers either a 5¾-hour day sailing or 7 hours at night. However, the night crossings have an advantage, arriving in Caen at 7.15am so you can be in *Disneyland Resort Paris* by 10am. There are up to four sailings a day (one a day with the high-speed ferry, from mid-March to mid-November), leaving Portsmouth at 7am (high-speed), 8.45am, 3.15pm and 11.15pm, and the port facilities are all new and well organised. *Normandie Express* features a self-service café, a

*Caen is about 2 hours from Paris*

*Brittany Ferries sail from Portsmouth*

bar, shop and open viewing deck, with reclining seats and a video games room, while the older *MV Normandie* has the extra facilities of a cinema, children's entertainment, a full-service restaurant, a second bar and a coffee shop, plus 2 and 4-berth cabins.

**BRITTIP**

There is a Carrefour hypermarket in Caen and also one in Herrouville, not far from Ouistreham, if you need to do some last-minute shopping before your return trip home.

The Caen terminal is actually located at Ouistreham, the newest ferry port on the Channel, 15km (9 miles) to the north of Caen (open 6.30am–11pm), and is well designed to provide a smooth return journey, with easy access and good facilities. To reach Paris, simply follow signs to Caen along the D514 and D515, then pick up the city ring road (N814) and go south-east for 3.5km until you hit the A13. Then it is autoroute all the way to Paris (210km; 131 miles), with 16.90 in tolls. Stay on the périphérique and skirt the city to the south, then pick up the A4 to Disneyland Resort Paris. On the return to Caen/Ouistreham, follow the signs for 'Car Ferry'. For more info, call 0870 907 6103 or visit **www.brittany-ferries.co.uk**.

**LD Lines** also offer an overnight sailing (11pm daily) from Portsmouth, to the port of Le Havre on their comfortable, modern Norman Spirit, arriving at 8am. They dock at the exclusive, modern Citadelle terminal, from where it is only 200km (124 miles) to Paris, using the N15, A131

# Thank you ferry much

We asked Britain's leading cruise and ferry website, Seaview (**www.seaview.co.uk**), to pass on their top tips for getting the most out of your cross-Channel journey – at the best price. Here's what they said:

*Don't leave your booking until the last minute. Prices rarely improve by waiting.*

Don't try to pull a fast one by buying a day-trip ticket when you plan to stay longer. Ferry operators have a knack of finding out and take a very dim view.

*Most ferry companies make it easy to book online and offer discounts for doing so.*

If you book online, keep the confirmation e-mail with its unique reference number. Short crossings are often ticketless, so a booking reference is vital. And look after it – you'll have to produce it at the ferry terminal.

*Read the reservation details carefully – twice! Mistakes do happen.*

Make sure you give the correct details when booking, such as names as they appear on passports, exact length of car, etc. It can save vital minutes at check-in.

*If there is a person with disabilities in your party, enquire about priority on-and-off arrangements.*

Try to book a sailing time that you can make without having to dash. However, don't panic if you miss it. Nowadays, there's usually room on the next sailing. If you are ahead of schedule, there's a chance you'll be put on an earlier sailing.

*If you are taking your dog on holiday, the train is best. Eurotunnel has areas for dogs to excuse themselves before travelling and, unlike the ferry, they have the pleasure of their owners' company on the journey.*

If you sail with SeaFrance, go for the new *Berlioz* or virtually new *Rodin*, by far the best ships in the fleet.

*If you prefer P&O Ferries and can afford the extra, treat yourself to the Club Lounge. It's comfortable, usually quiet, and soft drinks, coffee and tea, etc. are complimentary. You can also pamper yourself with a meal at Langan's Brasserie.*

Be aware that, should an emergency arise, Apex bargain tickets are non-refundable, while full-price tickets usually are.

*Remember you lose an hour on arrival in France, so take this into account when you are considering sailing times.*

and A13. For more info, call 0870 428 4335 or visit **www.ldlines.co.uk**.

Portsmouth (**www.portsmouth-port.co.uk**) itself is also served by excellent road links, with the port at the base of the M275 having its own exit on to the motorway. It is actually closer to London than either Dover or the Channel Tunnel and is arguably Britain's best-connected ferry port. The new Newbury bypass on the A34 has also cut down the journey time from the Midlands, West and North.

For websites to help you with ferry crossings and road access after you arrive, the following are helpful, starting with the essential **www.seaview.co.uk**. Then there's **www.ferrybooker.com** (with lots of useful info on driving in France, the ports and working out your route). When it comes to driving, **www.auto routes.fr**, **www.viamichelin.com** and **www.sytadin.tm.fr/** (for Paris traffic reports) are extremely useful and worth checking in advance.

*SeaFrance's* Cézanne

# By Eurotunnel

Need to get to Calais fast, conveniently and with a choice of services 24 hours a day? Well, Eurotunnel is the answer. This versatile shuttle service from Folkestone in Kent has up to four departures an hour at peak times, with a crossing time of just 35 minutes. In fact, it can take just 45 minutes from the time of loading to driving off at the other end, making it easily the quickest vehicle crossing time of any cross-Channel service. Finding Eurotunnel also couldn't be easier as the terminal is just off Junction 11A on the M20, about a 45-minute drive from its intersection with the M25, and is well signposted.

**BRITTIP**

For the latest travel, weather and road news for the area, call Eurotunnel's information line on 0800 096 9992.

After arriving at the Eurotunnel terminal, proceed straight to check-in and quote your booking reference number (or use their new self-check-in facility, which you can practise online). You can just arrive on spec, but you will be allocated a space on the next available shuttle, and may have to wait a while. It will also usually be more expensive than booking in advance. In busy periods a booking is highly advisable to avoid a wait of more than an hour. You are

*Eurotunnel*

*Fun awaits at Buzz Lightyear's Laser Blast*

requested to arrive at least 35 minutes before your booked departure time. You can stop off in their extremely smart and spacious main terminal building, grab a bite to eat and do a bit of pre-trip shopping. Once checked in, you drive through both British and French passport controls (there are no checks on arrival, as with the ferry). Please note LPG vehicles are NOT allowed on Eurotunnel trains.

Eurotunnel recognises it is not always possible to plan your arrival time accurately. So, if you arrive late but within 2 hours of your booked departure time, they transfer you to a space on the next available shuttle at no extra charge (although this could take a while if it's busy). If you arrive 2–24 hours after your departure time, you will be charged only the difference between the price paid originally and that applicable to your new departure. If you arrive more than 24 hours late, you will need to buy a new ticket.

**BRITTIP**

Don't forget the necessary documentation for your vehicle, insurance and any breakdown cover you have for the journey.

For an even quicker and smoother passage, travel **FlexiPlus** and benefit from a priority lane at check-in and a guaranteed space on the next available shuttle. There is an exclusive

© Disney

*Mickey in Adventureland*

lounge (open 6am–10pm) to allow you to freshen up, enjoy a light meal, complimentary tea, coffee and newspapers, and use the phone/fax. There is even a free take-away snack service. The extra speed, convenience and service that this provides is highly worthwhile, especially on a short trip.

For direct access to the lounge, go straight to passport control, then follow the FlexiPlus signs (in the UK, keep to the right-hand lane, in France, keep to the left). Stay in the respective lane until you reach the Eurotunnel FlexiPlus barrier, then use the token given to you at check-in to gain access to car parking for the lounge. You will also be given a paper hanger at check-in, which you need to display on your rearview mirror. From the lounge, you will be given priority boarding on the next available shuttle.

Once you're ready to board, you just drive straight on to the shuttle where you stay in your car. You can get out to stretch your legs in the carriage (and there are toilets, usually in every third carriage). On arriving at the other end, you drive off (in Calais/Coquelles) practically straight on to the A16 autoroute. From there, you head for the A26 (signposted initially to Calais and then to Saint-Omer, Arras, Reims and Paris) before picking up the A1 at Arras (see map on page 42).

On the return journey, you come off the A16 at Junction 13 (look for the signs for Tunnel Sous La Manche). If you have time to spare here, you can visit the huge **Cité Europe** shopping mall, which has some 200 shops and offers the usual great deals on things like wine, beer, spirits and food. Plus there are clothing stores such as Etam, Naf Naf, H&M, Sergio Tacchini, Zara and Quiksilver, as well as other well-known chains such as Footlocker, Toys R Us and even a Disney Store.

## BRITTIP

Check out **www.day-tripper.net** for more details on Cité Europe, the bargains to be had and an excellent map of the area.

All in all, the Eurotunnel operation really is as simple as it sounds, and the ease with which you are suddenly off and running in France comes as quite a surprise the first time, so don't forget to drive on the right! It is also a relatively cheap option, with Short Stay Saver fares (2–5 days) from £78/car (at 2007 prices) and Standard Fares (more than 5 days) from £98. A 5-Day FlexiPlus costs £149 each way and a standard FlexiPlus £199 each way (you can also 'mix and match' FlexiPlus and Standard fares).

The other great benefit of Eurotunnel as opposed to the ferries (apart from it suiting more independent-minded travellers) is the fact that the shuttle service is never affected by the weather and you are certainly not likely to get seasick on a train! For more info, visit **www.eurotunnel.com** or call 08705 353535.

*Eurotunnel trains*

**BRITTIP**

An excellent route-planning facility can be found at the website **www.eurotunnel.com**. Just type in your route details and you get easy-to-follow instructions to your destination. It even provides the total cost of the tolls en route. Click on 'Passenger Travel' and then 'Travelling Abroad'.

# By rail – Eurostar

The fastest direct route from London to Paris these days is via the smooth Eurostar operation from the new St Pancras International station. There are up to 17 services a day to the Gare du Nord station in Paris, with a fastest journey time of 2 hours and 15 minutes (quicker than flying, once you take into account time negotiating the airports to get into the city centres). You can go to Gare du Nord and then use the RER rail service to get to *Disneyland Resort Paris* (at the Marne-la-Vallée station). But you are much better off waiting for the daily direct service – 2 hours 34 minutes from London to Mickey! This is literally the fast-track service – at up to 300kph/186mph – especially as it's just 2 hours from Ashford International station in Kent. It is a high-speed link with great comfort, style and convenience.

*Waiting for Eurostar*

*Eurostar*

Put aside any preconceptions (and real misgivings) of the British rail system, because this is how modern rail travel really *should* be. You are guaranteed a seat (no mean feat for some regional rail services), the trains are clean and comfortable and their time-keeping is second to none in the UK (okay, the latter is not saying a lot, but Eurostar really does have an excellent punctuality record). The opening of the final section of the new high-speed rail link trimmed almost 30 minutes off the rather pedestrian journey from London to the tunnel itself, while the whizz through northern France remains a breathtaking experience. The move to the new home at St Pancras in November 2007 brought a wonderful range of purpose-built facilities to this high-quality experience.

Add to this the excellence of all the other terminal facilities – at the brand new Ebbsfleet Station in Kent (although this is not on the direct route to *Disneyland Resort Paris*), Ashford, Gare du Nord and Marne-la-Vallée – and you have an operation of the highest order and user-friendliness. For anyone living within 2 hours' drive of Ashford, this is a highly worthwhile alternative to the London station, as the ease and efficiency with which you can park and walk across to your train makes for a hassle-free journey, especially with children.

## Super St Pancras

The original Victorian structure of St Pancras station has been given a major contemporary makeover – inspired by New York's iconic Grand Central Station – to accommodate the Eurostar trains and their facilities. The array of shops, bars and restaurants include a world-class brasserie, Europe's longest champagne bar (all 90m/295ft of it!) and a daily farmer's market. The shops alone are a mixture of one-off boutiques and big-name brands, making for a retail selection unequalled at any station in Europe. There is WiFi connectivity, including an exclusive lounge for Business Premier customers. In all, there are six platforms for the Eurostar services, instead of five at their old Waterloo location, with the capacity to operate far more services. There are also outstanding connections to St Pancras International, with six underground lines and seven rail companies operating from here or nearby King's Cross and Euston.

Eurostar operates a daily service direct to Marne-la-Vallée, departing St Pancras at 8.53am and Ashford at 9.26am, arriving in the heart of the Disney Magic at 12.27pm. There are also direct services to Lille, Brussels, Avignon and the French Alps, while connections are possible to more than 100 destinations in France, Belgium, Germany and Holland (NB: there are no Eurostar services on Christmas Day. Sunday train times also vary slightly – consult **www.eurostar.com** for the latest timetables).

If you choose the Gare du Nord route (or are unable to take advantage of the Disney direct service), you should find it relatively easy to transfer to Marne-la-Vallée via the RER train link on Line D (although the trains are seriously crowded in the morning and evening rush hour). Just follow the (Green) signs to Melun. From Gare du Nord, you change trains at Châtelet Les Halles to switch from Line D to Line A for Marne-la-Vallée.

Another alternative (and a worthwhile tip if you miss the direct service) is to take one of the Eurostar trains to **Lille** and change there for a TGV train to Marne-la-Vallée (about 65 minutes). You do not even have to change platforms at Lille, just wait (usually no more than half an hour) for the French high-speed train and you're off to the heart of the Magic once more.

## RER-ing to go

Using the RER system to get to and from *Disneyland Resort Paris* is a doddle. This largely overground train link takes about 35–40 minutes to get from the resort into central Paris and runs until after midnight. While the trains may not be the cleanest (the graffiti menace has been here with a vengeance!), they run at regular intervals every hour and scrupulously to time. The RER goes underground through central Paris, where it links up with the Métro underground system. You do not need to use the **Métro** – or the well-organised bus system, which links with both – unless you are on a serious sightseeing tour of the city.

**Marne-la-Vallée** is at the end of the (Red) Line A4, which runs basically east–west through Paris. Gare du Nord is at a junction of the (Green) Line D, which runs largely north to south and (Blue) Line B, which bisects the city from north-east to south-west, and has the **Charles de Gaulle Airport** at the end of the B3 link (north-east). **Orly Airport** is on a special branch line – the Orlyval – connecting to the Antony station on the (Blue) Line B4.

*The new St Pancras station*

service to Paris and Lille (or any of their other regular destinations), you have the choice of three classes, **Standard**, **Leisure Select** or **Business Premier**. If you are used to using your local train service, Standard will feel like travelling first class – the individual seats are all comfortable, with decent elbow room, carriages are roomy and there is easy access to the two buffet cars. With Leisure Select and Business Premier, the service is seriously upgraded.

### BRITTIP

A special fare applies for both wheelchair users and a travelling companion on Eurostar – priced at the lowest available Standard class fare – and there are toilets and an area adapted especially for wheelchairs in Leisure Select or Business Premier. Blind people travelling with companions also benefit from the same deal.

Leisure Select fares offer a three-course meal at your (extra-width, reclining) seat and complimentary newspapers and magazines. There is plenty of space if you need to work en route (or keep the kids amused with board games etc.) and uniformed staff are always on hand.

Business Premier, as you would expect, is the most expensive and affords complete flexibility for travel any day of the week from London to Paris, as well as other perks like a 10-minute check-in and exclusive lounge

access. However, if you are interested only in the direct service to *Disneyland Resort Paris*, your choice is restricted to just Leisure Select or Standard fares. There are always two buffet cars per train and a smattering of Disney fun to whet your appetite, with Disney Cast Members onboard to assist with hotel arrangements and provide some entertainment for the children, ensuring your visit gets off to a flying start. Baby-changing facilities and bottle-warming are available, along with activity packs for children if you ask at the terminals. Plenty of ramps, passenger conveyors and lifts are provided as well.

### BRITTIP

Using the RER from Gare du Nord to get to *Disneyland Resort Paris*? Change at Châtelet Les Halles, as you simply need to switch platforms rather than go up and down a potentially confusing set of escalators – the RER signposting takes a bit of getting used to.

On the direct St Pancras–Ashford–Marne-la-Vallée route, Standard fares start from £59 return for adults and £44 for children under 12. Leisure Select fares start from £139 and £94 (children under 4 travel free without an assigned seat). Their cheapest fares are also *non-flexible*, which means there are no refunds or exchanges; you need to choose a (more expensive) *semi-flexible* ticket for leeway with exchanges and

*Marne-la-Vallée station*

## A Disneyland day-trip?

The high-speed nature and regularity of the Eurostar service means you could opt for just a **day-trip** to *Disneyland Resort Paris*. Taking the 5.27am from London would put you in Paris by 8.50am. Taking the RER to the resort would get you to the theme parks by around 10am.

The direct return service is at 7.25pm from Marne-la-Vallée, arriving back in Ashford at 8.37pm and St Pancras at 9.13pm. But, if that does not suit you, the last train from the Gare du Nord station in Paris to London is usually at 9.13pm, which means you could still have until 7.30pm in the parks before catching the RER service into Paris.

refunds. With the London–Paris Leisure Select variety, all trips (except the Weekend Day Return) must include a Saturday night stay. But there is NO stay-away condition if tickets are booked more than 21 days in advance.

Eurostar fares compare extremely favourably with airline prices (even the low-cost carriers) and, for the extra convenience of arriving right in the heart of the Disney fun, they take some beating.

**BRITTIP**

It is possible to travel one way in Leisure Select and the other in Standard. It is definitely worth travelling in Leisure Select on the way home to give yourself room to wind down after all that exhausting fun!

**Eurostar services:** At the main Eurostar **terminals**, you should find everything efficient and easy to use. At London's **St Pancras International** mainline station, the Eurostar services operate on the main level from platforms 5–10. The departure terminal is built into an upper level in the old station's undercroft and here you will find the impressive range of purpose-built facilities – shops, cafés and bars, along with a cash machine

that dispenses both euros and sterling. There is not much car parking nearby, though, and it's expensive at £16 a day. At **Ashford International**, the main concourse offers a pleasant café, plus shops, currency exchange and left luggage, while passing into the departure lounge gives you more chances to grab a drink or bite to eat, another shop and currency exchange, plus a Eurostar information desk. The multi-storey car park here holds 2,000 cars and parking is £11.50 a day (an alternative, open-air car park is available nearby at £9.50 a day, although it involves about a 100m/109yd walk to the station). To plan a rail journey to Ashford (or any other UK station), look up details on **www.nationalrail.co.uk** or **www.thetrain line.com**.

If you are returning from **Gare du Nord**, the Eurostar service is upstairs on the first level (it's surprising how many people don't notice this when they arrive), where there is again a good range of cafés and shops once you pass into the departure area. You have to check in at least 30 minutes before your departure to allow plenty of time for security screening.

**BRITTIP**

At Ashford International, go through to the second café as you enter the departure lounge as it is usually less congested.

*Gare du Nord*

**Marne-la-Vallée** is the least exciting of the main Eurostar terminals (but then it can afford to be with its situation). You arrive at the lowest level of the station and take the escalator or lift up to the main concourse. If you are heading straight for the theme parks, there should be a Disney Cast Member to direct you to the nearest exit. If you are heading for your hotel first, go out of the main doors straight ahead of you, and the bus stop for all the Disney hotels (except *Disney's Davy Crockett Ranch*, which does not have a bus service) and those of the four Selected Hotels (the Explorers, Vienna International Dream Castle, Holiday Inn and Kyriad) are immediately in front of the station.

### ✠ BRITTIP

If you haven't already bought your RER ticket to get from Gare du Nord to Marne-la-Vallée (which you can do at any Eurostar station), avoid the often crowded main ticket offices on the Paris station concourse. Instead, wait until you reach the last, smaller ticket office just before the entrance to the (Green) Line D of the RER as there is rarely much of a queue here.

The Eurostar service includes the considerable bonus of the **Disney Express** baggage arrangement, which enables you to go straight to the theme parks on arrival while your bags are taken to your hotel. This has

*Triumphal arch outside the Louvre*

© Disney

*Phantom Manor*

to be organised before you travel either through your tour operator or at the St Pancras terminal if you have booked Disney accommodation independently (you need to be able to show confirmation of your hotel booking to do this at St Pancras).

Once you have the correct baggage tags (and Disney Cast Members will be on the direct service to assist you and provide the right tags if you have not been sent them with your tickets), you simply attach them to your luggage and take them to the first-floor *Disney Express* baggage office when you arrive at Marne-la-Vallée.

For our money, this is the most efficient and stress-free form of travel we have encountered, especially in Europe. When travelling with children it provides much to ease parents' minds (as well as the bonus of children's general fascination with trains). The onboard buffet food could be better (especially for children) and smokers will not be happy to know that Eurostar is a completely non-smoking service, but those are extremely minor quibbles.

Eurostar also now features **packages** to *Disneyland Resort Paris*, with a full range of Disney hotels and others nearby on the RER line to Marne-la-Vallée. Go to **www.eurostar.com** and click on the *Latest Deals* link, but you must add Disneyland tickets to your booking as they are not included automatically.

*Meet Captain Hook!*

# By air

If the Eurostar route is the most time-efficient way of getting to the heart of the Magic, where does that leave air travel? Well, if you live anywhere outside the South East, it provides the best alternative, especially using the two main Paris airports of Charles de Gaulle and Orly. The proliferation of low-cost airlines in recent years has broadened the choice considerably.

**BRITTIP**

Beware the low-cost carriers who use Beauvais as their 'Paris' airport. Beauvais is more than 60km/37mls north of Paris and the only way to get to Marne-la-Vallée is rather convoluted. The airport provides a shuttle bus to Porte Maillot RER and Métro station in west Paris for €13/person. You then need to take the Metro Line 1 (Direction Chateau de Vincennes) to Charles de Gaulle Etoile and change there for the RER Line A to Marne-la-Vallée.

All of the regional airports around the UK have at least one daily service to the French capital and, with the likes of EasyJet (Luton, Liverpool, Bristol, Belfast, Glasgow, Edinburgh, Newcastle), KLM (Aberdeen, Birmingham, Bristol, Edinburgh, Heathrow, Manchester, Newcastle, Southampton), flybe (Belfast, Norwich, Edinburgh, Manchester, Birmingham, Cardiff, Exeter, Southampton), Ryanair (Glasgow

Prestwick, Dublin and Shannon to Paris Beauvais), Jet2.com (Manchester and Leeds Bradford) and bmi baby (East Midlands) all offering variations on the low-cost alternative, it means your choice of flights has never been greater. Add the scheduled services of Air France (from nine UK airports) and British Airways (who fly from four) and you have almost 20 regional flight gateways to Paris.

**Paris Charles de Gaulle Airport** (CDG) is by far the bigger (and more complex) of the two Paris airports (it is the main international terminus, whereas Orly has more domestic flights). Situated some 23km/14mls to the north-east of the city centre, it actually consists of no less than three main terminals – CDG 1, CDG 2 and the smaller satellite arm CDG 3. The CDG 2 hall is subdivided into Terminals 2A, 2B, 2C, 2D, 2E and 2F, with the RER and TGV stations situated between 2C–2D and 2E–2F. At CDG 1, the RER station is located next to Terminal 3. A new Satellite 3 (S3) next to 2E and 2F is due to open in June 2008 to handle the giant Airbus 380, while a 2G terminal (purely for local traffic) is due to open in late 2008.

**BRITTIP**

It's about a 10-minute walk from the RER station to the Air France departure gates in Terminal 2F at CDG 2 and from the station to Terminals 2A and 2B.

*CDG Terminal 2F*

While both CDG 1 and CDG 2 have their own RER stations, the T3 terminal is linked to CDG 1. There is also a new (in 2007) automated shuttle train that links all three main terminals, in a straight line fashion, from CDG1 to Parking PR, CDG 3 (for RER), Parking PX and CDG 2 (for the TGV station), then back again. It covers the full 3.5km/2¼mls distance in 8 minutes and the service runs every 4 minutes.

The **VEA Navette** shuttle offers a direct service from CDG (all terminals) to the hotels of *Disneyland Resort Paris* 8.30am–7.45pm (10pm on Fridays) daily, either to the six Disney hotels and the Marne-la-Vallée bus station OR (four times a day) to the four partner hotels of the Val de France area (if no direct Val de France service is scheduled, take the Disney hotels service and change at the bus station for the free shuttle bus). It is a fairly plodding coach service, taking a good 45 minutes to reach the first stop, but it does have the great benefit of being door to door and runs at 20–40-minute intervals throughout the main part of the day. It costs €16/adult and €13/child aged 3–11 (under 3s free). To contact the VEA service, call 00 33 1 53 48 39 38 or visit **www.vea.fr/uk/index.asp**. From CDG 1, you get the VEA shuttle at Level 3, the departure level, Gate 20. Using CDG 2A, the shuttle is at Gate A11; CDG 2B and 2D at Gate D12; CDG 2C at Gate C1 and CDG 2E and 2F, at Gate 5 of the Gallery, Level 0 exit 0.09.

*Adventureland in spring*

© Disney

*The TGV*

Alternatively, you can take the **RER** service on Line B all the way in to Châtelet Les Halles (about 40 minutes), then change there for Line D to Marne-la-Vallée (another 35–40 minutes). It is a simple enough route at off-peak times but much harder to negotiate with luggage in the morning or evening rush hour. For RER info, call 00 33 1 58 76 45 91 or visit **www.ratp.fr** and click on the UK flag for the English version.

**BRITTIP**

The VEA Navette shuttles will take credit card payment, so don't worry if you don't have any euros to hand yet.

Another alternative is to take the **TGV** train from the airport to Marne-la-Vallée, which can work out slightly cheaper than the VEA shuttle (although services are fewer). There are six trains between 6.54 and 11.50am, then basically one an hour 1–6pm and another seven up to 9.54pm. At off-peak times the ticket is €14.90 one-way but it rises to €23.20 at peak times. The big benefit though, is that it takes just 12 minutes and you can walk out of the station to pick up the shuttle bus to any Disney hotel right outside. For the return journey to the airport there are ten services from 7.29am–12.22pm, then another 12 from 3.11–23.04pm. (Be warned – if you miss the Charles de Gaulle stop, you will end up in Lille or even

*Indiana Jones and the Temple of Peril*

Brussels!). You can also get taxis outside all the terminals, although it will cost around €80 one-way to any Disney hotel.

**Paris Orly Airport**, 15km/9mls to the south of the city centre, is divided more simply into Sud (South) and Ouest (West) terminals, and there is a free shuttle service operating every 5 minutes or so over the 2-minute journey between the two (from the South terminal, look for Exit K and from the West terminal, go to the departure level and Exit W). With good direct links into the city, Orly makes a reasonable alternative to Charles de Gaulle, although the **RER** route is a little more complicated (take the airport link to Antony on Line B, then go to Châtelet Les Halles and change to Line A for Marne-la-Vallée). At Orly South, take Exit G on the ground floor (platform 1 to Paris), and at Orly West, take Exit G also.

## BRITTIP

For information on both Paris airports – including terminal maps, flight times and services – visit **www.aeroportsdeparis.fr** and click on the Union Jack/British symbol in the top right-hand corner.

However, the best choice is to use the direct **VEA Navette** shuttle bus service to all the Disney hotels (8.30am–7.30pm daily, journey time 45–50 minutes) for €16/adult, €13/ child 3–11 (under 3s free). At Orly South, head for the Bus Station, platform 2 for the VEA bus and at Orly West, go to Level 0, Gate C. A taxi from Paris Orly to any of the Disney hotels will cost about €40–45.

When it comes to the airlines themselves, **Air France** (**www.airfrance.co.uk**) is, not surprisingly, the biggest carrier in terms of daily flights, using both main Paris airports. At Charles de Gaulle, they fly into CDG 2F. **British Airways** (**www.britishairways.com**) flies to CDG 1 (from Birmingham, Edinburgh and Manchester) and CDG 2B (from Heathrow), while **flybe** (the old British European; **www.flybe.com**) also uses CDG 1, as does **bmi baby** (**www.bmibaby.com**). **EasyJet** (**www.easyjet.com**) and **Jet2.com** (**www.jet2.com**) fly into CDG T3 and

*Navette shuttle buses*

**KLM** (**www.klm.com**) operates at CDG 2F. You could also try **Alitalia** (**www.alitalia.com/gb_en**), which flies from Aberdeen, Birmingham, Edinburgh, Manchester, Newcastle and Southampton to CDG 2F and **American Airlines** (**www.american airlines.co.uk**) which flies from Heathrow to CDG 2B.

There are few direct flights to **Orly** from the UK, although Air France flies there from London City Airport and budget airline **Thomsonfly** (**www.thomsonfly.com**) fly daily from Coventry. **EasyJet** also uses it as a base, but only for operations elsewhere in Europe, not the UK.

## Choosing a tour operator

While it is perfectly possible – and sometimes cheaper – to book a DIY holiday by putting together your own hotel and travel arrangements, the tour operators to *Disneyland Resort Paris* have developed an extremely sophisticated, not to mention exceptionally good value, raft of packages that make booking with them (especially if you book direct) highly worthwhile. Add in the number of internet travel companies like **ebookers.com** and **lastminute.com**, and there is a bewildering variety on offer for you to choose from.

The first thing to do is to shop around and get an idea of the prices for the different types of package. Most tour operators in this market are the big,

*Disney's Hotel Cheyenne*

well-known brands, who all feature some of the keenest pricing thanks to their ability to deal in bulk (notably Leger Holidays, Cresta and Thomas Cook), but several out-and-out Paris specialists are worth considering.

When it comes to simple price comparisons, it is more the method of travel that makes the main difference, hence a coach-based trip is usually the cheapest on offer, followed by Eurotunnel or ferry self-drive, then Eurostar and finally flying. But there are often special deals to be found – particularly at off-peak times – and it definitely pays to keep your wits about you when looking for a bargain. So you need to know what the general going rate is before you plunge in!

Look for the *Kids Go Free* season (usually January–March) when under 12s travel, stay and play for free

*Disney Village*

*Leger Holidays luxury coach*

(return travel, hotel accommodation with continental breakfast and park tickets); or the more limited season for *Kids Under 7 Free*, when children aged 4–6 benefit from free accommodation and park tickets (in 2008, this extended until 5 January and 20 March–27 April), plus periodic extra days for free.

Here is a look at the six main national tour operators on the Disneyland beat. With all of them, Disney accommodation usually comes with theme park passes for the full length of your visit.

**Leger Holidays:** The biggest coach-tour operator to *Disneyland Resort Paris*, and voted by Disney as the best UK group operator in 2006, Leger have a countrywide network of routes, with more than 400 joining points in England and Wales, taking customers to Dover and crossing the Channel for the 4-hour drive to the resort (with one refreshment stop). They operate a mixture of their own branded coaches plus those of well-known companies from all over the country. All are modern and comfortable, with toilets and drinks facility and they reduce travel hassles to the minimum, which goes down well with families.

The 3-day coach package offers a 2-Day Park Hopper ticket; the 4-day package features two full days in the parks, with departure after breakfast on the fourth day and the 5-day trip offers two park days and a full-day Paris tour on the fourth day, or the option to stay in the parks (extra day's park admission not always included). Leger are the only coach company offering Disney rooms during Christmas week, with their 5-day coach departures having a 3-Day Park Hopper ticket. Arrival time aims to be between 8 and 10pm on the first evening. The return journey usually leaves after breakfast on the last day (early evening on 3-day packages).

Leger produced their largest programme to date for 2008 and are the only UK tour operator to offer all four modes of transport, with increased departures of coach, self-drive, Eurostar and air packages, and a huge choice for all budgets. Included is a range of early booking offers – from room discounts, hotel upgrades, single parent discounts and grandparent savings – to enhance their value-for-money family prices. They also package it extremely well, using their most popular hotel, the 3-star Explorers Hotel (see page 94), which is wonderfully family-friendly and is the only hotel to accommodate six to a room. The Explorers is Leger's base price accommodation and comes in slightly cheaper than Disney's most budget-orientated offering, the *Hotel Santa Fe*, which is 2-star. They have the option to upgrade to *Disney's Hotel Cheyenne, Sequoia Lodge* or *Newport Bay Club*. The Kids Go Free season (for 3- to 11-year-olds, from January–March) is available with all four transport options (based on one adult to one

*Disney's Hotel Santa Fe*

child). The self-drive alternative is to *Disney's Davy Crockett Ranch*, which offers self-catering accommodation. Their brochures also highlight special events like Bonfire Night, Halloween and Christmas extremely well.

Leger's innovative flight programme features scheduled and low-cost airlines from 20 UK airports, including Birmingham, Manchester, Newcastle, Southampton, Aberdeen and Liverpool, with new departures from Glasgow, Belfast and Cardiff for nationwide coverage. Transfers are provided with all flights to Paris Charles de Gaulle Airport, but not from Beauvais (although a taxi can be arranged).

Summer is easily their busiest period and the 5-day package has caught on really well since the opening of the *Walt Disney Studios Park*. The Explorers Hotel always proves popular but Leger have also added the 4-star Holiday Inn and Vienna International Dream Castle hotels in recent brochures as both offer large family rooms and are located just 8 minutes (by the free shuttle) from the parks. These two reflect a demand for quality hotels that are still well priced compared to Disney's 3-star range, with higher standards of service and the bonus of swimming pools.

*Enjoying the pool at the Dreamcastle Hotel*

*Dreamcastle Hotel*

Leger have a year-round programme to Disney. The majority use P&O Ferries from Dover but some dates are served via Eurotunnel. We describe a typical Leger 5-day break in Chapter 2 (see page 21), which shows how hard it is to fit everything in! Call Leger Holidays on 0845 4080781 or visit **www.get2magic.co.uk**.

**Transport:** Coach via P&O Ferries or Eurotunnel; Eurostar; self-drive with P&O Ferries or Eurotunnel; flights (Air France, BA and various low-cost carriers).

**Cresta Holidays:** One of the biggest of the mainstream operators who offer the full range of options, Cresta have frequently been voted the Top Short Break Specialist by the UK travel trade, so they have a good idea of what they're about. They also aim to be one of the most flexible outfits in the business, hence they can combine just about any aspect of the resort, hotels and travel arrangements to suit your requirements. Their brochures are also among the clearest and most readable on offer.

Cresta features the full range of Disney accommodation, six Disney Selected or Associated Hotels and six off-site hotels, all of which offer 'free night' bonuses, and many of which are chosen for their proximity to the RER line that takes you directly to the station at Disneyland Resort Paris. They also have a few great little extras, like a Planet Hollywood privilege card, entitling you to a 20% discount from your total bill and a special voucher offering an extra 10% discount at the La Vallee outlet shopping village.

*The pool at the Explorers Hotel*

The smart Explorers Hotel (see page 87) is heavily featured in Cresta's 2008 programme and their lead-in price for the excellent value hotel (based on a 2-night stay) is an eye-catching £187 per person, inclusive of breakfast and Theme Park tickets. Two great kids offers are available – the Kids Go Free deals from January–March and the Disneyland Resort Paris 15th Anniversary Kids Under-7 Stay & Play Free. Other extras include free autograph books for the kids and free tickets to the Sea Life centre at certain times. Contact Cresta on 0871 664 7812 or **www.crestaholidays.co.uk/disney**.

**Transport:** Eurostar; flights (Air France, British Airways, flybe, bmi baby and easyJet).

**Thomson:** A member of the TUI travel group (that also includes travel agent Thomson Retail, formerly Lunn Poly), this company is well organised and extremely knowledgeable, with a keen reservations team. There are some great special offers (notably 3 nights for 2, 4 for 3 and 5 for 4, all including

breakfast and an extra day to explore both Disney parks), free child places at selected times of the year and early booking offers and discounts, including a free extra day in the parks when you buy a 3- or 4-Day Park Hopper ticket with selected Near The Magic hotels. They stress that with the increasing popularity of the resort, early bookers will get the best deals and advise to book early for school holidays. They offer meal vouchers as an optional extra, which helps with your pre-holiday budgeting and you can pre-book character meals and shows, which is extremely handy.

**BRITTIP**

The main Disney tour operators advise: 1 – Book early (essential for high season); 2 – Use Disney's FastPass system in the theme parks (see page 109); 3 – Plan your day with the aid of park maps (and this book!), which give you all the show times, parades, etc; 4 – Book your meals on arrival.

An immensely readable brochure contains all the Disney hotels and the full range of travel options, including scheduled flights (from seven airports), low-cost carriers (from 14 regional airports), Eurostar, fly-drive (with Europcar car hire) and self-drive options. For those who prefer to arrange their own travel, Thomson offer accommodation only, with Disney park tickets included. Disney's Half-Board Meal Plans are also

*Disneyland Park entrance*

© Disney

available at £14/adult and £8/child (£17 and £9 for Half Board Plus at *Disney's Hotel New York, Newport Bay Club* and *Sequoia Lodge*).

A selection of Near the Magic hotels are also available on a self-drive basis offering free child places year-round and free night offers at certain times of the year. These are situated either 5–20 minutes' drive from the Disney parks or close to the RER line into Marne-la-Vallée. Call Thomson direct on 0870 050 1505 or visit **www.thomson. co.uk** (again, one of the better websites, with good info).

**Transport:** Eurostar; flights (Thomsonfly, bmi, Air France, British Airways, bmi baby, EasyJet, Ryanair, Jet2 and flybe); self-drive via Eurotunnel, P&O Ferries and SeaFrance.

**Thomas Cook:** This famous name in the travel agency business operate an extremely well-run *Disneyland Resort Paris* programme. From the clarity of their brochure to the quality of their ticketing material – which includes a 36-page information booklet – Thomas Cook live up to their reputation as one of the originators and innovators in the tour operating business. Their free kids' pack – for all children aged 3–11 (but not on accommodation-only bookings) – is one of the best we've seen, with a J-bag containing a disposable camera, ripper wallet, activity book, crayons, a pen and an autograph book.

*The pool at Disney's Hotel New York*

© Disney

© Disney

*Disney's Newport Bay Club*

Their booking staff are extremely switched on when it comes to advising guests with disabilities. Again, you can pre-buy meal vouchers to use in the hotels, parks and *Disney Village*, and book character meals in advance (especially during peak periods), which can help with your budgeting. They also offer free nights at Disney resorts periodically, some Kids Go Free deals and a free kids' character breakfast and Buffalo Bill's show ticket with every adult booking (for under 12s). Plus there are exclusive offers such as free Sea Life Centre tickets and Earlybird Money Savers.

Thomas Cook feature the full range of Disney hotels and the usual off-site options (these vary little between operators). Aimed at self-drive customers (or fly-drives, with Avis car hire), the off-site hotels are near RER stations. There are also some 'free night' deals to be had at various times. On P&O Ferries, kids eat free with a paying adult in the International Food Court.

The flight options are extremely well detailed, from no less than 17 UK airports (although Aberdeen and Belfast flights go via either Gatwick, Heathrow or East Midlands). For more info, call Thomas Cook on 0870 750 5711 or visit **www.thomascook.com**.

**Transport:** Eurostar; flights (Air France, British Airways, EasyJet, bmi baby); self-drive via Eurotunnel, P&O Ferries.

© Disney

*Newmarket do special Halloween packages*

**Newmarket:** A specialist tour operator that you won't find in any travel agency. You will find their Magical Breaks packages in many local and national newspapers, plus a new range of direct-sell holidays. From Aberdeen to Plymouth, you are likely to see their newspaper-endorsed reader offers and usually at eye-catching prices (even for Eurostar packages). They offer mainly off-site hotels (hence the budget-orientated operation) with good, reliable coach services (most of which use P&O Ferries from Dover).

Their Paris expertise dates back to the opening of *Euro Disney*, hence they have a knowledgeable staff (including their own in-resort reps), and also do big business with special interest groups and schools' Study Experiences (for students of information and communications technology, plus other curriculum-driven subjects). With their coach tours (the vast majority), they have some 500 pick-up points all over the country and the coach is your mode of transport throughout the trip at the off-site hotels, which tend to be in the greater Paris area (usually of the Campanile, Ibis, Novotel standard – a basic but comfortable 2- and 3-star). The only drawback is you're restricted to the coach's one trip to and from the hotel (you have to make your own way back if you want to return from the parks earlier).

All are on a bed and breakfast (continental) basis, and they feature either 3- or 4-day trips. On coach tours, the 3-day trips feature two 1-Day Passports for the theme parks (you arrive mid-evening on the first day, have one full day there, then return early afternoon on the third day), while the 4-day version has a 3-Day Passport included (as you have two full days for the theme parks, plus part of the final day before an afternoon return; Scottish departures leave earlier on the final day).

They also offer a good range of Disney breaks for specific events such as New Year, Bonfire Night and Halloween.

Going by Eurostar, Newmarket offer 3- and 4-day trips, arriving in the early afternoon on day one and

*Chinese New Year at Disney Village*

© Disney

departing in the evening on day three or four. They also now sell a selection of similar breaks in conjunction with the low-cost airlines from a wide range of regional airports, with accommodation provided at the Kyriad Hotel at *Disneyland Resort Paris*. For more information, call 0845 226 7766 or see **www.newmarket holidays.co.uk**.

**Transport:** Coach via P&O Ferries or Eurotunnel; Eurostar; flights (various low-cost carriers from range of regional airports).

**Harry Shaw:** Another popular and busy Midlands coach-tour specialist, this company's speciality is 2- and 3-night trips, with either one or two full days in the theme parks while you are there. They feature primarily Disney accommodation at the *Santa Fe, Cheyenne, Newport Bay* and *Sequoia Lodge* hotels, inclusive of park tickets and breakfast. The 2-day tour picks up during the morning at 22 points in the Midlands (variously from Tamworth to Newport Pagnell) and three in the South East, arriving in *Disneyland Resort Paris* in the evening. You then have one full day in the parks before returning in the afternoon of the third day after more park time (arriving back in the

*Disney's Hotel Cheyenne*

Midlands in the early hours). The 3-night option adds a second full day in the parks before returning on the morning of the fourth day. For more details, call 024 7645 5544 or visit **www.harryshaw.co.uk**.

**Transport:** Coach via P&O Ferries or Eurotunnel.

There are other regional companies who all feature *Disneyland Resort Paris*, including: Midlands specialists **Travelsphere** (0870 240 2426, **www.travelsphere.co.uk**), **Applebys** of Lincolnshire (01507 357900, **www.applebystravel.co.uk**); East Anglia operator **Galloway Travel** (01449 618077, **www.galloway-travel.co.uk**); Yorkshire's **Gold Crest Holidays** (0870

*Midsummer event at Davy Crockett's Ranch*

## Top 10 romantic options for Disneyland Resort Paris

Although it's well known as a family destination, *Disneyland Resort Paris* is also popular for honeymoons, anniversaries and other special 'couples only' celebrations. Here is our guide to the best things to do when it is just the two of you, so that you can really make the most of your visit.

1 Stay in one of the Tinker Bell suites at the *Disneyland Hotel*.

2 Or stay in the Roosevelt Suite at *Disney's Hotel New York*.

3 Failing either of those, *Disney's Newport Bay Club* offers a genuinely lovely Honeymoon Suite.

4 Take one of Cityrama's Illuminations evening tours of Paris.

5 Have dinner at the California Grill at the *Disneyland Hotel*.

6 Take an evening stroll around Lake Disney and stop for a drink at the Redwood Bar at *Disney's Sequoia Lodge*.

7 Have lunch at the wonderful Blue Lagoon restaurant inside the Pirates of the Caribbean ride at the *Disneyland Park*.

8 Enjoy a drink in the Fantasia Bar at the *Disneyland Hotel*, listening to the relaxing sounds of their pianist.

9 Try the dinner buffet al fresco at the Vienna International Dream Castle Hotel.

10 In winter, stop at *Disney's Hotel New York* to watch the ice-skating and grab a mug of hot cocoa from the nearby drinks stall.

70000 007, **www.gold-crest.com**); Leeds Co-op agency **Sundeal** (0800 953 0431, **www.sundeal.co.uk**); York-based **Superbreak** (0871 221 3344, **www.superbreak.com**); Middlesbrough-based **Siesta International Holidays** (0845 217 2443, **www.siesta holidays.co.uk**) and Gloucestershire's **Travelscope** (0870 380 3333, **www.travelscope.co.uk**).

Finally, to use some of the best online search engines (that seek out deals and special offers from a wide range of tour operators) for flights or holidays, try any of the following: **www.lastminute.com, www.expedia.co.uk, www.travelocity.co.uk, www.opodo.co.uk, www.ebookers.com**.

## Book direct

Of course, you can always book directly with Disney if you have an idea of what you want to do. The resort offers a full range of packages with all the usual methods of transport and they even feature a good range of off-site accommodation, with the nine

nearby hotels in Val D'Europe and Val de France. Disney's brochure is worth getting just for all the lavish photography and large-scale maps, and they highlight all the extras, free nights and Kids Go Free deals. The pricing system and dizzying array of supplements for the different forms

*At the top of Notre Dame*

*Try to fit in a tour of the* **grands boulevards** *of Paris*

of transport can take some deciphering, but basically every possible permutation is open to you.

The brochure is designed so that you begin by choosing your

*Take a promenade by Lake Disney*

© Disney

*accommodation* (inclusive of local taxes, breakfast and park tickets in most cases); then *how long* you want to stay (from 1–5 nights, with discounted extra nights possible); decide your mode of *transport* (from Eurostar, flights or self-drive using P&O Ferries or Eurotunnel); whether to opt for the *Half Board Meal Plan* if you wish (which adds a lunch or dinner a day for the duration of your stay, see also page 77) and finally select any *additional features* (such as character meals, shows, excursions or even birthday celebrations). You can even pre-book pirate and princess costume packs for your kids (at £31 and £38 respectively) with a stay at any of Disney's hotels! For details, call their hotline on 08705 030303 or visit **www.disneylandparis.co.uk**.

**Transport:** Eurostar; flights (Air France, British Airways, bmi baby, EasyJet, Ryanair, Thomsonfly, Jet 2 and flybe); self-drive via Eurotunnel or P&O Ferries.

But wait, before you can make a fully informed choice, you need to have a good idea of the array of accommodation that awaits you, both in the form of the Disney resorts themselves and the usually cheaper alternatives for staying off-site. So, read on and we will reveal all about how to choose your hotel…

**W**hen it comes to where to stay in and around *Disneyland Resort Paris,* you will not be surprised to know that there is a bewildering variety. Disney alone has six very different and entertaining hotels on site, while *Disney's Davy Crockett Ranch,* about a 15-minute drive away, offers an alternative for those with a car. There are another seven hotels 'Near the Magic', which benefit from being close to the resort, and several dozen more within a 15- to 25-minute drive.

The key is the combination of location and price. All the Disney resorts offer the huge convenience of being just minutes from the essential theme park Magic, but their hotels do tend to be on the expensive side. If you are staying on-site, the chances are you won't need any other form of transport. But a car is not always necessary if you stay off-site, as the easy-to-use RER rail line makes staying in somewhere like Bussy-St-Georges, Noisiel or even Bercy, towards the centre of Paris, a perfectly viable proposition.

The section on the various tour operators in the previous chapter shows the great range of packages on offer. Many operators feature off-site hotels, as the demand for the Disney hotels is high and they are at virtually 100% capacity in peak periods like summer and Christmas. The area along the RER corridor makes a handy base for tackling Disney (and Paris, for that matter), and the general standard of hotels is sound if unspectacular. Their star-rating system is pretty accurate and virtually every hotel works on a bed and breakfast basis (a continental breakfast with cereal, pastries, cold meats, cheese and tea/coffee – the Holiday Inn at *Disneyland Resort Paris* is a rarity in that it charges extra for breakfast). It is advisable to stay off-site during the summer when Disney's prices are at their highest, while the price difference between on- and off-site properties is less in the winter months.

**BRITTIP**

The quoted price rates of hotels in France are always per room and not per person.

*Characters at Disney's Hotel Santa Fe*

© Disney

Staying **off-site** can actually provide you with more flexibility if you want to use the hotel just as a base and not part of the holiday itself (the Disney hotels play an important role in the holiday experience). You'll have more incentive to get out and about if you stay off-site and it's convenient for seeing more of Paris, while many hotels offer 'extra night free' deals.

You should certainly check in advance, however, whether or not you'll need a car. If you are not close to an RER station – or the hotel does not have a shuttle service to the nearest station – you will struggle without your own transport. However, many of the tour operators (notably Thomson, see page 67) now offer travel to the resort by Eurostar, with off-site hotels near RER stations.

### BRIT TIP

As of January 2008, France is officially a **No Smoking** zone. All public places have been declared smoke-free, which means all restaurants, bars, museums, offices and shops – and the theme parks – are off limits to smokers. However, hotel rooms are excluded from this law, so you still need to specify if you want a non-smoking room.

*Disneyland Hotel*

© Disney

© Disney

*Disney's Newport Bay Club*

## Disney hotels

When it comes to getting the maximum out of your trip, you can't beat the full and all-encompassing experience of staying **on-site** (see maps on pages 81 and 92). The majority of Brits choose this option; yet, curiously, only a small percentage of other nationalities do, so Disney hotels are often mainly occupied by British guests. Just the simple fact of being able to walk into the parks in the morning, through *Disney Village*, is one of the great pleasures of staying here. Even from *Disney's Hotel Santa Fe*, which is the furthest away of the six on-site resorts, it is no more than a 20-minute stroll and, on a sunny morning, it is a true delight. The old estate agent adage of 'location, location, location' is just as true here!

There are also other significant benefits to staying *chez* Mickey for the duration of your visit, most notably the **Extra Magic Hour** perk. This allows Dream Annual Passport holders, guests staying in a Disney hotel and Hotel L'Élysée Val d'Europe to enjoy specific attractions at the *Disneyland Park* on certain dates, 2 hours before park opening or (less often) 2 hours after park closing (depending on the day). On Extra Magic mornings, follow the signs for 'Extra Magic Hour' or 'Disney Hotel Guests' to bypass the regular queue. On Extra Magic evenings, collect a special wristband (from 5pm onward) under the Main Street Station. You

*Room at Disney's Hotel New York*

will be required to show your Hotel EasyPass or Dream Annual Passport to gain early entry or receive an evening wristband.

Another important perk, especially for families, is the excellent **character interaction** you get at all six hotels in the morning and evening. At least one character will always be 'on parade' in the hotel foyer and kids are virtually guaranteed to get their autograph books off to a flying start in this way. (Intriguingly, both the Explorers Hotel and the Dream Castle in nearby Val de France have developed their own popular characters, although they call them 'mascots', for guest interaction). Disney's **service and hospitality** adds significantly to everyone's enjoyment, while all resort guests get their own **Identification Card** that can be used as a charge card in both parks and at *Disney Village* (apart from the Rainforest Café, Planet Hollywood, McDonald's and the Gaumont Cinema complex).

Resort guests also benefit from **free parking** at the hotels, theme parks and *Disney Village*; the **free shuttle bus service**; **free entry to Hurricanes disco** in *Disney Village* and a whole range of **recreational activities**, from swimming and tennis to outdoor playgrounds, video games and even ice-skating (outside *Disney's Hotel New York*, but open to all Disney hotel guests for a small fee). There is a **shopping service** for hotel guests, whereby you can have anything you

buy in one of the theme parks delivered to the Disney shop in your hotel, for collection from 8pm that day. Each hotel also organises regular **children's activities** and all have Disney TV and a computer games console in their play area.

**BRIT TIP**

The character dining options can be booked through your hotel concierge in the foyer (see Brit Tip on page 80), and it is advisable to do this as soon as you check in.

Finally, and highly importantly for those with children, there is the option to have a **character breakfast** at one of three locations – the Inventions restaurant for guests at the *Disneyland Hotel* or either Café Mickey or The Steakhouse in *Disney Village* (there is, as you would expect, an additional charge for this). These feature an American buffet breakfast with breads, pastries, scrambled eggs, ham, sausages, cereals, fruit juices and hot drinks, and are priced at €16/adult and €12/child (3–11) for Disney hotel guests (it counts as a supplement against the normal hotel breakfast). They are also available for non-Disney hotel guests, but the prices are €25 and €17.

The two outdoor **tennis courts** at *Disney's Hotel New York* are available to all Disney hotel guests (there is a small fee for balls and racket hire), on production of your Disney resort ID card.

*City Bar at Disney's Hotel New York*

An additional (non-character) feature at peak times for guests at *Disney's Newport Bay Club, Disney's Sequoia Lodge, Disney's Hotel Cheyenne* and *Disney's Hotel Santa Fe* is the **Good Morning Fantasyland** breakfast, whereby hotel guests can opt to enter the *Disneyland Park* an hour early and board the Disneyland Railroad train (or just walk) to Fantasyland, where a basic continental buffet breakfast is served in one of the restaurants (usually Au Chalet de la Marionette).

### BRITTIP

Although there is no extra charge for the Good Morning Fantasyland breakfast, you need to specify whether you would like to do it when you book your package, as it is likely to be fully subscribed when you check in at the hotel.

If you arrive as early as possible, you will then be in pole position to ride the likes of Dumbo and Peter Pan or La Carrousel, up to 30 minutes before regular park opening, with little or no wait. This is especially useful on non-Extra Magic Hour mornings.

In nearly all cases, when booking a Disney hotel or one of Disney's partner hotels, you are obliged to accept a Park Hopper Ticket for the duration of your stay as part of the package (or a 3-Day ticket if you opt for the minimum 2-night/3-day package), which obviously suits most people as it keeps you up and running in the theme parks from first minute to last. However, it may not be suitable if you plan on doing some non-Disney sightseeing as well, so you need to weigh up whether an off-site hotel might be the better option. The main exception to the Disney hotel rule is if you are an Annual Passport holder, in which case you can book just bed and breakfast packages through the central reservations office on 00 33 1 60 30 60 69 from the UK.

Most **room sizes** will accommodate a family of four comfortably, but you are limited for choice with five or more (although some rooms can accommodate a cot if required). Basically, you have only three choices in this instance: *Disney's Davy Crockett Ranch*, where the cabins can house up to six people (but you must have your own transport); two connecting rooms in one of the six hotels; or one of the 15 family rooms, which can accommodate up to six at *Disney's Newport Bay Club*, although these rooms are more expensive and are at a premium, so you would need to book early. (Looking outside the resort, the Pierre & Vacances Residence Val d'Europe is an ultra-smart apartment block in the town which can accommodate up to seven, while the Explorers Hotel can take family groups of up to ten.) Rooms for guests with disabilities are available in all six hotels, but not *Disney's Davy Crockett Ranch*.

*Café Fantasia in the Disneyland Hotel*

## Disney's dining bonus

One new feature available for Disney's on-site resort guests (except at *Disneyland Hotel*) is the **Half Board Meal Plan** – pre-paid meal vouchers, which can be used in several Disney restaurants for a saving of up to 15% off menu prices. You must purchase the vouchers prior to arrival for all members of your party and for the duration of your stay. Each adult voucher is valid for a starter, main course and dessert *or* All-You-Can-Eat Buffet, plus one soft drink or mineral water. Children's vouchers are valid for a main course and dessert *or* All-you-Can-Eat Buffet, plus one soft drink. The **Half Board Standard** meal plan (for guests at *Disney's Hotel Santa Fe, Hotel Cheyenne* and *Davy Crockett Ranch*) includes seven resort restaurants and the restaurants at those three hotels at €19/adult per night and €9/child per night; **Half Board Plus** (at *Disney's Hotel New York, Sequoia Lodge* and *Newport Bay Club*) includes 14 resort restaurants and the restaurants at those three hotels (€24 and €10). Two Half Board Plus vouchers can be combined for the Grand Princess character lunch or dinner at Auberge de Cendrillon in the *Disneyland Park*. You can also upgrade a Standard voucher to **Plus** or **Gourmet** on any night during your stay if you would like to try exclusive dining not included in the plan (specific restaurants only), simply by exchanging your voucher for its face value when you dine. You can book vouchers up to 3 months in advance on 08705 03 03 03. NB: Half Board Meal vouchers do not guarantee a table reservation and restaurant reservations must still be made separately. See your Hotel Concierge desk on arrival or call the Dining Reservation Service (in France) on 01 60 30 40 50.

All rooms feature a telephone, international TV channels and radio, and a shower/bath. *Disney's Hotel Cheyenne, Disney's Hotel Santa Fe* and *Disney's Davy Crockett Ranch* do NOT have air-conditioning (although the former two have ceiling fans), while only the *Disneyland Hotel* and *Disney's Hotel New York* have hairdryers fitted as standard in the bathrooms (the others have hairdryers available on request). The *Disneyland Hotel, Disney's Hotel New York* and *Disney's Newport Bay Club* all have mini-bars, as does *Disney's Sequoia Lodge* in its Montana rooms only, while the former trio also have room safes. All offer non-smoking rooms and (except *Disney's Davy Crockett Ranch*) a left-luggage service.

When checking in, you will be given your park tickets, any vouchers for various options you might have booked (for meals or Buffalo Bill's Wild West Show), park maps, an information guide to the hotel (these are well written and highly collectable), a *Disney Village* programme and your Resort ID card, while children also get a name badge to wear (if they wish!).

### BRITTIP

If you arrive at the hotel between noon and 2pm, have lunch there before heading off to the theme parks; you will get served much quicker.

Each resort hotel should be able to supply a cot on request and all feature **children's menus** in their main restaurants. **Room service** is available at the *Disneyland Hotel, Disney's Hotel New York* and the Admiral's Floor of *Disney's Newport Bay Club*. There is no official in-house **babysitting** service for any of the hotels, although there is a private firm who can arrange in-room babysitting for you via the front desk.

*Babysitting is available at Disneyland hotels*

© Disney

In all cases, check-in time is 3pm (although rooms are occasionally available from 1pm. Take advantage of the left-luggage provision and you can still head straight for the theme parks), while check-out is 11am.

### 🇬🇧 BRITTIP

If you have booked Eurostar's Disney Express service (see page 60), you simply leave your bags, cases, etc. in the left-luggage office at your hotel when you check out, and they will be transferred for you to collect at the Disney Express office at the Marne-la-Vallée station. Whether or not you've booked, Disney Express labels ARE available for your return journey for a few extra euros from the hotel check-in.

The pros of staying on-site are substantial, but what of the cons? Well, the price difference is the obvious issue to highlight here. You can save a good 20–30% by opting for one of the smaller hotels nearby, and the six official nearby hotels (four in the **Val de France** area) all represent significant savings while offering much of the convenience, facilities and service. In fact, we rate the Explorers Hotel and the Holiday Inn Disneyland Paris as possibly the best all-round value of all.

Breakfast at the Disney resorts can also be something of a bunfight at peak periods. You are allocated a set time-slot (that may not be terribly convenient in the first place) but you may still find queues just to get in, even at more upmarket hotels like *Sequoia Lodge* and *Newport Bay Club*. If you're looking to be in the parks by 9am, you may struggle to get through breakfast in time, unless you have the 7.30am time-slot (not everyone's idea of a holiday rise-and-shine!). The off-site hotels are noticeably less frenetic (with the possible exception of the busy Explorers Hotel), and often provide a welcome break from the hustle and bustle in early evening.

Those in the Val de France area benefit from a beautiful countryside location, with a large lake that backs on to the four hotels, which provides a pleasant way to unwind after a day at the parks. However, the (free) shuttle bus service can be a bit of a trial at peak times (half an hour before park opening and at park closing). It calls at all four hotels in turn, which means either an uncomfortable 10–15-minute ride or, occasionally, having to wait for another bus if the first one is full. The Dream Castle in particular suffers from this as it is the last pick-up point on the four-hotel circuit.

Having underlined the price differential, Disney's six hotels (amounting to 5,200 rooms, plus the 535 cabins and 60 caravan sites of *Disney's Davy Crockett Ranch*) do offer a range of prices to suit most pockets, from the more budget-priced *Disney's Hotel Santa Fe* to the opulent 4-star *Disneyland Hotel*.

We at the *Brit Guide* have our own ratings system for the hotels, too, allocating €s in the following price ranges:

| | | |
|---|---|---|
| €€€€€ | = | More than €150/night |
| €€€€ | = | €100–150/night |
| €€€ | = | €75–100/night |
| €€ | = | €50–75/night |
| € | = | Less than €50/night |

*Disney's Sequoia Lodge*

© Disney

Disneyland Hotel

We also award CCCs out of five for the extra facilities at each property. Hence you can be sure a CCCCC hotel should have all the creature comforts you can think of, including a swimming pool and a choice of restaurants, while a CC would be of the more basic, motel-type. Here are Disney's magnificent seven in detail.

# Disneyland Hotel

The resort's signature hotel, right at the entrance to the *Disneyland Park* (and otherwise known as the Pink Palace), is a massive mock-Victorian edifice featuring the most comfortable and spacious rooms, sumptuous decor and one of the best restaurants in the whole area. The Disney theming is at its most discreet here (you have to look closely at the wallpaper to realise the built-in Mickey subtlety) and there is some elegant furniture sprinkled around (witness the four classic grandfather clocks along one corridor that display the times at each of the Disney resorts around the world – they also play Disney tunes on the hour and half-hour!). Standard rooms feature either a king-size bed and a fold-out or two doubles, plus a highly elaborate TV/video cabinet with mini-bar, and all have the high ceilings reminiscent of Victorian buildings.

The top two floors feature the exclusive **Castle Club**, with a private lift (straight to the theme park!) and reception desk, a lounge bar for breakfast, afternoon tea and light refreshments, plus a fabulous view out over the *Disneyland Park*. There are spacious Junior Suites (58sq m/624sq ft as opposed to the 34sq m/366sq ft of standard rooms), plus four Tinker Bell Suites (69sq m/743sq ft) with a lounge and a separate walk-in shower as well as a bath. In addition there are three one-off suites of truly exceptional order – Walt's Apartment, the (Cinderella) Vice-Presidential Suite and the (Sleeping Beauty) Presidential Suite.

From the three-storey lobby right through to the Celestia Spa, the period theming is impressive but not overwhelming. There is a **Galerie Mickey** selling souvenirs and travel essentials, the main bar area **Café Fantasia** (with inventive decor geared to the film of the same name) as well as two restaurants. **Inventions** is themed on the great technical creations of the 20th century and offers an excellent dinner buffet, in addition to the character breakfasts. The **California Grill** is the hotel's fine-dining option and the quality on offer is superb, with a conservatory-style motif and an open kitchen at one end. At the other end, a lounge affords more great views of the theme park.

The indoor pool area is equally smart, with a medium-sized pool, Jacuzzi, gym and massage treatment rooms,

Disneyland Hotel

## BRITTIP

Each Disney hotel has a concierge desk in the foyer specially for booking meals and shows in any of the hotels, parks or *Disney Village*. Try to plan day by day and visit the desk first thing in the morning to make your bookings – especially at peak times. If you can book for your whole stay straight away, you will be one step ahead of the masses.

as well as a sauna, steam room and solarium. The inevitable video games room is fully geared up for kids of the requisite age, while the Club Minnie activity centre includes TV, video and computer games. The only thing it doesn't have is an outdoor play area, but then the *Disneyland Park* is right on the doorstep! However, there is a supplement for a standard room with a park view. The Celestia Spa offers a fabulous array of spa, massage and beauty treatments, including couples treatments (at €190 for two hours) and adds the ultimate relaxation after the parks! Call 01 60 45 66 05 to book, or 6605 from a Disney hotel phone. In all, there are 496 rooms, plus 18 suites and it really is the pinnacle of the on-site accommodation. **Official rating \*\*\*\*; our rating** €€€€€, CCCCC.

*Disney's Hotel New York*

# Disney's Hotel New York

Welcome to the Big Apple! While this is a Disney hotel it is a wonderfully themed hotel in its own right, with an art deco, 1930s' view of New York that extends from the massive 'tower block' façade to individual touches in the rooms and the background jazz throughout the lobby and bar area. There is little overt Mickey-ness about it, but lots of grand style and clever imagery, with the bonus in some rooms of a fabulous view over Lake Disney. It also has, we reckon, the most amazing suite of them all, the two-storey Presidential Suite, with floor-to-ceiling windows, wonderful furniture, a living room complete with piano and a dining room for up to ten guests. The upstairs double bedroom has a separate lounge and Jacuzzi.

## BRITTIP

If you find *Disney Village* a touch too frenetic in the evening, head for the City Bar at *Disney's Hotel New York*, which offers the perfect surroundings for a relaxing and enjoyable drink or two.

Most standard rooms (31sq m/334sq ft), which have some lovely rosewood cabinets, sleep four comfortably, while others offer just one king-size bed. The Resort Suites (56sq m/603sq ft, one on each corner of each floor) have masses of space for a family of four, with a separate bedroom and living room. There is a beautiful Honeymoon Suite (62sq m/667sq ft) as well. With 565 rooms in all (including 27 spacious suites), the hotel features two restaurants (the intimate, formal atmosphere of the **Manhattan Restaurant** and the more relaxed, cosmopolitan style of the **Parkside Diner**), a delightfully elegant bar, a hair salon (the only one on-site), boutique and gift shop, two outdoor tennis courts (small fee for racket and ball hire) and an ice-skating rink (an eye-catching facility in winter).

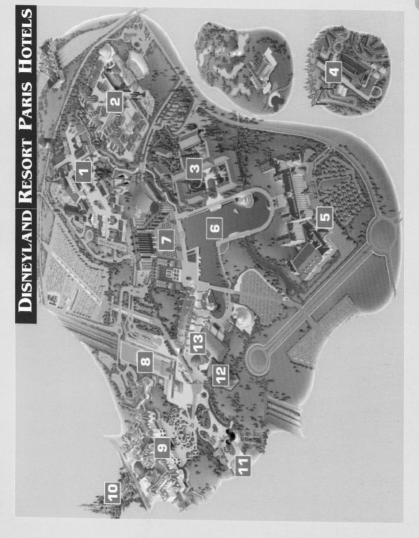

## Disneyland Resort Paris Hotels

1 Disney's Hotel Cheyenne
2 Disney's Hotel Santa Fe
3 Disney's Sequoia Lodge
4 Disney's Davy Crockett Ranch
5 Disney's Newport Bay Club
6 Lake Disney
7 Disney's Hotel New York
8 RER/TGV/bus station
9 Disneyland Hotel
10 Disneyland Park
11 Walt Disney Studios Park
12 Vinci Car Park
13 Disney Village

**BRITTIP**

*Disney's Hotel New York* is a product of American architect Michael Graves, who also designed the Swan and Dolphin Hotels in *Walt Disney World Resort in Florida*. So, if you enjoy the fun-style architecture of those two, *Disney's Hotel New York* is bound to appeal to you too.

For kids, there is the indoor **Children's Corner**, with themed activities at different times of the day, and the ubiquitous video games room. The one drawback here is that the hotel is also a big convention facility, and it can draw a sizeable business/conference crowd at times.

A bonus with *Disney's Hotel New York* is the swimming pool complex, which is among the best of the on-site hotels. The extremely large pool has both an indoor and outdoor aspect, while there is also a Jacuzzi, sauna, steam room and a good-sized gymnasium, plus a pleasant outdoor terrace. After the *Disneyland Hotel*, it is also the closest to the theme parks, situated at the opposite end of *Disney Village*, and is barely a 10-minute stroll from the gates of the *Disneyland Park*, slightly less for the *Walt Disney Studios Park*.

While it may be a touch too formal for some tastes (mainly due to the conference aspect), *Disney's Hotel New Yor*k does have an exciting feel, especially for young adults and

teenagers, and is in a perfect situation looking over Lake Disney but still within an easy stroll of *Disney Village*. **Official rating ****; our rating** €€€€, **CCCCC.**

## Disney's Newport Bay Club

Keeping with the American theme, *Disney's Newport Bay Club* has a New England seaside resort feel, with the largest spread of rooms of any of the on-site hotels (or any hotel in Europe, come to that). It may not appeal quite so much to children (it has possibly the most 'grown-up' style of all six hotels), but it is well equipped to cater for all the family. It has two excellent pools (a large one outdoors and an elaborate one, with a pirate ship centrepiece, inside), a Jacuzzi, steam bath and fitness room, an outdoor play area, the usual video games arcade and a Children's Corner play area with organised activities on certain days. There is also a convention centre here, but the business aspect is less intrusive than at *Disney's Hotel New York*.

**BRITTIP**

Hairdryers and irons are available on request, free of charge, from the front desk at most Disney hotels, subject to availability and sometimes a deposit, except for the *Disneyland Hotel* and *Disney's Hotel New York*, where they are provided in the rooms.

The two restaurants are semi-formal – the **Cape Cod** serves European cuisine with a touch of Mediterranean flair, while the similar **Yacht Club** specialises in fish, seafood and grilled meats (try the clam chowder for a true taste of New England) – and you are allocated either one for breakfast when you check in (if the hotel is full – if not, the Cape Cod is used on its own). There are two fine bars – **Fisherman's Wharf**, which opens from the foyer and the more

*Disney's Newport Bay Club pool*

© Disney

© Disney

*Captain's Quarters at the Newport Bay Club*

nautically themed **Captain's Quarters** piano bar – that both look out over Lake Disney. The large **Bay Boutique** offers a good selection of Disney merchandise and travel essentials.

The sheer size of the hotel (1,080 rooms, plus 13 suites) means the foyer can get terribly congested, especially from 9–10am when people are checking out. There is a separate reception desk for the **Admiral's Club**. The latter covers the lake side of the top two floors (giving wonderful views) and offers a more personal level of service, plus room service and a quieter, more relaxed atmosphere (quite a welcome bonus when the hotel is full). The majority of the spacious, two-room suites (55sq m/592sq ft) are at this level, too, with the unusual octagonal Honeymoon Suite (45sq m/ 484sq ft) being quite stunningly romantic.

The main suites also feature some lovely colonial-style furniture and extra nautical touches. Standard rooms (27sq m/290sq ft) continue the refreshing blue and white colour scheme of the rest of the hotel and all include mini-bars and room safes. *Disney's Newport Bay Club* is at the furthest end of Lake Disney, so it is a good 15-minute walk to the theme parks. But, on a pleasant morning, there is not a more delightful walk anywhere in the Ile de France. **Official rating \*\*\*; our rating €€€, CCCC.**

## Disney's Sequoia Lodge

If you like to be surrounded by gardens and greenery, head straight for *Disney's Sequoia Lodge*. Here you will be transported to one of the great American national parks. The main aspect of the hotel is a touch flat and monolithic but the interior and landscaping detail are quite breathtaking, with a fabulous use of stone and hundreds of imported trees and bushes for an authentic feel.

For the ideal warming winter retreat, the **Redwood Bar and Lounge** has a massive open fireplace and cosy furniture. The low, sloping, beamed ceiling and flagstone floor of the lobby set the scene for an outdoor adventure with all the comforts of a luxury resort (well above its 3-star rating, in our opinion). The judicious use of dark woods adds to the rugged feel and, when the weather is good, there is a lovely terrace overlooking Lake Disney where you can sit with a drink.

### BRITTIP

Not sure of where to stay at Christmas? *Disney's Sequoia Lodge* is the perfect choice during the winter. It takes on an enchanted atmosphere with all the festive decorations.

*Disney's Sequoia Lodge*

© Disney

The gift shop, **The Northwest Passage**, sells a standard range of toiletries, snacks, drinks and souvenirs, while the Little Prairie is the kids' corner, with a TV and video, games station and an elaborate character photo area (available 5 days a week to either take your own snaps or use the official Disney photographer). There is the usual video games room, plus an outdoor play area, with slides and a sandpit, set among some beautiful gardens, full of unique (for Western Europe!) foliage, a waterfall and even a mock beaver dam. Stroll the paths along the 'Rio Grande' and you come to the hotel's pool lodge, an indoor/outdoor facility that features a water-slide, freeform leisure pool (great for kids), large Jacuzzi, sauna, steam room and gymnasium. There is a solarium that may be pre-booked at €4 for 5 minutes, €8 for 10 minutes and €16 for 20 minutes, as well as massages (€70 per half-hour).

The 1,011 rooms (including 16 suites) are split between the huge main building and five lodges spread throughout the gardens. Standard rooms (22sq m/237sq ft) have either a Lake Disney or gardens/car park view, large windows and a few extra themed touches like rocking chairs and rustic light fittings, which combine well with the dark wood furniture and the dark bedspreads and curtains to provide that American backwoods ambience.

*Hunter's Grill*

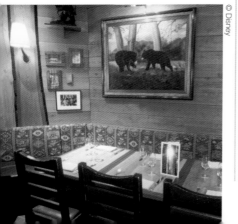

© Disney

The cabin lodges offer exactly the same room space and facilities as the main building (Montana) rooms, apart from a mini-bar (so they are slightly cheaper). A lake view carries a supplement but is well worthwhile (and should be requested when you make your booking). The spacious two-room suites (55sq m/592sq ft) all have a lake view, and the Honeymoon Suite features an open-plan arrangement with no door between the bedroom and living room.

**BRITTIP**

Our suggestion for the Hunter's Grill at *Disney's Sequoia Lodge* is the Ranger's Rotisserie – a Yosemite Salad, followed by a marinated roast chicken thigh, a herb sausage and prime roast rump steak, sliced at your table, plus dessert. Outstanding!

*Disney's Sequoia Lodge* has two mouth-watering diners, the **Beaver Creek Tavern** and **Hunter's Grill**. The former is the more family-orientated option, with a varied menu to suit those with a big appetite and includes a Mixed Grill Skewer of beef, lamb and sausage, with sautéed potatoes and spiced kidney beans. The dessert buffet is outstanding. Within the restaurant is a kids' area with a TV showing Disney cartoons.

The Hunter's Grill continues the hotel's outdoors theme in magnificent style, with a huntin', shootin', fishin' motif that boasts a feature kitchen serving up delicious rotisserie dishes. There are three main set options, including an excellent vegetarian menu, with a choice of desserts, all for €26 (without drinks). For both restaurants there is a separate children's menu (€12). Neither is open for lunch.

At a first look, *Disney's Sequoia Lodge* may seem more of an adult environment, but children usually love the 'outdoorsy' feel. The great extras of the pool, gardens and play area make it a great family base but

*Lake activities at Sequoia Lodge*

you may have trouble persuading the kids to leave when the characters are in residence! It takes 10–15 minutes to walk into the theme parks, or you can take the free 5-minute shuttle bus ride. **Official rating \*\*\*; our rating €€€, CCCC½.**

# Disney's Hotel Cheyenne

Howdy partners, welcome to the Wild West – or Disney's version of it at least (safer and a lot more comfortable!). This imaginative hotel is usually a huge hit with children and is therefore a popular family choice (although it can be a little raucous at times when the kids re-enact Custer's Last Stand at regular intervals, armed with rifles and bows and arrows from the hotel shop!). The theming is comprehensive and convincing, from the wonderful period-style entrance lobby (complete with two striking bronze horse and rider statues) to the rooms and their rustic, kid-friendly bunk-beds. It is also quite extensive, as all the rooms are low-rise (no more than two storeys) to give the feel of a Wild West town.

The level of creature comforts is not quite the same as elsewhere – no swimming pool or air-conditioning, no luggage delivery to the rooms and only a self-service restaurant. But, there are some significant extras aimed at the kids – optional pony rides and mechanical buffalos (spring and summer, for a small fee) and a Fort Apache outdoor play area.

The lobby is themed like a Goldrush-era claims office, with a Land Claims desk instead of a reception area, a huge stone fireplace and a mock hotel entrance at the opposite end of the vaulted-ceiling foyer. The foyer has a kiddie corner (with organised colouring, face-painting and drawing on certain days) that has mini-saddles instead of chairs! **The General Store** is the standard gift shop and there is a video games room next door.

Western paraphernalia abounds and the cowboy theme continues into the bar and restaurant areas, with saloon-style doors, wooden tables, chairs, balustrades and ceiling beams. The **Red Garter Saloon** features live country music in the evening and has an outdoor terrace.

The 750-seat **Chuck Wagon**, which also has its own **Saddle Bar** and wagon play area, is a cafeteria-style eaterie dressed up like a Texan pioneer marketplace. It serves a good mixture of international dishes, from barbecue-smoked chicken and beef to salads, pasta, risottos and fresh wok-fried Chinese specialities (set meal €22/adult and children's menu €10).

Step out of the main building and you are in a true cowboy town, with raised, boarded sidewalks, dirt streets and blocks of hotel rooms all disguised as various buildings, such as the Guest House, Blacksmith and Sheriff's Office. The 14 blocks are each named after a famous character like Doc Holliday, Jesse James, Calamity

*Disney's Hotel Cheyenne*

Jane and Running Bear. Blocks 17–19 (they are actually numbered from 10–25, omitting 13), Sitting Bull, Wyatt Earp and Billy The Kid are closest to the main building and the bus stop for the free shuttle to the theme parks and *Disney Village*. There are 1,000 identical rooms (all 21sq m/226sq ft) spread out through the 14 blocks, which have internal access only and most feature a double bed and two bunks. The two guest launderettes are free to use, although you need to buy washing powder from the General Store.

### BRITTIP

If the bus queues are too long when you want to return to *Disney's Hotel Cheyenne*, take the short cut back in less than 10 minutes. Walk out past the train station, cross the bridge to the main road, turn right and you will be able to enter the hotel's main gate (along a walkway), entering from the car park. You may need to show your hotel ID, but it will save you having to deal with full buses.

The in-room theming is more limited here and the bathrooms slightly more spartan compared to the other resorts, but then it is designed for more budget-conscious visitors (no air-conditioning, just ceiling fans). The regular shuttle bus to the theme parks, *Disney Village* and RER station takes about 5 minutes (queues permitting) or you can walk it (in 15–20 minutes) along a pathway under the main road and past *Disney's Hotel New York*. **Official rating \*\*; our rating €€, CCC½.**

*Inside Disney's Hotel Cheyenne*

*A room at Disney's Hotel Santa Fe*

## Disney's Hotel Santa Fe

Right at the budget end of the six-hotel spectrum is this extensive *pueblo*-style resort decked out in best American South West fashion, with Native American, Spanish and Mexican cultures providing the decorative motif, and a giant Clint Eastwood billboard (like a drive-in movie screen) welcoming you 'into town'. In truth, this is a glorified motel, but that doesn't stop it being fun for kids, good value for money and still well situated to enjoy all the Disney Magic. It gets extremely busy in high season (breakfast sittings are pre-allocated from 7am) and is popular with coach operators, so it gets congested in the morning with large numbers of guests arriving and departing at the same time.

### BRITTIP

As at *Disney's Hotel Cheyenne*, breakfast at *Disney's Hotel Santa Fe* is of the most basic continental kind – cereal, croissants, pastries, juice, tea/coffee – but you can pay a supplement to add bacon, eggs and fresh fruit.

On first impressions, the hotel looks rather dreary with its collection of square, concrete blocks up to five storeys high, but the Imagineers have been at work here, even if the fanciful 'volcano' is now a derelict grey hulk. There are four 'trails' through the resort (corresponding to the four different room sections – Artefacts, Water, Monuments and Legends), each with their own symbols and icons scattered around – from rusting desert 'vehicles' to outlandish meteorites, water trails, a geyser and even a crashed flying saucer! The smattering of desert scenery is also quite eye-catching.

**BRITTIP**

You need to request a room with bunk-beds when booking accommodation at *Disney's Hotel Santa Fe* if that is what your children want (and which is usually a lot more comfortable for children aged 6 plus).

The main facilities are in the reception building, while the 1,000 rooms are spread out over 41 blocks surrounded by small car parks, so if you are driving, this is the only hotel where you can more or less park outside your room. The 700-seat **La Cantina** serves up a Tex-Mex dinner buffet in a food-court-style servery. You can make up your own meals (salads, tapas, fajitas, nachos, roast pork, chicken, beef, spaghetti and meatballs) or choose one of the set meals (€22/adult and €10/child), and there is an ice-cream and coffee bar. Imaginative touches have food served from the back of a flat-bed truck and drinks dispensed from 'petrol pumps' – worth highlighting as so many people miss them in their rush to get to the parks. The children's corner, with organised colouring and drawing activities (in the evenings), is also here, with a computer console and Disney TV.

Next door to La Cantina is the **Rio Grande Bar**, with live entertainment and karaoke on certain evenings. **The Trading Post** is the Disney gift shop, with a good range of souvenirs, snacks, drinks and basic toiletries. A video games room is available for the kids, plus an outdoor playground, the Totem Circle, which is handy if they have any energy left at the end of the day! Back in the lobby, characters meet 'n' greet in the morning, which is the ideal way to start the day if you have young autograph hunters.

**BRITTIP**

The petrol station next door to *Disney's Hotel Santa Fe* is one of the few places on-site where you can buy fresh milk and other handy groceries.

The identical rooms (21sq m/226sq ft) are cheerfully decorated, if a little sparse by comparison with the other hotels, but many also come with bunk-beds instead of two double beds. As with all Disney accommodation, they can house a family of four (or four plus one in a cot), although they are a little short of drawer space.

Like *Disney's Hotel Cheyenne*, there is no in-room air-conditioning, just a ceiling fan. The two hotels are adjacent to each other, so it is perfectly permissible to pop 'next door' to enjoy some of the facilities there too, notably, the Fort Apache play area for kids, the pony rides and the Red Garter Saloon. The hotel is a good 20- to 25-minute walk from the parks, but once again, if the weather is fine, it is a lovely way to start the day as you stroll alongside the 'Rio Grande' and up by *Disney's Hotel New York*, around Lake Disney and through *Disney Village*.

*Disney's Hotel Santa Fe*

© Disney

Alternatively, the shuttle bus takes about 10 minutes and, while there is usually quite a queue in the morning around the parks' opening times, they run several buses at once on this route (as they do at all the bigger hotels). **Official rating \*\*; our rating €€, CCC.**

## Disney's Davy Crockett Ranch

If you drive down to *Disneyland Resort Paris* and are happy to use your car to get to the theme parks every day, staying at *Disney's Davy Crockett Ranch* is the best value way to enjoy all the fun and still have a taste of Disney imagination in your accommodation. Here, in 'trapper country', are 535 cabins with one or two bedrooms accommodating up to six, plus 60 caravan and camper van sites. The sites all have water supply and connections for electricity and water drainage, plus their own picnic bench and open-air barbecue.

Set in 57 hectares/140 acres of pretty woodland about a 15-minute drive from the theme parks (where parking is free with your resort ID card), you do get the feeling of being out in the wilds (see map on page 81). The woods are dotted with imaginative touches such as Native American tepees, while all the main services and facilities are located in a wonderfully fun cowboy 'village' at the heart of the ranch. Here you will find a host of great activities and

*Disney's Davy Crockett Ranch*

*Disney's Hotel Santa Fe in summer*

amenities, from the **Alamo Trading Post** (the gift shop and grocery store, 8am–11pm) to the great children's play area. There is even a farmyard and mini-menagerie featuring reindeer and wolves.

### BRITTIP

The camping sites are particularly popular with the Brits and the Dutch. They sell out well in advance at peak season, so you need to book EARLY in summer.

The 'village' is actually a fully fledged resort in its own right, centred on the Trading Post and **Crockett's Tavern**, a log-cabin restaurant serving lunch (12.30– 2.30pm) and dinner (6– 10.30pm), with a take-away service, too. The buffet-style servery offers up a good variety of dishes, from salad, fish and chips, roast chicken and pasta to entrecôte steak and even a vegetarian meal, while there is a choice of four kids' meals (€10). Across the street is the authentic (if rather small) **Saloon** (5pm–midnight) serving beer, wine and cocktails, with live entertainment and karaoke at peak times, plus outdoor seating and a large-screen TV in summer.

**Bowie's Bike Barn** (8am–6, 8 or 10pm seasonally), the information centre, houses the children's activity corner, with a computer play station, video console and organised face-painting and colouring, all set up around a large table with clever mini-saddles to

*Tepees at Disney's Davy Crockett Ranch*

sit on. Disney characters make an appearance every evening, while there is grown-up entertainment too, with themed evenings, line dancing and discos, plus organised sports, from jogging and aerobics to *petanque* and archery.

**BRITTIP**

It is advisable, especially in summer when the resort can hold around 4,000 people, to book a table for dinner at Crockett's Tavern. Lunch is rarely over-subscribed.

The **Lucky Raccoon** video games room adds that essential amenity for kids, and they are then spoiled for choice with the likes of horse and pony rides (ages 4–11 only; €9), Davy's Farm (a petting zoo with goats, sheep, rabbits, birds and ducks), an outdoor play and climbing area, table tennis, volleyball, basketball, archery and mini-golf (the latter for €6 for nine holes). There are two free-to-use indoor tennis courts (one of which is used alternately for archery, table tennis and volleyball in winter) and a nature park with the Indian Meadows village and trails to see the reindeer park and wolf enclosure.

**BRITTIP**

The reindeer actually 'work' in Disney's Christmas Parade at the *Disneyland Park*, but they get 10 months off, which they spend at the ranch!

Cycling is another activity for children and adults, with a huge range of bikes and quadracycles for hire at €20 for an hour, to be used on the cycle trails throughout the resort and woods.

The final outstanding element of the resort is the **Blue Springs Pool**, an extensive indoor water park (8.30am–10pm) with a semi-circular paddling pool for toddlers, a large, free-form leisure pool that has a waterfall, long water-slide, fountains, squirt pond and a huge Jacuzzi. You can rent towels for a small fee. Under 12s must be accompanied by an adult at all times in the pool area. It is an exceptional facility and you may struggle to get the kids out, even with the lure of the theme parks!

Eight circular 'trails' house all the accommodation. Each trail has its own take-away 'cottage', where breakfast is served (7–11am) for you to take back to your cabin, caravan or tent. The one-bedroom cabins (all 36sq m/388sq ft) feature a spacious lounge with TV, a kitchen complete with two hot-plates, dishwasher, fridge, microwave, kettle, coffee machine and all the necessary cutlery, crockery and cooking utensils. There is also a breakfast bar area. The bathroom (fully stocked with towels) includes the toilet but the two are separate in the two-bedroom cabins. Some have a pull-down double bed in the lounge, others a convertible sofa, while the bedroom has a double bed and two bunks. Many of the one-

*Indian Meadows*

bedroom cabins do look their age (more than 12 years old), hence it is a basic 2-star property. Outside, they all have their own brick-built barbecue and picnic bench, plus parking.

### BRITTIP

The ranch's 60 two-bedroom cabins are all newer than the one-bed ones, and come at a slight premium. They also go quickly (although more are due to be built), so it's best to book early.

The two-bedroom cabins (39sq m/ 420sq ft) have the two bunk-beds in their own room, giving mum and dad a little peace and quiet. The living quarters are arranged slightly differently and the general fixtures and fittings are that bit smarter. The difference in price is minimal, so these are the better option. The caravan and camp sites are on Moccasin Trail (the others are named after similar cowboy icons – Wagon Wheel, Big Bear, Tomahawk, etc.) and you'll find toilets, showers and a launderette at the centre of this area. At peak times, a mini-train/tram runs around all the trails, ferrying people between the accommodation units and village area.

The site is completely secured against non-visitor traffic. You check in at the reception area at the main entrance, much as you would for a hotel, and they provide you with your keys, the all-important Disney resort ID cards and the security code to access the

*A winter landscape at Disney's Davy Crockett Ranch*

site, which you punch in at the gate just past reception. Then, when you depart, you just drop the keys off in a deposit box, so you need not go back into reception.

The parks and *Disney Village* are about a 15-minute drive from the ranch, which is about 3km/2mls off Exit 13 of the A4 autoroute. To get there, simply come out of the property, take the second exit from the roundabout (signposted A4 Reims) and continue along the A4 to Exit 14 for 'Les Parcs Disneyland'. **Official rating \*\*; our rating €€, CCCC.**

**Davy Crockett's Adventure** (see also page 205) is an adjacent forest park, open to the general public, with a series of five tree-top adventure trails of varying difficulty for all ages from 8 up. It promises up to 3 hours of challenging tree-climbing, rope bridges, giant swings, obstacle courses and the feature 16m/52ft Tarzan Tree Jump. It costs €25 for those over 1.40m/4ft 6in tall and €15 for those under. Look up more (in French only) on **www.aventure-aventure.com**.

*Aerial view of Disney's Davy Crockett Ranch*

### BRITTIP

To call ANY of Disney's hotels, simply dial the main switchboard – 00 33 1 64 74 40 00 from the UK, 01 64 74 40 00 in France – and ask for the hotel you require.

© Disney

# Beyond Disney

Once you move beyond Disney for your choice of accommodation, things become simpler. There are few grand theme hotels (the Holiday Inn, Dream Castle and Explorers Hotel at Val de France are the only exceptions) and no great variation in style or facilities (almost all are 2- or 3-star). Rooms tend to be small but comfortable and the majority will provide a good, basic continental breakfast. We have toured the Seine-et-Marne region extensively and looked at most of the hotels on offer and have been impressed by the generally high standard of cleanliness and friendliness.

A lot of hotels in the immediate vicinity of Marne-la-Vallée are quite smart and pleasant, while all hotels are inspected regularly to ensure they conform to their star rating. Quite a few have swimming pools, but you need to decide if you are likely to use a pool after a long day at the parks to make it worthwhile paying extra.

We have subdivided the off-site hotels into those that are Near the Magic (including the new sub-region of Val de France), those that are a short drive away, and hotel chains that have accommodation in Paris itself (which is not necessarily a bad idea if you want to see a lot of the city, as it is only 35–40 minutes to *Disneyland Resort Paris* by RER).

# Near the Magic

When it comes to hotels that are within a figurative stone's throw of the theme parks, there are nine contrasting choices in the Val d'Europe area. These include four hotels in an associated development just off the main ring road (which Disney refers to as its Selected Hotels). One of these, the Explorers Hotel, is primarily for the UK market, while all usually host a high percentage of British guests. Looking at them in detail, they are:

**Hotel du Moulin de Paris:** Built in 2001, this smart, well-run hotel in Magny-le-Hongre (a 5- to 10-minute drive from the theme parks) has been extensively refurbished, with all the 82 identical bright, clean rooms getting a fresh, new look. They comfortably accommodate four, with a double bed, a single and a pull-out, or a double and two bunks (you need to request a room with bunks in advance). Cots are also available on request but maximum occupancy for each room is four. The bathrooms have a shower only, no bath. Breakfast and dinner are served in the airy conservatory-style restaurant (and sandwiches at the bar) and, in summer, an outdoor patio makes a lovely place to sit for a drink. A heated outdoor pool (May–September), sauna and small fitness room are free to hotel guests.

If you arrive early and want to head to the theme parks, you can leave your bags in a luggage room.

A daily shuttle runs to and from the theme parks (returning half an hour after closing time) for €2/person, while there is also a public bus to Marne-la-Vallée station. The hotel is on the Rue du Moulin á Vent, just off the Boulevard de l'Europe, the ring road that goes around *Disneyland Resort Paris*. More importantly, most packages here include your theme park tickets. Call 00 33 1 60 43 77 77 from the UK. **Official rating \*\*\*; our rating €€€, CCC.**

*Hotel du Moulin de Paris*

# Off-site hotels

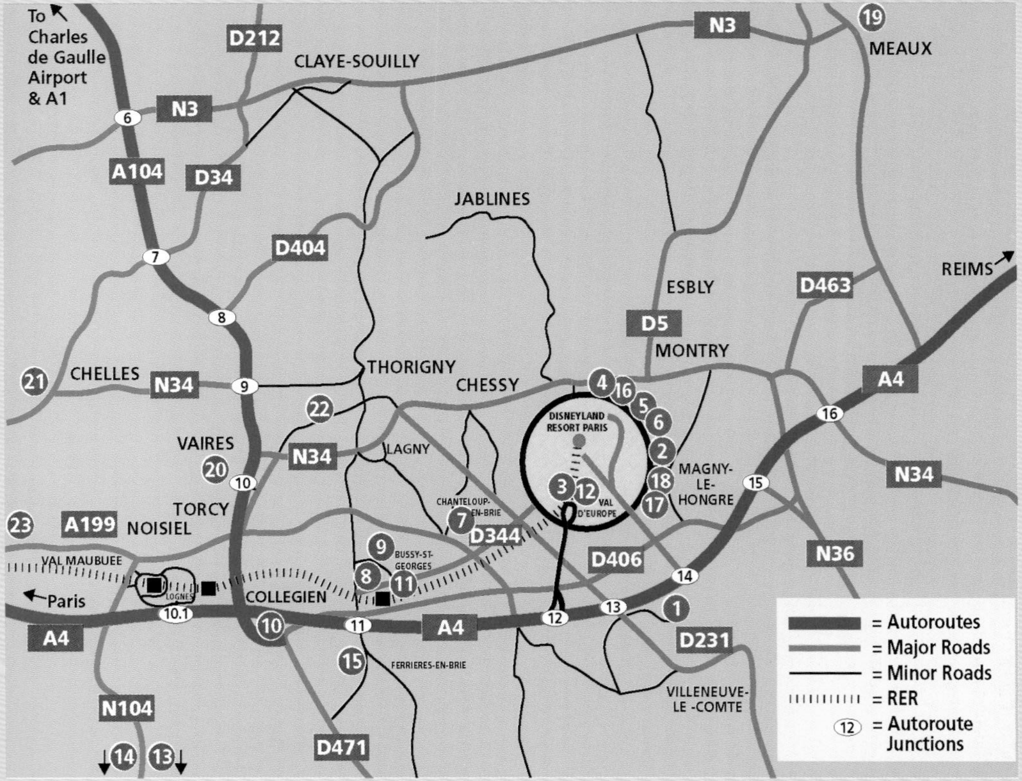

1 *Disney's Davy Crockett Ranch*
2 Hotel du Moulin de Paris
3 Hotel l'Elysée
4 Explorers Hotel
5 Holiday Inn at *Disneyland Resort Paris*
6 Hotel Kyriad at *Disneyland Resort Paris*
7 Chanteloup Hotel
8 Best Western Marne-la-Vallée
9 Golf Hotel
10 Novotel Collégien
11 Tulip Inn
12 Pierre & Vacances Residence Val d'Europe
13 Hotel Saphir
14 Best Western Abbay du Golf
15 Hotel St Rémy
16 Vienna International Dream Castle Hotel
17 Marriott's Village d'Ile de France
18 Radisson SAS Hotel at *Disneyland Resort Paris*
19 Camping Le Parc
20 Parc de la Colline
21 Kyriad Chelles
22 Comfort Inn Lagny-sur-Marne
23 Novotel Atria Marne-la-Vallée

Key:
= Autoroutes
= Major Roads
= Minor Roads
= RER
(12) = Autoroute Junctions

*Radisson SAS Hotel*

**Radisson SAS Hotel at Disneyland Resort Paris:** Opened in December 2005, this smart property in the Radisson group stands right on the edge of the Golf Disneyland complex in Magny-le-Hongre (and has impressive views over the three nine-hole courses). The hotel has 250 fully air-conditioned rooms, including 20 suites and 139 family rooms for up to four people. It is set up, to a large extent, as a convention hotel with excellent business facilities, so you can expect a busy but elegant style. But there is also plenty to attract the Disney holidaymaker. There are two restaurants – the cosy **Brasserie Birdie** and the gourmet dining of **Pamplemousse Restaurant, The Chardon bar** (also serving snacks), a Play Club for children, and a Wellness & Fitness Centre, including a swimming pool, fully equipped gym and a variety of treatment and massage rooms. Call 00 33 1 60 43 64 00 or visit **www.golfresort.paris. radissonsas.com. Official rating****; our rating €€€€, CCCC.**

**Hotel l'Elysée:** At the heart of the Val d'Europe development, and therefore just a 5-minute RER ride to the theme parks, this rather chic 3-star property opened in July 2002. The Hotel l'Elysée features a grand reception lobby and underground parking. It has an extremely quiet ambience, which is a nice contrast after the hurly-burly of the Disney resort. The 152 rooms all accommodate four, in a double bed and two single sofa beds (made up ready for your arrival), while there are four spacious junior suites and five rooms adapted for the disabled (two persons maximum). The rooms all have a mini-bar and safe and the marbled bathrooms are extremely smart. Cots are available on request, but they can't add up to a fifth person. However, there are inter-connecting rooms for larger families.

The hotel has a left-luggage room, free shuttle service to the Disney theme parks, a video games room for kids, an elegant bar and a high-quality restaurant, while 24-hour room service is also available. Most packages here include park tickets and either a free parking pass or daily RER tickets (which are €21.50 each way). An extra bonus is the fact that the hotel also benefits from the **Extra Magic Hours** programme. The last train from Marne-la-Vallée back to Val d'Europe is at 12.12am each day. Call 00 33 1 64 63 33 33 or visit **www.hotelelysee.com. Official rating ***; our rating €€€€, CCC.**

**Hotel Ibis Paris Marne La Vallée:** One of the newest hotels in the smart, budget Ibis chain, this is right in the middle of Val D'Europe and just a short walk from the RER station. With 100 air-conditioned rooms (four of them disabled accessible), it offers a budget choice in an ideal 'near the Magic' location. With a continental breakfast served from 4am–noon you will not go hungry and the Ibis chain also feature 'anytime snacks' just to

*Hotel l'Elysée*

make sure! The hotel is fully WiFi accessible and, while the facilities consist of a simple Pasta Café restaurant (open 7–10.30pm) and bar, it is hard to fault their eager-to-please attitude. It is just a 5-minute walk from the big Val D'Europe shopping centre, with its cafés and restaurants. Call 00 33 1 60 36 20 06 or visit **www.ibishotel.com. Official rating \*\***; **our rating** €€€**, CC.**

**Pierre & Vacances Residence Val d'Europe:** Opened in 2003, this stylish apartment complex from the French chain of holiday residences has a good array of flexible accommodation that makes it an ideal base for a longer stay in the region. With 290 apartments and studios, sleeping from two to nine (at a squeeze), this is a modern and well-furnished offering. All feature a fully equipped kitchenette (cooking hob, fridge, microwave and dishwasher), a living room and either a one- or two-bedroom option, plus what they call a 'cabin' that has additional bunks. The studios offer living/sleeping space for up to three, while the largest apartments can sleep three in the living room, four in the two bedrooms and two in the cabin. All have a bathroom and the larger ones have a shower room too.

### BRITTIP

Towels are only provided in Pierre & Vacances properties for a fee, so it is advisable to bring your own. You are also required to pay a €200 deposit when checking in.

*Crew room at the Explorers Hotel*

*Room at the Hotel l'Elysée*

The resort-style set-up offers a launderette, indoor car park, luggage room, small gym and an outdoor heated swimming pool open May–September. A separate charge (on check-in) is made for TV, WiFi and phone use. Continental breakfast is served daily in a corner of the big reception area. Call 00 33 1 60 42 82 82 (in France) or 08700 267 144 (in the UK), or visit **www.pv-holidays.com. Official rating \*\*\***; **our rating** €€€**, CC.**

## Val de France

This region consists solely of four neighbouring hotels that are well worth considering. Disney counts them as official partner hotels, tour operators call them 'Near The Magic' and they can be found just off the Boulevard de l'Europe, about a 10-minute drive from the Marne-la-Vallée station hub for drop-off to the theme parks and *Disney Village* (with a regular free shuttle bus service). It is possible to walk from here, but it takes at least half an hour.

**Explorers Hotel:** This highly imaginative 390-room hotel – one of the real highlights of this area – was built for tour operator MyTravel and is used primarily by their affiliate companies (including Cresta Holidays) and coach-tour specialists Leger Holidays. It is designed with the British visitor in mind (some 70% of guests are usually from the UK), hence there are some smart touches

*The back of the Explorers Hotel*

for families. It was the first fully themed off-site hotel (followed by the Holiday Inn and Dream Castle) and offers both extra-spacious rooms (with families of six to ten in mind) and some superb children's facilities, although only a handful of rooms have air-conditioning. It is much the same price to eat and drink here as in the parks or *Disney Village*, however, and their fine-dining restaurant can be a touch expensive.

**BRITTIP**

The shuttle bus serves all four Val de France hotels and runs every 15 minutes (10 minutes at park opening and closing times). It operates 6.30am–11.30pm September–June and 6.30am–1am July–August, and stops at all four in turn (Explorers – Kyriad – Holiday Inn – Dream Castle). This means the trip to the parks from the first stop can take a good 20 minutes when it's busy and vice versa on the return journey.

Designed like a grand French manor – the preserve of mythical explorer Sir Archibald de Bacle (ouch!) and his various 'discoveries' – it is a fun and spacious creation, from the busy lobby area (complete with a Kids Corner with mini-cinema and two rides, plus a novel fountain) to the buffet-style restaurant with its outdoor terrace (wonderful on a sunny morning). Walk through the lobby and you have a startling view over the **Tropical Atrium** at the heart of the hotel, which is also home to the

Secret Lagoon Swimming Pool, a 20m/66ft heated indoor pool with a separate toddlers' area. The wreck of the Seven Seas Raider pirate ship is beached at one end of the lagoon, allowing kids the chance to explore the decks and passageways or take to the water-slide. A second, more elaborate, dragon-themed water-slide was added in 2005, making this guaranteed fun for kids of all ages. Work will be under way late in 2007 to create a new **mini-water park** for younger children, with smaller slides and water games, which should be open in early 2008.

**BRITTIP**

Surprisingly, there is a €1 charge for a pool towel at the Explorers, so take your own towels. The pool also gets VERY busy in late afternoon.

The **Plantation Restaurant** is the main diner, a market-style emporium offering breakfast (7–10.30am) and dinner (6–10.30pm). The plentiful continental-style buffet breakfast offers a good selection for all the family (or you can choose a cooked breakfast for a few extra euros), while dinner is an elaborate all-you-can-eat buffet (salad bar, cooked meats, grills, fish, pasta, vegetables and rice) including soft drinks, at €21/adult (€28 with wine or beer) and €11/child. The salads and desserts are especially good.

*Kids' play area at the Explorers Hotel*

**BRITTIP**

Like the Disney hotels, you are given a time-slot for breakfast each day. You collect these from reception when you check in and it is advisable to pick your times for your whole stay as the best ones go quickly.

For more informal dining there is **Marco's Pizza Parlour** where you can order a take-away if you prefer and **Traders Café Bar** for snacks and a drink or two (both 5–11pm). The new **Brioche Doree** café (5–11pm) offers an elevated view of the Atrium and the chance to sip a speciality tea or coffee and grab a pastry or sandwich. You will also find three **internet** terminals here (although much of the hotel is also WiFi compatible). The **Captain's Library** (6.30–10pm) is a themed full-service restaurant, once again offering children's meals, and with a small play area to keep them amused while mum and dad finish dinner. While it is a touch expensive for an off-site restaurant (featuring salads, chicken, salmon, mixed grills and mussels, with kids meals from €6.70–12), the food here is outstanding for what is, in theory, a 3-star hotel. Finally, **Smugglers Tavern** (6pm–11pm; 6pm–1am in high season) is the hotel's main pub-style bar, with a corner given over to a large-screen TV for sports events. There are pool tables and dartboards, and snacks are available here too. It is highly popular most evenings (you

*Special suite at the Explorers Hotel*

*Explorers Hotel pool*

might want to request a room in a different block to the Tavern if you are early-to-bed types).

Traders Café is also brilliantly designed for parents to be able to sit back and watch their offspring expend some energy in the activity areas. **Scally Wagg's Jungle Adventures** is the big indoor soft-play area (in two sections, for 2–4s and 5–12s), with all the requisite ladders, ropes, slides and ball pools, while the Seven Seas Raider is also nearby. Then there is a two-part arcade/games room, the Kids Club for younger children (with ride-on toys and basic arcade games) and Harry's Action Zone for older kids, with the usual (noisy!) video games.

**BRITTIP**

The Explorers' room configurations are the most family-friendly of any hotel here. The use of the 'bunk cabins' and single beds (instead of two doubles) give them huge flexibility, especially with older children.

The room choice is definitely a cut above the usual accommodation. Standard rooms, called 'Crew rooms', feature one double bed and two singles, with a bath, shower and separate toilet (a useful idea), plus interactive satellite TV with video games, pay-per-view programmes and films, room safe, hairdryer and ceiling fan (no air-conditioning), plus tea- and coffee-making facilities.

*The Explorers Hotel*

Each Crew room can be connected to a 'bunk cabin' for two children. Extended families or groups of friends can take two interconnecting Crew rooms with the bunk cabin in between and sleep up to ten (the bunk cabin doors can be closed).

There are seven 'Captain's Suites' sleeping up to six in two bedrooms, plus three imaginative Themed Suites (Planet Hollywood, Jungle and Sweets), which have superbly equipped kids' quarters (you may struggle to get your youngsters out of this suite!). All ten suites have a lake view and air-conditioning for the hot summer months. An additional suite on the top floor is classified as an executive room, and features a plasma TV. Finally, nine rooms are fully fitted out for guests with disabilities (arguably the best of their kind in the whole area).

Additional features include free parking at the hotel, the parks and *Disney Village*, picnic lunches, currency exchange facilities, an outdoor kids' playground, a Disney store, a concierge and information desk. However, the Explorers is a non-smoking hotel, apart from areas such as Smugglers Tavern.

The hotel is situated just across the resort-encircling Boulevard de l'Europe from *Disney's Hotel Santa Fe* and is the first of the four hotels of the Val de France district. Call 00 33 1 60 42 60 00 or look up **www.explorers hotels.com** (with some online discounts for booking direct). **Official rating ***; our rating** €€€€, CCCC½.

**Holiday Inn at Disneyland Resort Paris:** If you prefer a more upmarket touch, look no further than the newest Holiday Inn in the Seine-et-Marne region. Designed in French manorial style with a circus-themed flavour throughout (that is quite stylishly done), this is a cut above the usual tourist fare (and, indeed, many other hotels in this well-known chain) and it scores high marks for families, too. At once both chic and cheerful, the hotel comes as a refreshing change from the usual identikit styling. It will appeal to all ages and boasts the extra service touches you would expect from a 4-star property, such as 24-hour room service and a business centre.

**BRITTIP**

Don't overlook the value of the Holiday Inn's family rooms and Kidsuites. If Simon's boys are anything to go by, you'll have difficulty getting your offspring out of the room because of 'their' area!

The 325 standard rooms (many interconnecting) feature a double bed and a curtained-off section (like a circus big top) with bunk-beds and a separate TV/games console for the kids. The 23 Kidsuites rooms have children's areas built into them in a more elaborate fashion. All rooms come with a main TV with international channels and internet access, plus room safe, hairdryer and tea- and coffee-making facilities. They are also fully air-conditioned.

*The pool at the Holiday Inn*

The hotel offers a sophisticated indoor leisure pool (with toddler area), smart fitness club and an extensive outdoor playground in the park-like gardens for the young 'uns, where they can burn off any excess energy. The main restaurant, **L'Etoile**, serves a pleasing mix of traditional French and international cuisine, while their buffet breakfast (with an extensive array of cereals plus hot and cold dishes) is possibly the best in the area – including Disney's hotels. The inner courtyard features an adjoining terrace to the restaurant and, for breakfast, this makes a wonderful start to the day if the weather permits. There is the inevitable Disney Store and an excellent bar/lounge, **Bar des Artistes**, which also serves a good array of family-orientated snacks (salads, sandwiches, omelettes, baguettes) for lunch and dinner.

## BRITTIP

If the parks are especially hectic or you just want a quiet break for lunch, head to the Holiday Inn and take advantage of their relaxed and friendly service in Bar des Artistes.

The hotel has its own bureau de change, and the overall value for money here is top notch. As with the other hotels of Val de France, the VEA Navette airport shuttle for both airports calls three times a day and is available without reservation. Call 00 33 1 64 63 37 37 or look up **www.ichotelsgroup.com**. **Official rating \*\*\*\*; our rating €€€€, CCCC.**

*Holiday Inn family room*

© Disney

*There are plenty of options for some peace and quiet*

## BRITTIP

If you sign up online in advance (for free) for the Holiday Inn's Priority Club programme, you qualify for early check-in if you arrive before the official 2pm opening time.

**Hotel Kyriad at Disneyland Resort Paris:** Right next door to the Holiday Inn is the flagship hotel of the budget Envergure group. With a lovely country house style, it is an excellent option for those who want to watch the pennies but still get a taste of the Magic. The 300 airy and spotlessly clean rooms are all air-conditioned, which is a bonus at this end of the scale, and come with tea- and coffee-making facilities, hairdryer and room safe.

The standard room features a double bed and two bunks, while the twin room can be either two singles or a double bed. No room can accommodate more than four, but there are various connecting rooms, bringing the number up to six or eight. The rest of the hotel is equally straightforward, with one restaurant and two bars in a friendly, relaxing ambience. The small children's play area in the lobby can get quite crowded in the morning. Although it is French owned and run, up to 60% of guests can be British at peak times. The overall feel is fresh and cosmopolitan. Call 00 33 1 60 43 61 61 or visit **www.envergure.fr/kyriadfr.html** for more details. **Official rating \*\*; our rating €€€, CC½.**

*Sanssouci at the Dream Castle Hotel*

**Vienna International Dream Castle Hotel:** This pleasant option opened in August 2004 and is now part of the Sterling Hotels group, who specialise in independent hotels worldwide aimed at a fully international market. Next door to the Explorers Hotel and similarly on the free shuttle bus route to the parks, the 400-room property (250 family rooms, 43 'Double Queen' rooms, 86 'King' rooms, including 10 fitted for disabled guests; and 21 Baron Munchhausen suites) exhibits a beautiful castle style, from the elegant lobby (complete with twin 'thrones', a sword-in-the-stone replica and suits of armour) to the well-fitted rooms (200 of which feature curtained-off bunk-beds – a great family touch). There is also a neat children's play area in the lobby, complete with ball pool, plus pool tables. The restaurant choice is impressive, with the more standard offerings of **Sanssouci** augmented by the expansive style of **The Musketeers**, which features a spectacular themed buffet each evening (the desserts alone are worth stopping in for!). There is also a charming outdoor terrace that makes a lovely setting for dinner on a summer evening. Both restaurants serve breakfast at busy periods, meaning there are no frustrating queues in the morning, as there are at some hotels. Their regular rate also includes a full American-style buffet

breakfast (quite a rarity) and, as Dream Castle set great store by the quality of their cuisine, it is a real highlight. The fully themed **Excalibur Bar** is a great place to enjoy a drink after a day in the parks and also serves light lunches and snacks.

**BRITTIP**
We rate the Excalibur Bar at the Dream Castle one of the most enjoyable places to relax with a drink or two, and at a good price – their alcohol tariff is almost half that of bars in the *Disney Village.*

Other notable features of the Dream Castle include a fun swimming pool with a Jacuzzi, smart fitness facilities, video arcade and a garden overlooking the lake, which backs on to the other hotels in Val-de-France. They also have an array of their own

*The garden at the Dream Castle Hotel*

characters, or 'mascots', which seem to keep children entertained in the lobby and at mealtimes. The hotel also boasts its own sauna, steam bath, Jacuzzi and solarium, with a range of massages, manicures, facials and other beauty treatments – a blissful tonic after a day pounding the parks! Call 00 33 1 64 17 90 00 from the UK or visit **www.dreamcastle-hotel.com**. **Official rating \*\*\*\*; our rating €€€€–€€€€€, CCCC.**

# A short drive from the Magic

**Chanteloup Hotel:** Tucked away in the pretty little village of Chanteloup-en-Brie, just to the west of Val d'Europe, is this small, family-run hotel. With just 64 small but smart rooms, each with a double bed and two fold-up bunks, plus a fitness centre, Jacuzzi and sauna, this is an ideal retreat after a day of frenetic theme-parking. It has a pleasant restaurant and a little foyer bar, and that's about it for the creature comforts, although there is a daily shuttle bus to Disney for €29/person return. To reach the hotel, turn off the A4 at Exit 13 and take the D231 past Val d'Europe for 4.5km/3mls, then turn left into Chanteloup-en-Brie. For more info, call 00 33 1 64 30 00 00. **Official rating \*\*; our rating €€€, CC.**

*A room at the Dream Castle Hotel*

*Chanteloup Hotel*

**Best Western Marne-la-Vallée:** One of the few 4-star hotels in the area, this former Holiday Inn is situated at the entrance to the modern town of Bussy-St-Georges, handy for both road and RER links to Marne-la-Vallée. It is a quiet, rather unprepossessing property, but it has real charm and style. The light, airy foyer opens up to reveal a smart restaurant with a conservatory annexe and a small, intimate bar, with a couple of video games and a pool table. The outdoor (unheated) swimming pool is open until the end of September (it closes sooner if it turns cold) and has a lovely patio area that allows guests to dine outside when the weather is fine.

The 120 rooms are extremely comfortable, even for four, with the choice of a double, triple and quad (two doubles) configuration, plenty of cupboard space and a marbled bathroom with hairdryer. Many rooms interconnect for larger family accommodation. They include satellite TV, internet connection, a trouser press and a kettle (but you need to buy tea and coffee sachets from reception).

The hotel hosts a lot of business conferences, so it can be busy during the week. It is only a 5-minute walk to the RER station (which is then 10 minutes to Marne-la-Vallée) and 10 minutes to the theme parks by car.

To get there, take Exit 11 off the A4 and follow the signposts to Bussy-St-

*Best Western Marne-la-Vallée*

Georges, go straight across two roundabouts and the Best Western is immediately on your right. Call 00 33 1 64 66 35 65 or visit **www.bestwestern-marnelavallee.com** for more info. **Official rating ****; our rating €€€€, CCC.**

**Tulip Inn:** Right opposite the RER station in Bussy-St-Georges (just two stops from Marne-la-Vallée) is this smart hotel. It has 87 non-smoking rooms, all with high-speed WiFi connection and air-conditioning. The brightly decorated rooms come with a king-size bed, two singles, or a double and two singles for a family of four. The hotel's facilities include restaurant L'Olivier for breakfast daily and lunch and dinner Mon–Fri, with French specialities, pizza and pasta, and the Cotton Bar for drinks and snacks in a relaxed setting. There is also a variety of shops and cafés within short walking distance. There is a fee for their car park. Call 00 33 1 64 66 11 11 or visit **www.tulipinnmarne lavallee.com**. **Official rating ***; our rating €€€, CC½.**

**Golf Hotel:** On the other side of Bussy-St-Georges is this distinctly countrified hotel, with a genuinely welcoming aspect, set on the edge of a golf course and with obvious benefits for the sporting fraternity. However, you don't need to be a golfer to stay here. The 93 light, airy rooms cater for everyone, with double, triple, twin and family rooms, the latter with a double bed and two fold-down or fixed bunks. Mini-bars and hairdryers are standard, as is internet access, and there is plenty of storage space.

The large restaurant has big picture windows and an outdoor terrace, while there is a children's play area to the side and a large green for kids to expend any remaining energy on. The outdoor heated pool is open from May to mid-September, and there are two private tennis courts available for hotel guests. There is a small lobby bar where you can have a quiet drink.

Given the surrounding greenery you could easily think you were a million miles from the hectic Disney whirl, but you are only 10–15 minutes' walk from the RER station or 5 minutes on their free shuttle bus (on request). To get to the hotel, carry on past the Best Western (see above), cross the Place du Clos-St-Georges, then turn right at Boulevard du Golf and the hotel is along on the left. Call 00 33 1 64 66 30 30. **Official rating ***; our rating €€€, CCC.**

**Novotel Collégien:** Slightly off the beaten track lies this smart hotel in the business-like Novotel chain (see page 108). Just south of the A4 and the town of Collégien, it is tucked away on a mini-industrial estate. It has some surprisingly family-friendly touches, with babysitting on request and an indoor play area. There is table football in the lobby, a heated outdoor pool (mid-April to end of September) and an extremely pleasant bar and lounge area (open until midnight). The 195 rooms (with

*Novotel Collégien*

one floor designated non-smoking) are all brightly furnished and feature a double bed and a fold-out sofa that will sleep two (smallish) children. Each room has a mini-bar, WiFi access and TV with English channels and pay-per-view films. There are two pairs of connecting rooms and six adapted for guests with disabilities. Usefully, the toilet is separate from the bathroom.

A busy convention hotel for much of the year, it is given over completely to the tourism business in July and at weekends. You can find it just past the junction of the A104 and A4; heading south (to Croissy-Beaubourg), turn left off the D471, straight over at the traffic lights and it is on the right. You really do need to have a car here as it is 3km/2mls from the nearest RER station. There is a free, secure parking area. Call 00 33 1 64 80 53 53 or visit **www.novotel.com**. **Official rating \*\*\*; our rating** €€€€, **CCC.**

**Hotel Saphir:** This one-off property, just to the south in Pontault-Combault, has 179 exceedingly smart rooms for two to four people, with the family rooms consisting of a double bed plus a single or a double sofa bed. While not the prettiest of hotels, it maintains a high standard of interior decor and service. The heated indoor pool is an excellent (and rare) amenity, along with a sauna and fitness centre for an additional charge. The family-friendly restaurant is well priced and there is a pleasant

*Hotel Saphir*

*Best Western Hôtel Abbay du Golf*

bar. Call 00 33 1 64 43 45 47 for more info or visit **www.saphir-hotel.fr**. It can be found just off the N104 travelling south at Exit 15, about 20 minutes' drive from *Disneyland Resort Paris*. **Official rating \*\*\*; our rating** €€€, **CCC.**

**Best Western Hôtel Abbay Du Golf:** Further south, in the older confines of the town of Lésigny, this 12th-century former monastery has been tastefully converted to hold 48 immaculate rooms and a wonderful restaurant. The hotel is right on the edge of a beautiful golf course yet it is still under half an hour's drive from the theme parks. It makes a great base for exploring some of the other villages in this area, but it is some way off the RER routes.

Family rooms offer an extra bed or bunks for children, and all feature satellite TV, mini-bar and hairdryer, while the superb traditional-style restaurant has a children's menu. To get there, take Exit 18 off the N104, then continue south on the Avenue des Hyveneaux and turn left after 1km/½ml at the signpost for Golf du Réveillon. Call 00 33 1 60 02 25 26 from the UK or visit **www.parisgolf hotel.com**. **Official rating \*\*\*; our rating** €€€, **CC½.**

STAYING THERE

## Our top 10 places to enjoy a drink at Disneyland Resort Paris

1  The Redwood Bar – *Disney's Sequoia Lodge*
2  The Excalibur Bar – Vienna International Dream Castle
3  Fantasia Bar – *Disneyland Hotel*
4  Billy Bob's Saloon – *Disney Village*
5  The Bar at The Steakhouse restaurant – *Disney Village*
6  Captain's Quarters Bar – *Disney's Newport Bay Club*
7  Sports Bar – *Disney Village*
8  City Bar – *Disney's Hotel New York*
9  Smugglers Tavern at the Explorers Hotel
10  Rainforest Café bar – *Disney Village*

**Hotel St Rémy:** Finally, a hotel to suit couples. This is a touch more detached and romantic than most, set in the picturesque hamlet of Ferrières-en-Brie, but only 7km/4mls from *Disneyland Resort Paris*. Originally built in the 19th century, but tastefully restored and reopened in 2000, it has just 25 rooms (all en suite, with satellite TV and hairdryer) with some wonderfully elegant individual touches and style, wooden floors and antique furniture. Its fabulous restaurant offers a children's menu (not Saturday lunchtime or Sunday evening), but there is not a lot else to keep kids amused in this quiet location. A car is advisable, although Bussy-St-Georges is only 2km/1ml away. The hotel can be found just off Exit 11 from the A4 – follow the signs to Ferrières-en-Brie and pick up the main Rue Jean Jaurès. Call 00 33 1 64 76 74 00 from the UK or visit **www.hotel-st-remy.fr**. **Official rating ***; our rating €€€, CC½.**

# Camping

With the ease in which you can drive down to this region of France, it makes sense to look at camping alternatives. One new campsite near the village of Touquin (13km/8mls south of the town of Coulommiers) is worth highlighting in particular. **Camping Les Etangs Fleuris** is a wonderfully rural and secluded site with 170 pitches and a host of clean, modern facilities, including an excellent pool (with a separate pool for children), a games room, bar and take-away, plus showers, toilets and a launderette. Their sporting activities include table tennis, mini-golf, petanque and fishing, plus horse-riding and nature walks nearby. The site also offers two types of two-bedroom mobile homes, all well furnished and maintained. It is about 45 minutes from *Disneyland Resort Paris* and an easy drive along the D231. Canvas Holidays package the site with either a Channel crossing or flights to Beauvais or Charles de Gaulle, plus theme park tickets. For more details call 01 870 192 1154 or visit **www.canvasholidays.com**.

*The Redwood Bar at Christmas*

Other sites in the Seine-et-Marne region include **Camping Le Parc**, 20km/12mls from *Disneyland Resort Paris* in 10 hectares/24¾ acres of woodland just outside the town of Villevaudé to the north-east (near Meaux). With 330 tent, camper van and caravan pitches, prices start from €16.60/night for a two-person tent without electricity but including shower use. It has a bar-restaurant, TV room and facilities for volleyball, tennis and basketball. New in 2007 was Aquatic Park, with slides, lazy river and swimming lagoons. Call 00 33 1 60 26 20 79 or visit **www.camping leparc.fr**.

Even closer is **Parc de la Colline**, near Torcy to the west, which has a mixture of mobile homes and chalets for up to seven people as well as campsites, all with electric hook-ups. They even have their own shuttle bus to the Torcy RER station at €5/adult and €2.50/child, and direct to *Disneyland Resort Paris* at €14 and €7 (return). Call 00 33 1 60 05 42 32 or visit **www.camping-de-la-colline.com**.

For those looking to explore more of northern France, the popular and extremely well-appointed site of **La Croix du Vieux Pont** at Berny-Rivière (near Soissons, about 80km/50mls north of *Disneyland Resort Paris*) comes highly recommended. With three swimming pools, bar, restaurant and tennis court, plus a good range of mobile homes and pitches, as well as facilities for the disabled, it is featured

*Clévacances*

*Parc de la Colline*

by British tour operators such as Haven, Keycamp and Canvas Holidays. Call 00 33 3 23 55 50 02 or visit **www.la-croix-du-vieux-pont.com**.

## Gîtes and Clévacances

Two other notable local forms of accommodation are the individual B&B style of the Gîtes de France, with some 145 *gîtes* and 99 guest rooms in the Seine-et-Marne region, and the newer Clévacances, or town centre holiday homes.

Generally speaking, the village style of the **Gîtes de France** offers charming, rural tastes of the local area and their people, with anything from two to ten rooms available to guests who enjoy becoming 'part of the family'. With so many to choose from throughout France they have become a mini-industry and you can obtain a full guide to the area's *gîtes* from the Comité Departemental du Tourisme de Seine-et-Marne at 11 Rue Royale, 77300 Fontainebleau, France, tel. 00 33 1 60 39 60 40 or visit **www.tourisme77.fr**. Log on to **www.gites-seine-et-marne.com** for more info about *gîtes*.

**Clévacances** are apartments, flats or suburban detached houses to let when not in use by their owners – from fully furnished weekly rentals to guest rooms. Prices range from €320–480 per week and they can be found throughout the Seine-et-Marne region, many very close to *Disneyland Resort Paris*. Reservations are usually handled directly with the owners and

## Holiday ownership

Inevitably, the explosion in hotel accommodation and tourist interest in the resort area has created the opportunity to 'buy' a piece of the holiday dream and there are several timeshare companies who would love you to sign on the dotted line. However, the only one we believe carries the right seal of approval is the extensive **Marriott's Village d'Ile de France** property, less than 2km/1ml from *Disneyland Resort Paris*. The first phase opened in June 2003 and consisted of 141 two-bed/two-bath townhouses with around 105sq m/1,260sq ft of living space. The Marriott Vacation Club International has genuine international bona fides and strong Disney ties, so you can be sure of getting a quality product, with excellent back-up at a good price.

The Village has access to three nearby 18-hole golf courses, plus its own dazzling array of facilities, including two swimming pools (one indoor lap pool and one outdoors), children's pool, whirlpool, health club (featuring a gym and aerobics room, sauna and steam room), children's facilities (games room, activity centre and outdoor playground), a bar/restaurant featuring local cuisine, a lobby lounge and a convenience store and deli (the Market Place, with a full array of fresh produce, wines and spirits, plus other essentials and even branded apparel). There is also 24-hour security and full reception services, and a regular shuttle bus to the theme parks.

The two-storey townhouses offer possibly the most luxurious accommodation in the region, with a king-size bed in the main bedroom, fully equipped kitchen (including microwave and dishwasher), a spacious living room (with satellite colour TV, DVD player and stereo), a utility room with washer/dryer, an individual terrace and an additional TV in each bedroom.

With Marriott Vacation Club, you purchase weeks within a particular season and you are free to reserve weeks within that season. You may change dates within your purchased time period from year to year (and there are then more than 50 Vacation Club resorts worldwide you can exchange weeks for). For more details, contact Marriott in the UK on 0800 328 3152; in France on 00 33 1 60 42 90 00; by e-mail to **mvciparis.owners@vacationclub.com**; or visit **www.vacationclub.com**.

they are categorised for comfort by a number of 'keys' from one to five. To get a free booklet or request more information, write to Clévacances Seine-et-Marne, 11 Rue Royale, 77300 Fontainebleau, France, tel. 00 33 1 60 39 60 39, or visit **www.clevacances.com/UK**.

## Hotel chains

Several French hotel chains offer good, cheap, basic accommodation for those on a budget both in Paris itself and in the Marne-la-Vallée area. Most are in the 1- and 2-star categories but a few offer a greater level of creature comforts. Here is a rundown of the most notable ones:

**Formule 1:** This is a basic, motel-type chain that keeps things pretty much cheap and cheerful (okay, forget about the cheerful bit). Built in boxy, prefab units, they are

accommodation only (apart from an extremely simple continental buffet breakfast €3.90/person) but they are almost invariably the cheapest in any location, with around 65 in the Ile de France region. They are surprisingly high-tech, with automated check-in

*Marriott's Vacation Club*

and clean, functional but small rooms. However, the rooms do not have a shower or WC, there are communal facilities on each floor. Part of the huge Accor hotel group, this is not the ideal place to go with a family because their service is so limited (and most rooms sleep only three) but for couples on a strict budget, they might be worth considering. For more details, call 0870 609 0961 in the UK or visit **www.hotelformule1.com. Our rating €, C.**

**Etap:** Similar to Formule 1 (and with 58 hotels in the region), but better, with an in-room shower and WC. Non-smoking rooms are also available. Call 0871 222 2288 in the UK or visit **www.etaphotel.com. Our rating €, C.**

**Campanile:** Another motel-style group. They don't have meals or bar service, although there is usually a restaurant attached to the property. Again, their hotels are all pretty uniform and stylised, but they are ideal for those on a budget, offer plenty of rooms for guests with disabilities and usually serve a great buffet breakfast. The rooms themselves are small but clean and comfortable. Part of the Envergure group (the second largest in Europe), the hotels rate officially as 2-star in France but provide a few extra, more thoughtful touches, such as in-room

*Kyriad Disneyland Resort Paris*

*Hotel Kyriad*

tea- and coffee-making facilities, making them a worthwhile place to stay. Rooms usually sleep only three and you need to reserve a child's fold-out bed in advance. Breakfast is around an extra €5/person at the associated restaurant and there are children's menus too. Call 0033 1 64 62 46 00 or visit **www.campanile.fr. Our rating €, CC.**

**Kyriad:** There are a lot more variations within this generally 2-star chain (which is also part of Envergure and a half-step up from Campanile) but it is still a basic family-orientated hotel. They have decent rooms that comfortably sleep three and some that accommodate four (one double bed, two singles). Some hotels include mini-bars and hairdryers and provide pleasant individual touches such as a welcome snack tray. Their excellent-value restaurants all have children's menus. Call 00 33 1 64 62 46 46 in the UK or visit **www.kyriad.com. Our rating €– €€, CC.**

The Hotel Kyriad at *Disneyland Resort Paris* has already been noted (see page 98), but another to look out for is the **Kyriad Chelles**, which is a friendly 2-star property in the town of Chelles just 20 minutes' drive from the theme parks (tel. 00 33 1 60 08 54 27).

*Comfort Inn Lagny-sur-Marne*

**Comfort Inn:** A similar quality and style to the Kyriad and Campanile chains, the Comfort Inn hotels (part of the Choice Hotels International group) are mainly found in central Paris and offer an excellent-value selection. Their city location means there is quite a difference in the style of each property but the basic standard remains sound. To book, call 0800 44 44 44 (in the UK) or 08 00 91 24 24 in France, or visit **www.choicehotels.com**. **Our rating** €€, **CC.**

There are some 27 Paris Comfort Inns, with the closest to *Disneyland Resort Paris* being the **Comfort Inn Lagny-sur-Marne**, a good 15 minutes away. However, it is still a good choice, easily accessed via A104 and A4. Lunch and dinner are available Mon–Fri at the on-site Casa Flavio, with drinks at the hotel bar. Babysitting, car hire service and guest laundry are available for an additional fee. There are also rooms for the disabled. Call 00 33 1 64 30 44 88 from the UK.

The Choice Hotels group also has ten of their more upmarket **Quality Hotel** properties in the Paris area, with an official 3-star rating and some elegant touches.

**Ibis:** A more upmarket 2-star choice (in the Accor group), this chain is functionally comfortable in general, with standard rooms (international satellite TV is a bonus, as is in-room internet connection) that sleep three (with an extra fold-out bed) and compact bathrooms. All have a restaurant, bar and snacks available 24 hours a day (part of their commitment to a more personal service), with an outstanding self-service breakfast buffet from 6.30–10am and a drinks and pastries service from 4–6am and 10am–noon. The restaurant choice varies from hotel to hotel. There are 51 Ibis hotels in the Paris region, including four in Marne-la-Vallée (see also page 93). To book, call 0892 68 66 86 in the UK or visit **www.ibishotel.com**. **Our rating** €€–€€€, **CC.**

**Mercure:** This member of the Accor group has a 3-tier quality system, the basic Relais/Inn Mercure, the genuinely 3-star Hotel Mercure and the more upmarket Grande Hotel Mercure, with enhanced levels of service and comfort. Most rooms accommodate three, with some family rooms for four, all have mini-bars and hairdryers. Non-smoking and rooms for the disabled are also available. The **Libertel** chain is also a Mercure affiliate, with a similar 3-star-plus style to the Grande Hotels. All have a decent restaurant (with a range of regional specialities), bar and a full-service continental breakfast. Their wine list is usually outstanding. The lobbies all feature a reading room, with a choice of international newspapers and magazines. They also

*Mercure Marne-la-Vallée*

specialise in weekend breaks, and most of their 52 hotels are in central Paris. To book, call 0870 609 0965 in the UK or visit **www.mercure.com**. **Our rating** €€€–€€€€, **CCC.**

**Novotel:** More of a businessman's hotel (and another member of the Accor group), but full of mod cons to suit tourist tastes as well, this modern chain offers fresh, spacious and comfortable rooms (sleeping up to four), chic restaurants and bars, and extras like satellite TV, mini-bars and room service. Most feature outdoor swimming pools (although they close from the early autumn to the end of spring) and conference/meeting facilities. Conversely, while they can be busy during the week, they often offer some great weekend breaks when they are quieter. Children stay free with their parents, but breakfast is extra. Call 0870 609 0962 in the UK or visit **www.novotel.com**. **Our rating:** €€€€, **CCC.**

*Sofitel Paris*

*Novoel Atria, Marne-la-Vallée*

In addition to the Novotel Collégien (see page 101), look out for the large **Novotel Atria Marne-la-Vallée**, in Noisy Le Grand, just 11km/6¾mls from *Disneyland Resort Paris*. It features 144 rooms (32 non-smoking), a smart bar-restaurant and a nice outdoor swimming pool in the summer. Call 00 33 1 48 15 60 60.

**Sofitel:** The premium brand in the Accor group, each hotel is an individual, but all with a deluxe style in both the sumptuous rooms and the excellent restaurants, with the latter featuring some of the best cuisine in Paris. The full range of mod cons and facilities are accompanied by efficient, courteous service. However, the handful of Sofitel hotels (12 of them) in the Ile de France are either in central Paris, Versailles or by Charles de Gaulle Airport, hence their price reflects both their location and upmarket nature. To book, call 0870 609 0964 in the UK or visit **www.sofitel.com**. **Our rating** €€€€€, **CCCC.**

Well, that's about all the essential accommodation info you need for now. Having dealt with the preliminaries, it is finally time to… hit the theme parks!

# 5 Welcome to the Parks

## or Here's where the fun really starts!

**O**kay, it's finally time to deal with the main business of being in *Disneyland Resort Paris* – the theme parks themselves. There is a lot to take on board – the *Disneyland Park* alone boasts some 48 attractions on its 57 hectares/140 acres, and there is something for all tastes and ages. The *Walt Disney Studios Park* has added a wealth of film- and TV-orientated fun, although there is probably less here to captivate the youngest visitors.

In all, there is at least three days' worth of pure adventure-mania spread between the two parks, and you need to have a pretty good idea of what's in store to get the most out of it and ensure you don't waste too much energy in the process! It is easy to get sidetracked by some of the clever details or minor attractions and miss out on some big-time thrills, while

equally, there is a genuine treasure trove of small-scale Disneyana that it would be a tragedy to overlook. Therefore, the following chapters will provide all you need to know to draw up your own plan of campaign for visiting each one.

If you have never visited a Disney theme park before, it is probably fair to start by reminding you this is NOT a comparable experience to a day at any other European park. That is not to denigrate the likes of Alton Towers (which is pretty sizeable), Thorpe Park or Chessington World of Adventures. All three possess some wonderful rides and offer good value for money. It is just that Disney builds and creates with a detail and a sense of wonder and fantasy that no one else can match.

You enter a truly magical world when you pass through the gates reading 'Le Parc Disneyland' in 1m/3ft high lettering. For the duration of your

*Main Street vehicles*

stay, you will be beguiled by a realm that offers the most enchanting and thrilling range of attractions on earth.

Anyone who has already been to the *Magic Kingdom Park* in Orlando or *Disneyland* in Anaheim, Los Angeles, will have a good idea of what to expect. However, while the *Disneyland Park* bears a strong resemblance to both of those, a lot of the essential detail and many of the attractions are different. When the Walt Disney Company set out to build a new resort experience on the European mainland, they did not want a mere copy of existing ideas. Rather, they wanted to update, enhance and improve, go back to the Imagineering drawing board if you like, cherry-picking the best features of all their parks and re-inventing them in a dramatic, new setting.

The Paris version is, to our eyes, a more refined and artistic interpretation of the American examples. The Imagineers were well aware they were building for a European market and have tried to tailor their designs in a less overtly American way. Of course, much of the fundamental magic inherent in the parks is quintessentially American, hence they maintain a strong essence of Uncle Sam. But, there is also a greater awareness of Disney's

*Peter Pan's Flight*

European heritage (Walt Disney himself spent a good deal of time in France as a young man and his family traced their lineage back to French antecedents) and of the need to tell the stories in a way that makes sense to an audience consisting primarily of French, British, Germans, Dutch, Belgians, Spanish and Italians (and they are never just plain 'rides' in a Disney park – everything has to tell a story and add to the overall theme).

Therefore, the multi-lingual nature of the resort is a key component to the overall feel and style of what's in store. Some of the design influences of the various nations are also evident in the theme parks themselves (the Sleeping Beauty Castle in the *Disneyland Park* is partly modelled on Mont St Michel in Normandy, for example).

*St Patrick's Day Parade*

# What's new in the parks

Disney forever looks at new ways to engage visitors and provide additional experiences, so there is a constant flow of live entertainment and other changes. In 2007, the Resort celebrated its **15th Anniversary** in grand style with an array of festivities centred on the *Disneyland Park*. A high-energy new parade, **Disney's Once Upon A Dream Parade**, was the daily highlight, along with **Disney's Character Express** and a new night-time presentation over the re-decorated Castle, **Candleabration**. The Anniversary celebration runs officially until March 2009 but several elements, like the Parades, will stay after that date. Other surprises included the re-opening of the **River Rogue Keelboats** and a major make-over for the old Critter Corral petting zoo to make it **Woody's Round-Up** character meet-and-greet plus the **Father Christmas Village** during the festive period and extra theming for Halloween.

In 2007, the resort also unveiled two major new attractions, **Crush's Coaster** and **Cars Quatre Roues Rallye** (Cars Race Rally) to begin a revamp of the *Walt Disney Studios Park*. This continues in '08 with the opening of the biggest ride in the Resort's history, **The Twilight Zone Tower of Terror** and another makeover of the former Television Studios Tour, to become the all-new and highly interactive **Stitch Live**. Additional entertainment included the **High School Musical On Tour** and **Toon Train** starring Chip 'n' Dale. In fact, much of the focus in 2008-09 will be on the newer park, as the Tower of Terror opening will also see part of the Production Courtyard area re-named as **Hollywood Boulevard**, with a whole new look and dramatic theming. Fabulous façades, buildings and a revamped entryway for the Studio Tram Tour will all serve to give this originally rather bland space a vibrant new lease of life and serve to make the *Walt Disney Studios Park* a much more inviting place to visit.

Of course, there will be other changes that beat our deadlines, so we are developing a website at **www.askdaisy.net/paris** for updates and further information.

## BRITTIP

It pays to arrive a little early for the opening time at each park to put yourself in front of the crowds for the first couple of hours. This way you can enjoy some of the rides that attract serious queues later on.

## The language challenge

It is true to say that the need to think in several languages provided the Imagineers with additional challenges that they had to meet in different ways – using subtitles, translations and extra soundtracks. While this adds a unique feel to familiar attractions ('it's a small world' or The Adventures of Snow White, for example), it does irk a small minority of English-speaking visitors – although we have yet to meet any children who didn't enjoy Pinocchio's Fantastic Journey simply because the commentary happened to be in French!

In our view, we always need to remember that we Brits are the visitors, and it pays to try to remember those few words of French we learned at school. At the end of the day, the resort is trying to appeal to the widest possible audience and, by and large, they succeed with extraordinarily cosmopolitan ability.

*Adventureland Bazaar*

© Disney

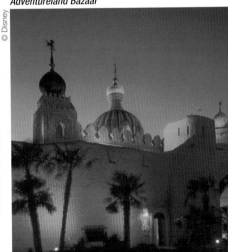

© Disney

*Eating at Annette's Diner in Disney Village*

## Set menus

A point worth highlighting for anyone unfamiliar with French restaurant culture is the usual provision of a fixed-price menu (*prix fixe*, in French) alongside the à la carte choice. Even at the standard counter-service burger-and-chips type diners, there is a Menu Mickey, consisting of a main course (burger, salad, pizza or pasta), a choice of dessert and a soft drink. At the full-service restaurants, the cheaper the set menu (starter, main course and dessert), the more limited it is.

*Legend of the Lion King at Videopolis*

© Disney

**BRITTIP**

If you fancy a beer at one of the counter-service restaurants around the theme parks, the best value is to choose the set meal option with beer instead of soft drink and you pay just €1 extra.

For both parks, we provide an At-A-Glance guide (on pages 124 and 162) that gives you some idea of what to expect to pay for food and souvenirs along the way. It is worth pointing out that your costs can quickly mount up if you buy numerous snacks – a small mineral water costs €2.40, a 25cl beer is €3.60, soft drinks variously €2, €2.60 and €3.40, three mini-doughnuts are €2.60 and a large portion of chips is €2.50. Kids' meals, which consist of a main course, such as chicken nuggets or pizza, chips, a small drink and a 'surprise' toy, are all €6. Even if you are totally unfamiliar with euros, you should be able to work out the kind of real cost you are looking at for a day in the theme parks.

Many of the outlets can provide something for the veggie appetite. The full-service restaurants all offer at least one vegetarian main course and good salads are not hard to find. They will also do their best to accommodate requests from guests

© Disney

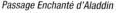
*Meet Aladdin in Adventureland*

## Character dining

Whether you are travelling as a family, a couple or on your own, some of the most magical memories can be made when you have a meal with Mickey and Co. Meeting the characters in a more intimate setting, with no long queues to navigate, is a real treat, with one-on-one interaction that is second to none. Watching Pluto colour with the children, seeing dad's reaction when Cinderella passes by or capturing Prince Charming kissing mum's hand are moments to be treasured for a lifetime.

Characters circulate inside the restaurant, stopping at each table for play time and precious family photos. The amount of time available to each group is dependent upon how busy the restaurant is (book off-hours, when things are quieter, for most attention). Don't forget to bring your autograph book and a fat pen, which is easier for the characters to hold. Some children may initially be put off by the size of some characters (who appear huge to little guests!), so you may want to see how your children react to them in the parks (from a 'safe' distance) before booking a meal.

Character meals can be booked as an add-on option to your package, when booking a room at a Disney resort, at City Hall or Studios Services or by

who have particular dietary requirements; don't be afraid to ask. Unlike the versions of the *Magic Kingdom Park* in American Disney resorts, this one does serve alcohol, but it is not cheap. A beer in one of the full-service restaurants is usually €4.20–5.50, while a bottle of wine can vary from €16–50.

Disney has also moved to make some of their food offerings – especially their kids' meals – a touch healthier by introducing more vegetables and fruit. Be sure to ask for these options when you order.

*Passage Enchanté d'Aladdin*

© Disney

calling the Reservation Hotline (from the UK) 00 33 1 60 30 40 50.

## The meals

*Disneyland Park:* **The Lucky Nugget Saloon** (usually with some characters from the following list: Chip 'n' Dale, Pluto, Goofy, Captain Hook, Tigger and Pinocchio); lunch (noon–3pm) or dinner (6.30pm–10pm, only available when park is open until 11pm, not available 31 December) buffet with international specialities, including starters, main courses and desserts; children have a special buffet with a drink and a surprise (cost €30 adults, €15 ages 3–11). Single Half Board Meal vouchers accepted as payment at this location only. **Plaza Gardens Restaurant** *Tea Party with Disney Characters* (usually with characters selected from Robin Hood, Minnie Mouse, Chip 'n' Dale, Donald and Daisy Duck and Tigger). Buffet selection of pastries, cakes, cookies, brownies, muffins, chocolate mousse and hot and cold drinks. Held every day, time confirmed upon booking (cost €13/person, under 3s free). Plaza Gardens also offers *Happy Birthday with Disney Characters* buffet of pastries and sweets, a slice of chocolate cake, plus a surprise present, a name badge and a birthday card for €18/person. **Auberge de Cendrillon** (with Disney Princes and Princesses, plus Suzy and Perla,

© Disney

*The Steakhouse in Disney Village*

Cinderella's mice). Set-price lunch or dinner featuring a cocktail for adults (soft drink for children), starter, main course and Cinderella Slipper dessert (cost €48/adult, €20 ages 3–11).

*Disney Village: Character Breakfast* at either **Café Mickey** or **The Steakhouse** (location varies; characters will include at least four of the following: Mickey, Minnie, Goofy, Pluto, Captain Hook, Tigger and Eeyore). Breakfast buffet of breads, cereals, scrambled eggs, pastries, fruit juice and hot drinks; two sittings – 7.30am and 9.30am (cost €17/adult, €12 ages 3–11 if you are staying at a Disney hotel – except *Disneyland Hotel*; €22 and €15 if you are staying at a non-Disney hotel – guests at Hotel l'Elysée, Pierre & Vacances Val d'Europe and Radisson SAS Hotel, second sitting only). **Café Mickey** also

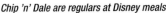

*Chip 'n' Dale are regulars at Disney meals*

© Disney

## Top 10 attractions

Here, purely for fun, is what we rate as our top 10 attractions, first for the *Disneyland Park*:

1 Pirates of the Caribbean
2 Space Mountain: Mission 2
3 Big Thunder Mountain Railroad
4 Phantom Manor
5 Indiana Jones and the Temple of Peril
6 Disney's Fantillusion Parade
7 Disney's Once Upon A Dream Parade
8 Star Tours
9 Legend of the Lion King
10 Buzz Lightyear's Laser Blast

And for the *Walt Disney Studios*:

1 Twilight Zone Tower of Terror
2 Cinémagique
3 Moteurs…Action! Stunt Show Spectacular
4 Rock 'n' Roller Coaster starring Aerosmith
5 Crush's Coaster
6 Disney's Cinema Parade
7 Armageddon: Special Effects
8 Animagique
9 Studio Tram Tour
10 Stitch Live

serves lunch and dinner continuously from noon–11pm, with the same line-up of characters present from 12.15pm–3pm and 6pm–10pm. With the characters here most of the day, you will usually benefit from some of the best character interaction at Café Mickey, which the kids will love.

*Disneyland Hotel:* **Inventions Restaurant** has a *character breakfast* – featuring selected characters from Mickey, Minnie, Goofy, Pluto, Tigger and Pinocchio – exclusively for *Disneyland Hotel* guests, but the *character dinner* (with some of Minnie, Mickey, Goofy, Pluto, Chip 'n' Dale and Eeyore) is open to the general public. Breakfast is a buffet with breads, hot meats, scrambled eggs, baked beans, potato, fruit and yoghurts, plus hot and cold drinks. Dinner buffet includes seafood, cold meats, salads, carved roast, desserts and more (cost €46/adult, €24 ages 7–11, €18 ages 3–6). Arrive at Inventions early for their dinner and you will benefit from some of the best character interaction as it is seldom busy early on.

## Ticket types

Moving along to more practical matters, you need to work out what type of ticket you should buy to make the most of your stay. With most packages that provide your accommodation, Park Hopper tickets for the length of your stay are included. That means you can enjoy both parks from the minute you arrive until the time set for your departure. It obviously provides the peace of mind and convenience of knowing that you do not need to worry about the mechanics of which park to visit when, as you have the benefit of being able to hop between parks at any time.

However, there is a range of ticket types, including annual ones, which are worth considering if you are staying off-site or visit regularly.

*Captain Hook's Galley*

© Disney

**1-Day Ticket:** This provides admission to either the *Disneyland Park* or the *Walt Disney Studios Park* for a full day's fun (which can be up to 11pm at peak periods). You may exit and re-enter the same park as many times as you wish throughout the day.

**1/2/3-Day Park Hopper:** This great-value ticket provides 1, 2 or 3 full days at the two parks, offering total freedom of movement between them on each day. The days do NOT need to be consecutive, which is invaluable if you are staying off-site and visiting other attractions and places in the region over, say, a week. Park Hopper tickets are also valid for a year from the date of purchase (but not if they are part of a package).

**Fantasy Annual Passport:** This provides entry to both parks, plus some useful extras like free parking, a free annual magazine, access to the official website with special offers and invites to special occasions (like new attraction previews), plus 25% off special event tickets (such as the Halloween party) and 10% off at Disney restaurants and shops. However, there ARE blackout days at both parks when the Passport is not valid for admission. In 2008 they are 23 March, 14–20 April, 2, 9, 11 May, 11–15, 30, 31 August, 26–31 October and 26–30 December. For 2009 dates, check out this website **www.disneyland paris.com/fr/passeport_annuel/nonadh/ hp.htm** (for some reason they give the information in French only).

*Hurricanes*

© Disney

© Disney

*Café Mickey*

### 🇬🇧 BRITTIP

You can save money if you are tempted to buy an Annual Passport after a visit to the theme parks, as the cost of a single day will be deducted from the cost of the Annual Passport. Visit the Annual Passport office at either theme park before you leave.

**Dream Annual Passport:** This version offers unlimited year-round access to both parks, access to Fantasyland in the *Disneyland Park* 1 hour before official opening and preferential rates on Disney hotel rooms at certain times, plus a number of exclusive advantages, discounts and events especially organised for Dream Passport holders. The bonuses include 10% off in most shops, restaurants and bars throughout the resort, 15% off up to four tickets for Buffalo Bill's Wild West Show, 50% off Disney's Halloween Party Night, free aperitif at table-service restaurants, free admission to Hurricanes nightclub in *Disney Village* for the passport holder and one guest, 50% off special event tickets, free parking for the theme parks or *Disney Village*, free pushchair and wheelchair hire in the theme parks, free luggage storage, 10% off *Golf Disneyland* fees, up to €4 off per person at Davy Crockett's Adventure, free annual magazine, priority information and reservation hotline, access to the official website with special offers and information and invitations to special occasions at the resort.

*McDonald's at Disney Village*

## BRITTIP

If just one family member buys the Dream Annual Passport, the whole party can still benefit from the many discounts at the shops and restaurants in the parks.

There is a substantial difference in price between the two Annual Passports (see At-A-Glance guides on pages 124 and 162), but you can save a good deal over the course of a year if you plan on visiting more than once, and the savings against the multi-day Hoppers should also be obvious.

## BRITTIP

Fancy a dabble on the stockmarket? All shareholders of Euro Disney SCA (the holding company that runs the resort) benefit from a range of hotel, park, shop and restaurant discounts similar to those of the Dream Annual Passport holders.

## Where to buy tickets

So, where can you buy your tickets, apart from joining the long early-morning queues at the ticket booths at the entrance to both parks? Well, you can call the UK booking line on 08705 030303 or the 7-day-a-week French centre on 00 33 1 60 30 60 30; visit any Disney Store in Britain or on the Champs-Elysées in Paris; any FNAC store in Paris; the Virgin Megastore on the Champs-Elysées;

the main RATP ticket offices on the Métro or RER; any Travelex Foreign Exchange Bureau (notably at the Eurotunnel terminal in Folkestone and at Portsmouth ferry terminal); on board P&O Ferries on Dover–Calais routes; or the Eurostar ticketing desks at the London St Pancras terminal or Ashford stations, or their Victoria station shop.

## BRITTIP

It is usually worth buying your tickets as far in advance as possible to avoid the probable annual price increase (usually in late autumn/early winter).

There are then the various official ticket brokers at travel agents and other outlets, some of whom can offer **4- and 5-Day Hopper Tickets**. Three companies we are happy to vouch for are Attraction Tickets Direct, Keith Prowse Attraction Tickets and Theme Park Tickets Direct.

*The Disney Store on the Champs-Elysées*

**Attraction Tickets Direct**, well known for being the UK's number one ticket broker for Orlando attractions, often run special offers on *Disneyland Resort Paris* 1-, 2-, 4-, and 5-Day Hopper tickets, and offer a unique Price Promise guarantee. They provide actual tickets, not vouchers, have free delivery within 7 days and their brochure is free upon request. Contact them on 0800 975 0002 (or visit **www.attraction-tickets-direct.co.uk**).

The **Keith Prowse** ticket agency (on 08701 232425 or online at **www.keith prowsetickets.com**) run occasional 'extras' with their tickets, plus a range of Paris city excursions, dinner shows (including the Lido de Paris, Moulin Rouge and Crazy Horse cabarets), sightseeing tours and cruises, and it is well worth getting a copy of their brochure. **Theme Park Tickets Direct** (on 0870 040 0210 or **www.themepark ticketsdirect.com**) are keenly priced, too.

🇬🇧 **BRITTIP**

Attraction Tickets Direct have some handy **discussion forums** on their website and we have been known to make an appearance there from time to time, so drop in and ask us a question or tell us your *Disneyland Resort Paris* stories!

*Keith Prowse also sell tickets to the Lido*

Once you have your tickets, you can avoid the first bugbear of visiting either park – the ticket booths. These are located prominently outside both parks but, however many windows are open, there is nearly always a slow-moving queue. If you can avoid them, you'll be a significant jump ahead of the crowds.

The final thing to remember before we get to the theme parks proper is that you can always escape the crowds – especially in the *Walt Disney Studios Park* – during the day by stepping out into *Disney Village* for a while. If the theme parks are heaving, the *Disney Village* and the hotels are probably a lot quieter. The great accessibility and convenience of the whole resort means that it IS possible

*Carrousel de Lancelot*

© Disney

## Rides for wimps!

For those who are reluctant to hurl themselves on to the fastest rides, here (by special online request!) is a guide to a walk on the 'mild side' with Disney. None of these will upset even the most sensitive of stomachs (although, with the exception of The Twilight Zone Tower of Terror, Crush's Coaster, Space Mountain, Indiana Jones, Mad Hatter's Tea Cups and the Rock 'n' Roller Coaster, there are few rides designed to be really dynamic):

1   Disneyland Railroad
2   'it's a small world'
3   Le Pays des Contes de Fées
4   Le Carrousel de Lancelot
5   Peter Pan's Flight
6   Flying Carpets Over Agrabah
7   Casey Junior
8   Autopia
9   Thunder Mesa Riverboats
10  Dumbo the Flying Elephant

to find places without queues to enjoy a meal, a drink or just recharge the batteries (and, at peak periods, you WILL need a breather at times) before you charge back into the hectic whirl.

## Ratings

All the rides and shows in the theme parks are judged on a unique *Brit Guide* rating system that splits them into Thrill rides and Scenic rides. Thrill rides earn T ratings out of five (hence a TTTTT is as exciting as it gets) and scenic rides get A ratings out of five (an AA ride is likely to be over-cute and missable). Obviously, it is a matter of opinion to a certain extent but you can be sure a T or A ride is not worth your time; a TT or AA is worth seeing only if there isn't a queue; a TTT or AAA should be seen if you have time, but you won't miss much if you don't; a TTTT or AAAA ride is a big-time attraction that should be high on your list of things to do; and a TTTTT or AAAAA

© Disney

*Thunder Mesa Riverboat*

attraction should not be missed! The latter will have the longest queues, so you should plan your visit around these rides.

## FastPass

Disney has a unique FastPass (FP) system for some of its most popular shows and rides worldwide and it is worth taking advantage of it in the *Disneyland Park* (it is not always available in the *Walt Disney Studios Park*, where queues tend to be shorter at quieter times of the year).

*'it's a small world'*

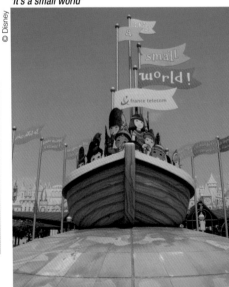

© Disney

## BRITTIP

Some rides DO run out of FastPasses before the end of the day, so it is advisable to grab one for the likes of Peter Pan's Flight and Big Thunder Mountain BEFORE early afternoon.

Here's how the FastPass works: at all attractions with the FastPass service (which is FREE – many people don't realise this), there are a series of kiosks next to the main entrance. Insert your park entrance ticket into a kiosk and it immediately spits your ticket out, followed by a separate slip with a time 'window' during which you should return to the separate FastPass queue (usually at least 1 hour later, occasionally 4 or more). When your 'window' is open, simply return to the FastPass queue and enjoy the attraction with only a minimal wait. You can only hold one FastPass per 2-hour period, although once you have used it you can get another. If your return time is more than 2 hours away, you can get a second FastPass after 2 hours have passed. For example, if you get a FastPass for Space Mountain at 9am with a return time between 1pm and 2pm, you can get a second FastPass for, say, Big Thunder Mountain at 11am. You need FastPass tickets for EVERY member of your party.

© Disney

*Star Tours FastPass outlet*

## BRITTIP

If you have young children, it is a good idea to put a note in their pocket with details of their name, your mobile phone number, hotel, etc. Cast Members are trained to take lost children to the Meeting Place and the provision of a note makes their job easier.

Some rides are restricted to children over a certain height and are not advisable for people with back, neck or heart problems or for pregnant women. Where this is the case, we have noted 'Restrictions: 1.32m/4ft 3in' and so on. Height restrictions (which are strictly enforced) are based on the average 5-year-old being 1.02m/3ft 3in tall, 6s being 1.1m/3ft 6in and 9s being 1.32m/4ft 3in.

*Big Thunder Mountain*

© Disney

## Pin trading

In addition to collecting souvenirs, you will probably also encounter the pin-trading phenomenon at some stage of your Disney adventure. This is hard to explain to the uninitiated as it has no real parallel in modern British culture. It is a particularly American idea and involves collecting – and trading – the many dozens of different enamel brooches that you can buy in almost every shop. They vary in price from around €8–15 and serious collectors carry them on lanyards around their neck, eagerly looking to barter and swap with other members of this not-so-secret society. Various Disney Cast Members also join in by displaying lanyards with pins to swap, and they are duty-bound to swap for anything they may be displaying. Children particularly appreciate this opportunity for a sure-thing, and Cast Members are usually gracious about waiting for youngsters to make a decision.

We have to say, pin trading rather baffles us, but those who get hooked on it will attest to having great fun looking for potential swaps with fellow devotees (as well as spending a small fortune on their collections!). For more info, log on to the UK-orientated discussion boards of **www.disboards.com** or **www.thedibb.co.uk** and ask one of the regulars to explain how to get suitably enthused!

Those with neck or back problems, or mothers-to-be, are advised to avoid the following rides: Space Mountain: Mission 2, Indiana Jones and the Temple of Peril, Big Thunder Mountain Railroad and Mad Hatter's Tea Cups at the *Disneyland Park* and The Twilight Zone Tower of Terror, Crush's Coaster and Rock 'n' Roller Coaster at the *Walt Disney Studios Park*.

## The 'baby switch'

If you have small children, but don't want to leave them while you have a ride, you DON'T have to queue twice. When you get to the front of the queue, tell the operator you want to do a 'baby switch'. This means mum can go on the ride while dad looks after junior and, on her return, dad can have his turn while mum does the babysitting.

**BRITTIP**
Many children also get a big thrill from collecting autographs from the various Disney characters they meet, and nearly all the hotels and shops sell some great autograph books.

If you have children of wide-ranging ages, check out the special section at the end of each park chapter to see which rides and attractions appeal most to which age groups. It is important in a resort of this size to concentrate on those areas that have the most appeal for YOU and, while it is not possible to be 100% accurate, the advice here is fairly tried and tested, so you can get a pretty good idea of what is most likely to be popular with your offspring!

*Space Mountain: Mission 2*

© Disney

© Disney

*Good Morning Main Street Parade*

A full **Baby Care Centre** is provided in the *Disneyland Park* next door to the Plaza Gardens Restaurant at the top of Main Street USA on the right, where there are nappy-changing facilities and a feeding room, with baby food (and nappies) on sale. **The Meeting Place for Lost Children** is also located here, with its own Disney staff. At the *Walt Disney Studios Park*

*The entrance to Adventureland*

© Disney

the Baby Care Centre is behind the Studio Services in the Front Lot, just inside the entrance on the right-hand side and you can find your lost children there, too.

**BRITTIP**

Kids, try to find the thickest pen you can for collecting autographs. Most of the characters find it a struggle to write with normal-size pens in their great big hands.

## Park etiquette

Some final words of warning. Picnics are NOT allowed inside the theme parks (although you can take bottles of water), but there is an area set aside for picnics outside at the exit of the moving walkway from the main car park. Appropriate clothing must be worn in the parks – which means shirt and shoes – at all times. No bare chests – even for women! Smoking, eating, drinking, flash photography and video lighting are not permitted on rides, during shows or in queues.

So what are we waiting for? First stop, the *Disneyland Park…*

# 6 The Disneyland Park

## or To all who come to this happy place, welcome!

It makes sense to start by taking an in-depth look at the original development here at *Disneyland Resort Paris,* the first Disney park in Europe, which opened its gates in April 1992. Although it is comparable to the *Magic Kingdom* in *Walt Disney World* (America's biggest tourist attraction), be prepared for some surprises in both scale and content from the US version. The *Disneyland Park* is bigger by some 17 hectares (42 acres) than its Orlando counterpart and, while there are fewer 'lands', the Paris version is more elaborate and involving.

The attractions range from the twee and fairly ordinary (Mad Hatter's Tea Cups and Autopia) to the wonderfully inventive (Phantom Manor and Pirates of the Caribbean) and on to the downright thrilling (Space Mountain and Indiana Jones and the Temple of Peril). The all-encompassing theming covers the Wild West (Frontierland), dark jungles and pirate caverns (Adventureland), film and storybook fantasy (Fantasyland) and a kind of retro future world (Discoveryland), possibly the most imaginative of the lot. There is at least one (depending on the time of year) unmissable daily parade and a range of other live theatrical productions that all carry the Disney hallmark of captivating family entertainment. In fact, there's plenty to make you go 'Wow!' plus a whole variety of attractions that will raise a big smile or two.

Prepare to be completely immersed in a convincing world of make-believe, where every tiny detail – from the uniforms of the Cast Members to the clever signage – conforms to that land's theme. But, be aware of some fairly blatant attempts to lighten your wallet along the way, notably at the many gift shops and especially after a number of the rides. By Disney's own reckoning, some 16,000 types of merchandise are on sale and, although 90% of it costs less than €15, it can quickly add up if you have children of the large-eyed variety!

*Sleeping Beauty Castle*

© Disney

Another slight negative to be aware of is the quality (or lack of it) in much of the counter-service dining. With only a couple of notable exceptions, the fare is not terribly imaginative nor is it particularly cheap (around €10 a head, even for the most basic meal). In the course of 3 days, that can be almost €190 just in meals for a family of four, eating twice a day at park counter-service restaurants (although the new **Half Board Meal Plan** can save as much as 15% off these costs if you are a Disney hotel guest – see page 77). Conversely, the handful of full-service restaurants DO offer some fabulous food – but at a price. Go for lunch at our favourite restaurant, the Blue Lagoon, and you could easily be €86 lighter with four to feed. A cheaper alternative is to stock up at breakfast, keep going with snacks from the many hot dog, popcorn, doughnut and drinks wagons around the theme park and have your main meal in *Disney Village* or at the hotel in the evening (where buffet options are often better value).

## The Disneyland Park at a glance

| | |
|---|---|
| Location | Off Exit 14 of the A4 autoroute, proceed to the clearly signed car park; or turn right out of the Marne-la-Vallée RER and TGV station; or through the *Disney Village* if staying at a resort hotel |
| Size | 57 hectares/140 acres in five 'lands' |
| Hours | 10am–6 or 7pm autumn and winter weekdays; 10am–8, 9 or 10pm spring, plus autumn and winter weekends, half-term holidays; 9 or 10am–10pm Christmas and New Year (until 1am New Year's Eve); 9am–11pm summer holidays (mid-July–August) |
| Admission | **Under 3** free; **3–11** €39 (1-Day Ticket), €49, €89, €111 (1-, 2- and 3-Day Park Hopper), **adults** (12+) €47 (1-Day Ticket), €57, €105, €131 (1-, 2- and 3-Day Park Hopper); **Annual Passports** (per person): Fantasy €129, Dream €179. *NB: All prices subject to increase from Easter 2008 (see **www.disneylandparis.com**)* |
| Parking | €8 |
| Pushchairs | €7.50 (Pushchair shop to right of main entrance, just under railway arch) |
| Wheelchairs | €7.50 (Pushchair shop) |
| Top Attractions | Space Mountain: Mission 2, Star Tours, Peter Pan's Flight, Dumbo the Flying Elephant, Big Thunder Mountain Railroad, Legend Of The Lion King |
| Don't Miss | Disney's Once Upon A Dream Parade, Fantillusion Parade and Wishes fireworks (summer and Christmas seasons only), The Tarzan Encounter, 'it's a small world', La Tanière du Dragon |
| Hidden Costs | Meals — Burger, chips and coke €9.95; 3-course meal at Blue Lagoon €28 (€15 for children); beer 25cl €3.60, 50cl €7.20. Kids' meal €9 (at all counter-service restaurants) |
| | T-shirts — €6.90–35 |
| | Souvenirs — €2.50–1,375 |
| | Sundries — Kids' autograph book €4.90 and €9.90; Space Mountain ride photos €15–20 |

# DISNEYLAND PARK

**Main Street, USA**
1 Main Street USA Railroad Station
2 Town Square
3 Disneyland City Hall
4 Main Street Transportation Company Vehicles
5 Liberty Arcade
6 Discovery Arcade
7 Central Plaza

**Frontierland**
8 Fort Comstock
9 Phantom Manor
10 Thunder Mesa Riverboat Landing
11 Rustler Roundup Shootin' Gallery
12 Big Thunder Mountain
13 Pocahontas Indian Village
14 River Rogue Keelboats
15 Woody's Round-Up
16 Chaparral Theatre
17 Frontierland Railroad Station

**Adventureland**
18 Indiana Jones and the Temple of Peril
19 Adventure Isle
20 La Cabane des Robinsons
21 Skull Rock
22 Pirates' Beach
23 Pirates of the Caribbean
24 Passage Enchanté d'Aladdin

**Fantasyland**
25 Sleeping Beauty Castle
26 Le Carrousel de Lancelot
27 The Adventures of Snow White
28 Pinocchio's Fantastic Journey
29 Dumbo the Flying Elephant
30 Peter Pan's Flight
31 Fantasy Festival Stage
32 Fantasyland Railroad Station
33 Alice's Curious Labyrinth
34 Le Pays des Contes de Fées
35 Casey Jr – le Petit Train du Cirque
36 Mad Hatter's Tea Cups
37 'it's a small world'
38 Royal Castle Stage

**Discoveryland**
39 Space Mountain: Mission 2
40 Les Mystères du Nautilus
41 Orbitron – Machines Volantes
42 Star Tours
43 Discoveryland Railroad Station
44 Honey, I Shrunk the Audience
45 Autopia
46 Buzz Lightyear's Laser Blast
47 Videopolis/Legend Of The Lion King
48 Arcades Alpha & Beta

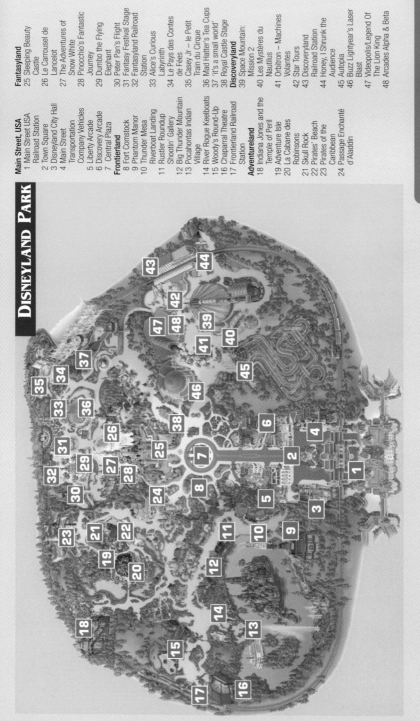

## BRITTIP

If you want a real budget option for lunch, nip out of the parks to the RER station of Marne-la-Vallée and grab a baguette, sandwich or Croque Monsieur at the station café. The beer alone is €2 cheaper!

You actually enter 'Le Parc Disneyland' underneath the *Disneyland Hotel*, the rather fanciful conglomeration of buildings known as the Pink Palace. You pass some extremely pleasant gardens (the whimsical Fantasia Gardens, with a number of character-shaped topiaries) and the inevitable fountains and ponds (good photo spot, this) before entering the main entrance plaza. The ticket booths are to the right of the entrance passage, but hopefully you already have your tickets and can head straight to the turnstiles. If you need Guest Relations or Left Luggage, bear to the right of the main hotel building and they are in front of you. Be aware there is quite a walk from the main car park to the theme parks, even with the moving walkways. You should allow 5–10 minutes to get there and pushchairs are a real boon if you have little ones.

*Disney & Co on Main Street*

*City Hall*

# Main Street USA

Once through the turnstiles, you enter a plaza in front of the main Disneyland Railroad station. Walk under the station and you are in **Town Square**, the main entrance to *Disneyland Park* proper and the lower portion of the first 'land', Main Street USA. This is a grand, turn-of-the-century version of small-town America, with a truly eye-catching array of shop and office façades all built in epic detail. It is not so much a thoroughfare as a living museum to generations of genuine Americana and it offers a fabulous glimpse into an idealised past of the United States.

Here you will get your first look at the most-photographed edifice in the whole resort – the Sleeping Beauty Castle (or Le Château de la Belle au Bois Dormant, to use its full French title). To your left is **Disneyland City Hall**, another guest relations office where you can pick up park maps (if you haven't already got one at your hotel or in the many cubicles underneath the Railroad Station), book meals at any of the restaurants or just ask any park-related questions.

## BRITTIP

Can't find the characters? Go to City Hall and they will tell you where they will be. City Hall is your best friend for a variety of queries – from the location of baby facilities (there are none here) to meal bookings.

## 15th anniversary fun

April 2007 saw the start of two years of birthday festivities centred on the *Disneyland Park*, with a lot of new decoration and live entertainment to mark the occasion. Some of this will be removed at the end of the Anniversary (March 2009), but key elements will remain to enhance the scene here. Look out in particular for **Disney's Once Upon A Dream Parade**, which has become the park's new signature daily highlight, the **Disney Character Express**, a cavalcade of character favourites, and **Candleabration**, a clever evening light-and-show spectacular in front of the heavily enhanced Castle.

To your right is the **Main Street Transportation Company**, where several vintage and horse-drawn vehicles can take you along Main Street USA to the Central Plaza, the theme park's hub, from which radiate the other four 'lands'. If you have time (or children), it is quite fun to take one of the horse-drawn trams or vintage cars (including a police paddy-wagon), but it's quicker to walk (especially if you use either of the two covered arcades that run alongside Main Street USA).

One of the most eye-catching features is the **Disneyland Railroad**, with a station (it has four; Adventureland is the only 'land' without a railroad

stop) well positioned to catch the unsuspecting visitor. The Victorian-style station provides an elevated view down Main Street USA, but the signature steam train ride, which circles the whole park and includes a clever 'Grand Canyon' scene en route to Frontierland (and a glimpse inside Pirates of the Caribbean), has long, slow-moving queues for much of the day. Be aware some stations may be used for offloading only during non-peak seasons. AAA.

### BRITTIP

The Disneyland Railroad is a relaxing ride when many of the others are showing long queues but DON'T join it at Main Street where few people actually get off. Instead, try the stations at Frontierland or Fantasyland for the shortest wait.

Main Street USA is basically the theme park's principal shopping area, with a whole range of stores (including the gargantuan **Emporium**, which stocks just about every kind of souvenir known to mouse-kind!) and cafés. Also here is **Dapper Dan's Hair Cuts**, a wonderfully atmospheric vintage barber's with the kind of furnishings you would usually find only in an antique shop (or an apothecary's). You can stop for a haircut or shave if the mood takes you (€20 or €14; €29 for both) or to get your child's hair cut (€10).

*Main Street USA*

© Disney

© Disney

*Liberty Arcade*

Main Street USA is full of clever Disney memorabilia – look for photos of Walt and his wife Lilly in Lilly's Boutique; the two murals of other Emporium shops in the Emporium; and the plates set into the street that bear the legend 'Elias Disney Constructions'. Many of the windows also bear witness to Disney Imagineers and VIPs down the years.

If you need any film or photographic equipment, Town Square Photography should be able to help you out (although beware the prices here – it is much cheaper to bring basics like film, batteries and flashcards with you). In all, there are 12 cunningly arranged shops along this 100m/109yd boulevard and it is worthwhile returning in the afternoon when the rides are busiest to check out some of the amazing detail here.

*Plaza Gardens Restaurant*

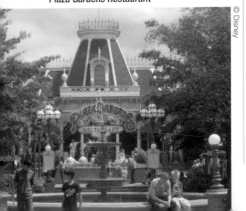

© Disney

You can also find ten different snack bars and restaurants to provide everything from breakfast, to a gourmet lunch, afternoon tea and evening dessert. Pick of the bunch is **Walt's – An American Restaurant**, which offers an elegant lunch and dinner (set menu €25 or €29, €12 for children, €15 teens). This fabulous diner, designed like a 1900s' hotel, is a tribute to Walt Disney himself, his ideas and creations, and features a wealth of personal detail, photos and memorabilia.

Hunting for bargains? Stop at the Plaza East and West Boutiques before you exit the park for special discounts. They stock a range of previous season's merchandise at greatly reduced prices.

At the top of Main Street USA, the **Plaza Gardens Restaurant** (11.30am–10.30pm) offers an excellent series of all-you-can-eat buffets for lunch and dinner in a plush, conservatory-style setting. The buffet is €20/adult, €10/child (and drinks not included) consists of a huge cold spread – salads, meats, bread and fruit – and a whole array of hot dishes – casseroles, pasta, roast beef, sausages, hot dogs and several types of vegetable and rice – plus a mouth-watering selection of desserts. There is also an excellent **character tea-time** (3–4.30pm) every day, featuring all the

*Casey's Corner*

Disney favourites, with a tantalising spread of cakes, pastries and desserts, plus one hot and one cold drink each (€13/person). For an extra €5 a head you can enjoy the even more fun-filled character Birthday Party.

### BRITTIP

Video camera battery running down? Don't fret – you can visit City Hall and they will be able to recharge it for you there and then.

Otherwise, your eateries are mainly of the counter-snack kind, with the **Market House Deli** (sandwiches, salads and pasta), **Casey's Corner** (all manner of hot dogs and soft drinks), **Victoria's Home-Style Restaurant** (pasta, quiche, pizza and salads), **The Coffee Grinder** (coffee, tea and cakes), **The Ice Cream Company** (hosted by Nestlé), **The Cookie Kitchen** and **Cable Car Bake Shop** (two sides of the same breakfast-orientated servery, with some delicious pastries and cookies) and the **Gibson Girl Ice Cream Parlour** (a full range of ice cream delights). Bear in mind not all of these are likely to be open at any one time (apart from the weekends in high season).

### BRITTIP

As an example of the Imagineers' art, listen carefully outside Victoria's Home-Style Restaurant and you will catch the distinct sounds of someone using the bathroom in the 'guesthouse' above!

For shopping, you should definitely check out the **Emporium** and **Lilly's Boutique** (glass and porcelain), as well as **The Storybook Store** (books, stationery, CD and audio cassettes), **Harrington's Fine China & Porcelain** (some lovely china, crystal and glass giftware), **Disney Clothiers Ltd** (adult and children's apparel) and **Main Street Motors** (more clothing).

As an alternative to walking up the middle of Main Street USA, pick one of the two arcades at either side (the **Liberty Arcade** to the left and the **Discovery Arcade** to the right) and wander right through away from most of the crowds. The Liberty Arcade features a clever tableau about immigrants arriving in New York (in French), while the Discovery Arcade is decorated with some clever period detail, which is worth a look later on.

### BRITTIP

Need to stay dry? Both Liberty and Discovery Arcades are fully covered and provide back-door access to most of the shops and cafés along Main Street USA. Very popular in winter!

At the top of Main Street USA on the right-hand side (just after the Gibson Girl Ice Cream Parlour) is a handy **Information Board** that displays the waiting times at the various attractions. Late arrivals should take note of this to get an idea of where to head first (and where to avoid for a while until the queues die down).

*Gibson Girl Ice Cream Parlour*

Main Street USA is also one of the prime locations to meet various **Disney characters**. Most days start with the official character 'opening ceremony', an early-morning cavalcade featuring Mickey, Pluto and various other chums. Many of them stop to sign autographs in three locations – on a platform outside the Liberty Arcade (just past Casey's Corner on the left as you come up the street), in the Central Plaza and on the Royal Castle Stage just to the right of Sleeping Beauty Castle.

For Halloween, Main Street USA is transformed into **Spooky Street**, with a major pumpkin-inspired makeover and some wonderfully clever visual touches. A giant pumpkin also appears in front of the Castle, with free face-painting for children under 11.

**BRITTIP**

Halloween is one of the most popular periods at the *Disneyland Park*, and you can expect some of the longest queues during the school half-term break and weekends in October.

*Halloween decorations on Main Street*

## Rope drop

If you arrive prior to the official opening time (either 9 or 10am), Main Street USA is not the place to linger as most of the crowd will flock to the **Central Plaza** in front of the Castle. This is REALLY where the action starts for a full day in the park, so don't be fooled into thinking they have opened early by letting you into Main Street USA. You need to have already planned your campaign from here to get a head start on the masses.

*Main Street has plenty of shopping opportunities*

© Disney

## Character carnival

Although the Disney characters appearing change from month to month, you can be fairly sure to catch them some of the time (especially 10am–midday) at the following locations:

**Town Square** (in corner by Liberty Arcade or under Gazebo in centre of Square): Any of Minnie, Pluto, Chip 'n' Dale, Donald Duck and Goofy.

**Main Street USA** (by Casey's Corner and Liberty Arcade): Mickey Mouse.

**Central Plaza** (Castle Hub): Disney Princesses.

**Royal Castle Stage** (in front of Castle): Winnie the Pooh (occasionally Tigger or Piglet).

**Fantasyland** (by Mad Hatter's Tea Cups): Some Alice in Wonderland characters, Pinocchio and Robin Hood.

**Discoveryland** (between Videopolis and Space Mountain): Any of Lilo & Stitch and Toy Story characters.

**Adventureland** (by Colonel Hathi's restaurant): Jungle Book and Lion King characters.

**Frontierland** (outside Cowboy Cookout Barbecue): some of Goofy, Pluto, Chip 'n' Dale, Country Bears and Pocahontas characters should be there.

Also, look for **Disney's Character Express** up to five times a day along Main Street USA, with the chance to meet a range of characters.

*Main Street characters*

Liberty Arcade and, at the top, wait to turn left into Frontierland. For the mysteries of Adventureland (including the wonderful Pirates of the Caribbean ride), move into Central Plaza and wait at its entrance on the left.

Those with children in tow, who will demand rides in the company of all their favourite characters like Dumbo, Peter Pan and the Mad Hatter, should wait in front of the Castle for the chance to get into Fantasyland first. Or, if the appeal of big thrill rides like Space Mountain: Mission 2 (an indoor, looping roller-coaster) and Star Tours (a brilliant simulator space ride) is highest on your 'To Do' list, then turn right in the middle of Central Plaza and await rope drop for Discoveryland.

*Toy Story Meet 'n' Greet*

© Disney

---

**BRITTIP**

If you are among the first to reach Central Plaza and you manage to get to the main rides first, you will enjoy the *Disneyland Park* at its best – with short or non-existent queues at the most popular attractions.

Depending on which of the 'lands' in front of you appeals most, head in one of the four directions and wait for the opening hour 'rope drop' by the Cast Members at each entrance.

If you fancy the appeal of cowboy country and the lure of a great thrill ride like Big Thunder Mountain or the scary fun of Phantom Manor, head up

**BRITTIP**

A perk with the Dream Annual Passport is entry to Fantasyland an hour before it officially opens. The Dumbo and Peter Pan rides often start half an hour early, so you can have a go on two of the most popular rides without waiting in long queues.

Once the ropes go down, the early-morning crowds will move (quickly!) in one of the four directions, so keep your wits about you. Study the park map for where you want to go and benefit from a first hour or so without lengthy queuing. It also pays (and royally so in peak periods) to avoid main meal times if you want to eat without more long queues and frenzy. It is a notable fact of *Disneyland Resort Paris* that people tend to pack out the counter-service cafés rather than the handful of full-service, sit-down restaurants. This means midday–2.30pm is a seriously bad time (unless it is an extremely quiet period of the year) to head for places like the Fuente del Oro Restaurante, Pizzeria Bella Notte, the Cowboy Cookout Barbecue or any of the other 14 counter-service diners in the park. Try to have a snack prior to midday or look to eat in mid-afternoon and you will benefit from slightly shorter ride queues during lunchtime.

*Silver Spur Steakhouse*

**BRITTIP**

Park too busy? Don't forget it is relatively easy to head back out to *Disney Village* and grab a bite to eat at places like Planet Hollywood and Annette's Diner.

Alternatively, you could book lunch at the start of the day at one of the four full-service restaurants (Walt's, Auberge du Cendrillon, Blue Lagoon or Silver Spur Steakhouse) to guarantee a pleasant sit-down and some rest – especially with children.

*Cowboy Cookout Barbecue*

*Once Upon a Dream Parade*

© Disney

## Pace yourself

The final piece of advice before we send you off on the great *Disneyland Park* adventure is to pace yourself. It is easy to try to do too much and end up a frazzled wreck by mid-afternoon! In summer, when the crowds are at their peak and the temperature can top 30ºC/86ºF, it can be a particularly tough business negotiating the rides, the long periods of queuing and the demands of tramping from one side of the park to the other in the name of entertainment. This is when you will most feel the benefit of a **solid plan**, booking your mealtimes in advance and giving yourselves a rest at strategic moments, whether it be finding a quiet corner for a drink or visiting a show that provides a welcome sit-down, preferably in the air-conditioned cool.

When it comes to eating, be aware that inclement weather quickly causes long queues to pile up in the restaurants, even in *Disney Village*. If you can pre-empt that sudden rain squall by getting to a café first, you will be well placed to watch the rush come in when the deluge starts. Equally, if you have brought some good **rain gear** with you, it is a great time to enjoy some of the rides while the majority seek shelter.

You will also need to **drink** a lot of water during the summer. The physical demands of the parks will quickly creep up on you unless you remember to rehydrate at regular intervals. It is, sadly, an all-too-common feature in mid-afternoon to see or hear grizzly children, often being berated by parents for not enjoying themselves (!), when all everyone needs is to just sit down for a few minutes, recharge the batteries and drink some water.

**BRITTIP**

Save euros by bringing a bottle of water with you and refilling it from the many drinking fountains around.

Most children (ours included) get a huge energy charge from being in the theme parks and the adrenalin keeps them going long after they should have keeled over. But that excited state can run out at a moment's notice and turn to angst if they are not regularly fed and watered – and it is easy to overlook the latter with so much going on.

In summer, it is advisable to carry a good **sunscreen** and use it liberally while you are queuing to prevent an unhealthy dose of the sun, which also exacerbates the tiredness factor – your biggest enemy.

*Fuente del Oro in Frontierland*

© Disney

# Frontierland

Okay, enough of the warnings – let's get to the fun! There is masses in store, so let us take you on a full tour of the remaining four 'lands' in the *Disneyland Park*. Starting immediately to your left from the Central Plaza brings you to Frontierland, a true rootin', tootin' cowboy town that oozes child appeal and has plenty of visual creativity and stimulation for grown-ups too. It is a realm of pioneers and gold diggers, the Wild West in vivid 3-D, with a big helping of some of the epic scenery that the real-life version possesses in places like Nevada and Arizona.

**BRITTIP**
Go to the top of Fort Comstock and you have a great spot to take memorable photos of Frontierland.

As in virtually all other areas of the park, Frontierland rewards the casual wanderer with some great little paths leading nowhere in particular but that reveal some interesting details or amusing scenery, such as the Indian village encampment or the hot springs (complete with Old Faithful geyser).

Once again, the loyal re-creation of the era can be seen in every building and façade, none better than the main entrance of **Fort Comstock**, which is an attraction in itself, where you can see scenes from Legends of

*Frontierland*

© Disney

*Phantom Manor*

the Wild West. Here, you can climb the wooden stairs to the ramparts, visit the US Marshall and Fort Jail, and peer into the offices (see if you can spot Buffalo Bill) and stables. Kids will want to roam the ramparts and scan other areas of the park through the telescopes provided. It is a good place to let youngsters explore on their own, too. AAA.

**Phantom Manor:** Turn left after coming through Fort Comstock and head along the plaza past the Silver Spur Steakhouse for one of the most clever and amusing rides in the Disney repertoire. This elaborate haunted mansion is a variation on the theme established in Anaheim and Orlando, with a ghoulish entryway leading to an underground ride of wonderfully creepy proportions. The introductory spiel is in French (while some aspects of the commentary are alternately in English and French). However, it needs little real explanation as the gloomy entrance parlour (watch for a remarkable trick here) takes you down to this spook-tastic world.

**BRITTIP**
Queues build up at Phantom Manor from mid-morning and, although they rarely top half an hour, this ride is a good one to do early or during a parade, when it's quieter. Or wait until the last hour before park closing when it rarely has a queue and is at its spooky best!

*Rustler Roundup*

Under 5s may find the mock-horror elements a bit too convincing but otherwise the whole experience is more fun than frightening. The story of an elaborate socialite wedding that went tragically wrong, leaving the bride as one of the 999 ghosts, is a bit hard to follow, but the ride takes you right through the manor and into a realistic haunted town in best graveyard fashion. In the queue you can study the elaborate terraces and gardens outside the manor, while you exit into Boot Hill and some more pun-laced scenery that includes various graves – such as 'Here lies Shotgun Gus, holier now than all of us'. The more attentive will also notice the sounds of knocking from the largest of the mausoleums in the graveyard. This can be a great source of amusement when people notice it for the first time on dark evenings! AAAA (TTTTT for youngsters).

**Thunder Mesa Riverboat Landing:** Backtrack slightly along the plaza and you can hop on a boat, offering a slow-paced and picturesque ride around much of Frontierland on the Rivers of the Far West, including several sections that can only be seen from the water. The commentary is bilingual and it is quite a capacious ride, so there is rarely much of a queue. The two boats, the *Molly Brown* and *Mark Twain*, provide an enjoyably authentic experience. This is a good ride to save for later in the day when both Phantom Manor and Big Thunder are busiest, but be aware the Landing may close earlier than other attractions. AAA.

Fans of the old-style arcade shooting ranges can get a quick 'fix' at the **Rustler Roundup Shootin' Gallery**, where €2 (the only additional charge for an attraction in the theme park) will give you ten shots at various audio-animatronic targets. TT.

**Big Thunder Mountain:** This is one of Disney's trademark roller-coasters. While others may thrill (or terrify!) with their topsy-turvy antics, Big Thunder sticks firmly to the straight and narrow and is as fun and inventive as most people desire, with this abandoned 'gold mine' showing it still has some life in it in the shape of its runaway train. Again, you get a different version from other Disney parks; this one starts straight away with a dive into the dark under the lake before whizzing around the mock sandstone monoliths and mine shafts in exhilarating fashion.

> ### BRIT**TIP**
> If you head to Frontierland first, Big Thunder should be your opening ride, followed by Phantom Manor. Then return to the mine-train coaster and grab a FastPass for another go later!

With three different ascents (and plunges), the proliferation of clever scenery all around you is never less than spectacular, so it usually needs at least two rides to take in all the detail (it looks great at night, too). This is one of the five FastPass (FP) rides, so it is well worth taking

*Thunder Mesa Riverboat*

advantage of, as the queues often top an hour at peak times. Afterwards, you can buy the souvenir photo of your ride (six package options, from €15–27.50). Restrictions: 1.02m/3ft 3in. TTTT. (FP).

**River Rogue Keelboats:** This river ride made a surprise return in 2007, having closed in 2001 because of operational difficulties. It features a gentle 20-minute tour of the Rivers of the Far West, following a similar path to the Thunder Mesa Riverboat, but providing a more up-close experience of some of the sights and a different perspective, close to the water. Set in Smugglers Cove, the Keelboats *Racoon* and *Coyote* are piloted by 'smugglers' who tell you stories of the Old West en route (mostly in French, unfortunately). The bad news is queues build up quickly here and move rather slowly, hence it is often a 45-minute wait, even at quieter times. The Keelboats are usually open only from 11am–6.30pm daily. AA.

**Pocahontas Indian Village:** If the youngsters are too short (or apprehensive!) to ride Big Thunder, head for this straightforward play area with a mixture of slides, swings and climbs geared towards under 6s. Unfortunately, this is one area that is affected by the weather as it closes when it rains, but, otherwise, it is a valuable place to allow the young 'uns to let off some steam. TTT (for the right age group!).

*The Tarzan Encounter*

© Disney

*Meet Jafar in Frontierland*

### BRITTIP

The back of the Pocahontas Indian Village originally housed the Indian Canoes ride, which closed after little more than a year because of operational difficulties.

**Woody's Round-up:** The former disused Critter Corral petting zoo has been reborn here as a smart new character meet-and-greet area, which features the stars of the *Toy Story* films for much of the year in this cowboy-style mini-village. Kids can enjoy rather more organised character interaction, plus extra fun at Halloween and the all-new *Father Christmas Village* for the full festive season, with the chance to meet Santa and his helpers

**Chaparral Theatre:** Opposite Critter Corral, this is one of the park's four main live entertainment venues. The attractions here are seasonal and Disney does tend to change them at regular intervals but, at the time of writing, the two offerings were: **The Tarzan Encounter**, a sensational 25-minute song, dance and acrobatic extravaganza showcasing the music from the animated film, with a cast of energetic 'apes' who find all manner of ways of leaping off, around and over the clever stage scenery. Tarzan and Jane (inevitably) make an appearance and, while it can be a bit loud for very young ears, it is a riot of colour and movement. There is also an audience participation section for

© Disney

*Mickey's Winter Wonderland*

establishment, designed like a classic Western hotel, using rich, dark wood and plush upholstery. The subdued lighting provides an intimate dining style and there is a display kitchen at the back. Steaks are their stock-in-trade, but they also do excellent salmon, chicken and pasta. A set, three-course meal is €25/adult, a two-course Menu Pony Express for children 3–11 is €12 and à la carte dishes range from €14.50–26.50. Superb desserts add to the high quality on offer here.

### BRITTIP

If there isn't a queue, take the Railroad steam train for the best short cut to Fantasyland or Discoveryland. However, it is usually quicker to walk if you need the fastest way back to Main Street USA.

children that is worth being ready for. AAAA (plus TTT). **Mickey's Winter Wonderland** takes over in the theatre from mid-November to early March, with an equally clever ice-skating show featuring Mickey and all the gang (including a suitably hapless Donald Duck) that will keep youngsters enchanted for the full 25 minutes. It is a fairly straightforward song-and-dance pastiche, but once again the staging and lighting are impressive and its bilingual style ensures English speakers are not left out of the picture. AAAA.

Next door is the **Frontierland Railroad Station**, which is often the best place to catch the theme park's steam train and take the slow chug all the way around.

Your dining options in Frontierland feature two outstanding opportunities. The **Silver Spur Steakhouse** is a truly deluxe

Character-seekers will want to make a beeline for the **Lucky Nugget Saloon**, which offers a fabulous Tex-Mex buffet lunch from 12–3pm with characters, plus 6–10pm for dinner in high season. The restaurant is wonderfully styled like a two-storey Western saloon, with a stage and a long bar. The food is a serve-yourself buffet (€30/adult, €15 for 3–11s) featuring assorted crudités, chicken wings, nachos, salsa, fajitas, spare ribs, chilli con carne, pasta, pizza and a large choice of desserts (drinks not included). The character interaction

*Silver Spur Steakhouse*

© Disney

here includes the seemingly omnipresent Chip 'n' Dale (or Tic and Tac as they are known in France), Pluto, Gideon (from Pinocchio) and Daisy Duck. If €90 for a family of four (plus drinks, which are not included in the set price) seems a touch expensive (as it does to us), check out the character tea opportunity at the Plaza Gardens Restaurant (see page 128).

Otherwise, your fast-food dining choices include the evocative **Cowboy Cookout Barbecue**, a counter-service barn of a place featuring spare ribs, burgers and smoked chicken. The lovely smoky barbecue smell, the cowboy ambience and the Country & Western twang (with live music periodically) add up to a memorable experience, even if the food is only average. **Fuente del Oro Restaurante** goes down Mexico way for more counter-service, cantina style, with tacos, chilli and other Mexican specialities such as fajitas and nachos (one of the better counter-service options, but very busy from midday–2pm). Finally, the **Last Chance Café** offers more cowboy fare with typical Western decor, serving turkey legs, chips and sandwiches.

Shopping is suitably cowboy orientated, with **Tobias Norton & Sons – Frontier Traders**, a leather emporium featuring hats, boots, wallets and belts; **Bonanza Outfitters**, offering the full range of Western apparel; and the **Eureka Mining Supplies**, which stocks a selection of typical cowboy-style foods and toys, including the inevitable hats and guns.

© Disney

*Stained glass window in Sleeping Beauty's Castle*

A unique feature of this section of the park is the latticework of paths that interconnect between Frontierland and Adventureland. This surprisingly small-scale landscaping is a notable element of the European influence behind the overall design, and the paths are almost interwoven to provide an alternative way of getting around as well as highlighting different aspects of the lands (but keep your map handy in case you get lost!).

**BRITTIP**

Try to get a view of the Castle from one of the small side paths between Frontierland and Adventureland, as there are a number of unusual perspectives offering good photo opportunities.

*Investigate the paths between Frontierland and Adventureland*

© Disney

© Disney

*A Halloween hair workshop*

## Halloweenland

If you are here in October, remember that Frontierland becomes Halloweenland for the month, with a dazzling array of spooky special effects, creepy scenery and haunted shows. A giant spider's web covers Fort Comstock, the Thunder Mesa Riverboat gets a ghoulish Mummy-style makeover, pumpkins, witches and scarecrows abound, various Disney characters turn up throughout Halloweenland's pathways and the daily Parade is taken over by Disney villains like Cruella De Vil, Ursula, Maleficent and Jafar. Children (under 12) can get into the 'spirit' with a makeover at the **Halloween Face Painting Workshop** in the Castle Plaza (with a choice of Witch Pink or Pumpkin Orange!) or the **Hairdressing Workshop** for a 'hair-raising' style at the Pumpkin Paint Pit near Big Thunder Mountain. The 2007 Halloween season added an amusing extra element with **Stitch** creating his comical brand of chaos, along with the **Pink Witches** staging a daily battle with the **Pumpkin Men** along Main Street USA and into Halloweenland (and on the Parade), with guests being invited to take sides in the amusing bickering. The **Pink Witches Convention Academy** and the **Pumpkinwood Forest** are set up in opposition, while the **Witches**

**Wake Stage** adds live music (near the Cowboy Cookout Barbecue) and kids are invited to grab some sweets at a traditional Piñata.

### BRITTIP

A special night-time Halloween Party event on 31 October is not widely publicised in the UK, so it is worth noting and seeking out if you are visiting at that time (call 00 33 1 60 30 60 53 to order tickets in advance).

The transformation of the whole 'land' – unlike anything attempted at the American parks – is hugely ambitious, but the Imagineers have pulled off quite a triumph here, making October a real must-visit month if you can.

*Halloween in Frontierland*

© Disney

# Adventureland

Africa, the Caribbean and the jungles of Asia combine to provide a host of contrasting – and thrilling – experiences, all with lush landscaping. This is the 'land' with the fewest attractions, but the whole area has such a wealth of detail and fine architecture (take a close look at Skull Rock and the castle façade of the Pirates ride) that it is easy to spend a good deal of time just wandering and admiring. Even if you don't eat at most of the counter-service diners, it is worth looking into places like Colonel Hathi's Pizza Outpost and Restaurant Hakuna Matata to appreciate the interior design that gives them a real storybook feel.

**BRITTIP**

Adventureland is the hardest 'land' to navigate, so hang on to your map to find your way from place to place.

**Indiana Jones and the Temple of Peril:** If you come from Frontierland, turn left by Colonel Hathi's for this 5-star thrill ride. Not content with creating a ducking and diving coaster that seems to zip along much faster when you're aboard than when you're watching, the designers added a brain-scrambling 360-degree loop and have reconfigured it twice to run either backwards or forward (in 2007, it was again going forward). The theming is wonderful, with the

*Indiana Jones and the Temple of Peril*

*Adventureland*

queuing area leading you through an archaeological dig in true Indiana Jones style, before you reach the temple and your rickety mine wagon.

Before you know it, you are being thrown around a tight, twisting track with its sudden loop and dramatic swoops, only to come to the end of the track all too soon once your body has got the hang of it! This is definitely not the ride if you suffer from neck or back problems as there is quite a bit of vibration along the way but it is also quite exhilarating and much more fun than it looks. Indiana Jones is a FastPass ride, which is handy for coaster lovers as queues can be slow-moving here. The first couple of hours of the day are rarely busy, but once the queues build up they stay fairly consistent until late in the day. Restrictions: 1.40m/4ft 6in. TTTT. (FP).

**BRITTIP**

The scary aspect of the Indiana Jones ride and its position at the innermost end of Adventureland means it is often overlooked by many park visitors, hence it is a good ride to do during the busier parts of the day.

Retracing your steps slightly and turning left brings you into the central portion of Adventureland, known as **Adventure Isle**. The Imagineers have worked overtime here to create something different

© Disney

*Le Pont Suspendu*

from existing themes in other parks. They opted for an overgrown adventure playground of the most elaborate kind. This is a delightful pot-pourri of attractions, mainly aimed at children but that are also eye-catching and detailed enough to appeal to adults as well.

> ### ✚ BRITTIP
>
> Adventure Isle is just about the only area of either park that is NOT accessible for guests with disabilities. It is simply not designed for the use of wheelchairs.

**La Cabane des Robinsons:** The Swiss Family Treehouse is the first attraction you come to on the Isle. The re-creation of the treehouse of the castaway Robinson family from the 1960 Disney film is only a walk-through attraction, and looks rather tired these days as the giant 'banyan tree' that was adapted to provide their shelter, food and running water is in urgent need of an overhaul. But queues are rarely a problem and there are great views from the top. AA.

Spinning off the treehouse is a high-level rope suspension bridge, **Le Pont Suspendu**, which takes you on to the five other sections of the Isle, **Skull**

Rock (a labyrinthine stone edifice that towers over one end of the lagoon), **L'Ile au Tresor** (a series of lookout towers and spooky secret caves), **Le Ventre de la Terre** (a series of galleries under the tree), **Captain Hook's Galley** (a rather tame pirate ship that actually has little to explore) and **La Plage des Pirates** (or Pirates' Beach, a clever play area of slides and climbs expressly for the little shipmates). Kids will want to dash off and explore Ben Gunn's Cave, Ambush Alley and Dead Man's Bridge, and it is a good area in which to let them loose for a while. TTT/AAA.

**Pirates of the Caribbean:** Coming off at the top end of Adventure Isle brings you to one of Disney's trademark and truly unmissable rides. The original version of this attraction was installed in *Disneyland California* in 1967 and remains an Imagineering gem to this day, highlighted by their pioneering work with audio-animatronics. These are a series of life-like figures that move, talk, gesticulate and, in this instance, lay siege to a Caribbean island! Your journey starts as you wind down inside the Pirate Castle, through secret streets and dingy dungeons, until you reach your boat

*La Cabane des Robinsons*

for a plunge into the darkness of this pirate realm.

There are two minor plunges (and slight splashes – front seat passengers may get a little wet), the first of which drops you into the middle of the island siege, with the clever – and distinctly amusing – action going on all around, and a second that drops into the pirate treasure caverns. Skeletons and dungeons abound, and it may be a little too intense for under 5s, but there is little that is genuinely scary and the whole effect is so amazing you will probably want to have several turns to appreciate all the detail involved. While it is a popular ride, queues drop off towards the end of the day and it is often possible to ride with very little wait (it is also a welcome place to cool down during the hotter months!). AAAAA (TTTT for under 8s). NB: See if you can spot some of the elements 'borrowed' when this ride was used as the inspiration for Disney's hit film *Pirates of the Caribbean* in 2003.

*Skull Rock*

*Passage Enchanté d'Aladdin*

If you enter Adventureland via the main entrance off the Central Plaza, you will come straight into the **Agrabah Bazaar** area. One of the scenic highlights here, the magnificent indoor/outdoor shopping and dining scenario (straight out of 1,001 Nights) of the **Agrabah Café** reopened in 2007 after a long hiatus but ONLY for Disney hotel guests on the Half Board Meal Plan (see page 77). We hope it will eventually reopen to all guests as it adds an imaginative dining location to the area, which otherwise hosts a couple of fairly humdrum gift shops. The **Passage Enchanté d'Aladdin** is a walk-through exhibit of the Aladdin story with some amusing tableaux and clever lighting tricks. AA.

**BRITTIP**

Plan a special meal, even with the kids, in the Blue Lagoon and you won't be disappointed. Book at City Hall or with your hotel concierge. A perfect pit stop in winter when it is heated to tropical temperatures!

Adventureland is also home to one of our all-time favourite Disney restaurants, the **Blue Lagoon**, which is actually set inside the Pirates ride (so there are usually a few shouts of 'Bon Appetit!' from people setting off on the ride as you dine). You enter just below and to the left of the ride entrance, and the setting alone is worthy of perusal. You eat on a mock

© Disney

*Colonel Hathi's Pizza Outpost*

### BRITTIP

A 'secret' route goes from the park's main entrance all the way to the heart of Fantasyland, mainly under cover. Take the Liberty Arcade up Main Street USA, turn sharp left into Frontierland, walk straight through Fort Comstock and follow the covered walkway into Adventureland, skirt round the side of Les Trésors de Schéhérazade (briefly in the open), then pick up the walkway alongside the restaurant Au Chalet de la Marionnette and you end up at the Peter Pan ride. It is also a quick way to get OUT of Fantasyland when the park is busy.

'outdoor' terrace under dim lights, authentically furnished, listening to sounds that evoke the feeling of an evening on some distant Caribbean island. The seafood-orientated menu is also a delight, with the likes of grilled swordfish with coriander, roasted prawns with basil, Jamaican pepper fillet of beef and chicken and seafood with Creole-style rice. The set menu is €28 (€15 for teens, €12 for 3–11s), while starters range from €8.90–16 and main courses from €14–28.50. The speciality set menu, Sea Treasures, features crab, scallops, tuna, ostrich steak, swordfish and grilled beef kebab for a princely €39. The kids' menu includes beef meatballs in a creamy tomato sauce, spaghetti bolognese or chicken kebab for €12.

Your counter-service options here include **Colonel Hathi's Pizza Outpost** (pizzas, salads, lasagne and spaghetti – set pizza menu at €9.95 – all in best *Jungle Book* style) and **Restaurant Hakuna Matata** (a decent African safari adventure, with spiced chicken, fish nuggets, lamb kebab and a shrimp and tuna salad). **Café de la Brousse** and **Captain Hook's Galley** offer sandwiches, hot dogs, ice creams and drinks.

Shopping brings an additional array of possibilities here, with **Indiana Jones Adventure Outpost** (safari accessories and Indy souvenirs), **Les Trésors de Shéhérazade** (magic lamps, dolls, clothes) and **Le Coffre du Capitaine** (as you exit the Pirates ride, with a suitable range of sea-themed treasures and toys) the pick of the bunch.

*Chalet de la Marionnette*

© Disney

© Disney

*'it's a small world'*

## Fantasyland

Having arrived in the theme park's largest 'land' via Adventureland, here you will find the biggest selection of rides and the most concentrated fun for under 8s. This is the stuff of pure fantasy and the whimsical creativity on show is first class, from the huge Castle down to the tiny detail of the clock façade on 'it's a small world'. Unfortunately, it is also the most crowded area, with queues building up quickly from mid-morning and rarely abating until early evening (when it is open until 11pm). Parts of the back of Fantasyland close from 9pm to prepare for the evening fireworks, so don't think you have the place to yourself all of a sudden!

*Mad Hatter's Teacups*

© Disney

If you have young children, Fantasyland should be your first port of call as it is likely to offer the most candidates for 'favourite ride' and it is not unknown for families to spend virtually all day here. If you come for 'rope drop' (highly recommended), you should head straight through the Castle and try to do the Carousel, Dumbo and Peter Pan in quick succession. These three are all terribly slow-loading rides where the queues build up almost immediately and remain painfully slow all day. Excluding Peter Pan but including the Mad Hatter's Tea Cups (another slow-loader), you might be inclined to say 'We waited for ages for THAT?' at the end of the ride as they are not terribly exciting for grown-ups, being basically re-themed versions of standard fairground rides. However, children will almost certainly demand to ride Dumbo at least once and, if you have managed to get it under

### BRITTIP

When Fantasyland is seriously busy, many people overlook the little area right at the back that is home to two excellent child-pleasing rides – Casey Jnr and Le Pays des Contes de Fées – where queues rarely build up but, if they do, move quite quickly. If these rides are packed out, you KNOW the park is crowded!

© Disney

*Blanche-Neige et les Septs Nains*

brimstone on all those who dare to disturb his slumbers. In the semi-darkness, it really is a convincing beast (watch its chest 'breathing'!) and is usually far too menacing for under 5s. TTT (for under 8s).

Stepping through the Castle's rear gate brings you to a courtyard and a great photo opportunity with the Sword in the Stone. Immediately in front of you is **Le Carrousel de Lancelot**, a standard horsey roundabout that youngsters love, even if queuing can take an age and mum and dad would rather be doing something (anything!) else. AA (TTTT for under 5s).

**Blanche-Neige et les Sept Nains (The Adventures of Snow White):** Right next door, this is a typically Disney kiddie ride that is a fairly dark journey into the cartoon world of the classic film. The soundtrack is in French, which detracts a little if you are unfamiliar with the story (but then, how many people is that likely to be?). All kids can relate to this mildly scary trip into the realm of the Wicked Witch, her evil plans and the suitably happy ending. Under 5s may find parts of it menacing, but Simon's then 4-year-old was okay once he had got over the initial worries of being in the dark and was happy to ride it again several times (shouting 'Boo!' at the witch!). AAA (or TTT for under 8s).

your belt without waiting half an hour or more (and the queue usually tops a mind-numbing hour), you will have done well!

Taking Fantasyland in a clockwise direction starting at the Castle, you have 12 main attractions from which to choose, plus seven restaurants and seven shops that include some of the most original gift items in the park.

**Le Château de la Belle au Bois Dormant (Sleeping Beauty Castle):** This is a draw in its own right, having two contrasting things to see. **La Galerie de la Belle au Bois Dormant** is easy to miss as you scamper through, but is actually upstairs in the Castle and tells the story in picture-boards and words (in French) of Sleeping Beauty. Check out the beautiful Renaissance-style tapestries that line the walls and the stunning (and highly photogenic) stained-glass windows. You can also walk along an external balcony that provides a great view from both sides of the castle. AA.

Underneath *le château* and accessible via three different portals (including a back door of Merlin's shop, down a winding stone staircase), is the magnificent **La Tanière du Dragon**, or dragon's lair. Here, the creature that turned many a would-be saviour of Sleeping Beauty to toast lurks in steamy, underground splendour, wrapped in reptilian fashion around the stalactites and stalagmites, occasionally rearing his audio-animatronic head to threaten fire and

*The Enchanted Fairytale*

© Disney

**Pinocchio's Fantastic Journey:**
Following on is another dark ride, this
time in the company of Jiminy
Cricket, showing his attempts to keep
the wooden puppet-boy on the
straight and narrow. Again, it is a
touch intense for the real young 'uns
(especially with the surprise menace
of the whale), but most kids find it fun
rather than frightening. The special
effect at the end with the Blue Fairy is
well worth seeing. AAA (TTT for
under 8s).

**Dumbo the Flying Elephant:** Needing
little explanation, this is a standard
fairground whirligig with elephants as
the flying 'vehicles' (albeit without the
requisite flapping ears which were, in
theory, Dumbo's trademark). The
front-seat passengers get to make the
elephant go up and down while
circling gently round and round, and
that's about it. There is little to look at
while you are queuing, the lines move
painfully slowly and the music is
horribly repetitive, but kids seem to
get a buzz out of piloting their
elephant and it is a highly visible ride,
so hard for parents to ignore! Head
here first thing or expect to queue for
ages (the crowds do ease off a little
during the parades, but there is no
substitute for doing this early on). TT
(TTTT for under 8s).

© Disney

*Pinocchio's Fantastic Journey*

**Peter Pan's Flight:** Next door to
Dumbo is Fantasyland's other serious
queue-builder, which has the saving
grace of being a FastPass ride (see
page 119). Once you get to board your
pirate ship, you rise up, up and away
over the streets of London, turn right
at the first star and straight on to
morning, all the way to Neverland
and a close encounter with Captain
Hook and his inept pirates. It is
another indoor dark ride (very dark as
you go through the star-lit portion),
but the overhead mechanism of your
'ship' and the elaborate scenery
combine to create the right illusion.
Usually a big hit with all the family
and a must-do ride as far as the kids
are concerned. Be aware that the
waiting time can easily top an hour

*Dumbo the Flying Elephant*

© Disney

© Disney

*Fantasy Festival Stage*

here and much of the queuing area is in the open, so your best bet is to try to take advantage of the FP. If the FPs have all gone (as often happens in high season by 2pm), leave it as late as possible or wait until a parade has just started. AAAA (TTTTT for under 8s). (FP).

Step out of Peter Pan, turn left and you come to the **Fantasy Festival Stage**, where the cute **Winnie the Pooh and Friends Too** stage presentation shows five times daily in peak season. Join Christopher Robin, Pooh and friends on a grand adventure to the end of the rainbow, where wishes come true. There is an element of menace (courtesy of the Heffalumps), which may unnerve some children, but courage wins the day and it all ends happily-ever-after. The show becomes **Winnie the Pooh and Christmas Too** for the festive season. AAA (AAAAA under 6s).

### BRITTIP

When not in use, the Fantasy Festival Stage makes a handy place to sit in peace and quiet with a drink or snack.

To the left of the Festival Stage is the entrance to the **Fantasyland Railroad Station**. This will usually get you back to Main Street USA much quicker than walking, if there isn't a serious queue. Now, all of these attractions so far are relatively faithful copies of Disney rides in other parks, but the

next one is a true *Disneyland Resort Paris* original.

**Alice's Curious Labyrinth:** An interactive maze leading up to the Queen of Hearts' castle, this seems to have almost universal appeal for children up to about 12. There is a range of *Alice in Wonderland* tricks and motifs along the way, including amusing signage, squirting fountains (kids *really* gravitate towards these, trying to catch the water as it 'jumps' from bush to bush), an encounter with the hookah-smoking Caterpillar and several scrapes with the Queen of Hearts and her guards (in various audio-animatronic guises). It is gentle stuff but keeps youngsters (and their parents) amused for a good 15–20 minutes and is an ideal place to visit when waits at Peter Pan and Dumbo hit an hour. AAA.

Passing further along and under the railway bridge brings you to the little area right at the back of Fantasyland that gets overlooked by some (although it is often closed at quieter times of the year). But, if you have young children this is somewhere you won't want to miss, both for the instant kiddie appeal and the shorter queues. Both rides are copies from the original *Disneyland Park* in California, but they possess a timeless charm for children.

*Alice's Curious Labyrinth*

© Disney

**Le Pays des Contes de Fées:** This is a gentle boat ride into a fairytale world, with miniature depictions of stories like *Snow White, Peter and the Wolf, The Wizard of Oz, Beauty and the Beast* and *The Little Mermaid.* For the Aladdin section, your boat is 'swallowed up' by the giant lion's-mouth cave from the story, which can be a little daunting for the youngest passengers, but the whole thing proceeds at barely walking pace, so you have plenty of time to ease any apprehensions. Closed October to March. AAA.

© Disney

*The White Rabbit at Alice's Curious Labyrinth*

> ### BRITTIP
>
> If you are at Le Pays des Contes de Fées out of peak periods, the boat ride is usually a walk-on attraction and has the great benefit for youngsters of being able to take them straight back on for another go.

**Casey Jr – le Petit Train du Cirque:** Another guaranteed hit for the under 8 brigade. In reality, it is a fairly tame, junior-sized coaster, themed in eye-catching style after the circus train in Dumbo. Some of the cars are designed like animal cages, others are open and, of course, two can sit up front in the 'engine'. It glides along for some 5 minutes, encountering a couple of mild dips and gentle bends, but it gives just the right illusion of

excitement to those of the requisite age (and any nervous parents!). Indeed, Simon's youngest – then aged 4 – must have set a record for riding this countless times in a row with great glee, delighting in trying to sit in a different seat each time! Closed October to March. AAA (TTTT for under 5s).

As you exit this two-ride mini-land, you pass the disused Les Pirouettes Du Vieux Moulin, a big-wheel type ride that proved unworkable with even moderate queues and that has quietly been abandoned. It still looks good in non-working mode but sadly that is all you get from it.

**Mad Hatter's Tea Cups:** Another standard fairground ride, this has been given a bit of *Alice in Wonderland* top-spin to make it seem

*Le Pays des Contes de Fees*

© Disney

© Disney

*Mad Hatter's Teacups*

more than it actually is. Kids all seem to love the chance to ride in these manically whirling cups, which have a wheel to make them spin counter to the main rotation (Uuurgghhh! we say). We have to admit, going round in never-decreasing circles (or so it feels) was never our cup of tea at all, but it remains a seriously popular ride, so it is best to do this one early in the day or later in the evening. TTT.

Continuing our clockwise tour of Fantasyland brings you next to one of Disney's signature rides.

**'it's a small world':** Designed under the direction of Walt himself for the New York World Fair in 1964, this ride has stood the test of time amazingly well for children under 8 and remains a big hit to this day. The exterior façade is one of the most eye-catching in the park, with all manner of moving and static elements that add up to a wonderfully artistic collage. Inside, all it really consists of is a slow-moving boat ride through a colourful series of scenes featuring audio-animatronic dolls singing and dancing in various national-themed displays, from Britain to Brazil and Africa to the Arctic. It has an insidiously catchy theme tune (we challenge you NOT to be humming it when you exit!) and a fabulously imaginative winter wonderland final scene, but otherwise it just highlights the clever way in which Disney's Imagineers can take a routine ride and give it a whole new style and appeal.

Once again, it proves that if you give it the right scale and a proportionate amount of detail (with a little sprinkle of Disney 'pixie dust'), the ordinary can become quite extraordinary. Many adults are even captivated by the spirit and vivacity of this attraction, and it is one that bears multiple visits. Queues rarely top 20 minutes and move quite steadily, so this is a good ride to do at most times, but especially in the afternoon (and when it's hot). AAAA.

**BRITTIP**

Hang around outside 'it's a small world' on the hour and watch the wonderful clock (you can hear it ticking from quite a distance) come to life with a display of moving figures in best Toytown tradition.

When it comes to mealtimes, Fantasyland has a gourmet offering in **Auberge de Cendrillon**, with an elegant ballroom-type setting and an excellent continental menu. Open for lunch 11.30am–4pm and dinner 5.30–9.30pm, it features ravioli, risotto, roast salmon, entrecôte steak and duck pâté as well as regular burger fare. The set meal is a hefty €48 (€20 for 3–11s), but the big attraction here is the character interaction. 'Suzy and Perla's Fantasies' features the two mice from Cinderella and a host of Disney princes and princesses,

*Auberge de Cendrillon*

© Disney

dancing and interacting with guests (reservations strongly advised, on 01 60 30 40 50 or from any Disney hotel concierge desk). There is also a pleasant outdoor courtyard, **La Terrasse** (where Cinderella's carriage stands), that offers a limited but tasty menu for dining al fresco, including soups, sandwiches and some delicious desserts.

The other outlets are all counter-service and fill up quickly for lunch at even mildly busy times: **Au Chalet de la Marionnette**, which has a rear entrance opening into Adventureland, serves roast chicken, burgers, salads and chips, plus a range of German desserts; **Toad Hall Restaurant**, modelled in mock English country house style, à la *Wind in the Willows*, serves fish and chips, pies, sandwiches and cakes, and **Pizzeria Bella Notte**, an Italian diner modelled on *Lady and the Tramp*, offers pizzas and pasta.

### BRITTIP

Of all the counter-service restaurants in busy Fantasyland, the Pizzeria Bella Notte is likely to have the shortest queues, as it is slightly off the beaten track.

© Disney

*Flora in the Fantillusion Parade*

More venues for a snack, ice cream or drink include **March Hare Refreshments**, **The Old Mill** and **Fantasia Gelati**. For shopping, the interlinked group in and around the Castle offers worthwhile browsing, with **Merlin l'Enchanteur** (a clever little 'rock-carved' boutique featuring fine crystal, glassware – hand-made while you watch – and porcelain statuettes), **La Boutique du Château** (a Christmas-orientated offering), **La Confiserie des Trois Fées** (a great sweet shop in the company of the good fairies Flora, Fauna and Merryweather from *Sleeping Beauty*), and the epic **Sir Mickey's** featuring cuddly toys, jewellery, glass and ceramics, and children's clothes, toys and games.

*La Confiserie des Trois Fees*

© Disney

*Entrance to Discoveryland*

# Discoveryland

When the Imagineers set about designing the park's fifth and final 'land', their challenge was to come up with a new variant on a fairly well-worn theme. In both Anaheim and Orlando, this area had been developed as Tomorrowland, an unabashed attempt to predict and present the future in an amusing way. There is a mock retro styling about the previous examples, but that was felt to be an over-used idea when it came to *Disneyland Resort Paris* and the call went out for something new.

So, the Imagineers studied their European history and literature and came up with a new motif, that of a future world inspired by technology derived from historical luminaries such as Leonardo da Vinci and Jules Verne. This helped to determine the overall look and feel of Discoveryland (a new title too, as Tomorrowland was felt to be too narrow a definition), hence the styling is a kind of 'antique' future, with much of the architecture borrowing heavily from Verne's 19th-century images of the future.

The two principal icons – Space Mountain: Mission 2 and the Café Hypérion – are magnificent re-creations of Vernian visions and help to create a visual stimulus that is both bold and exciting (can you tell we quite like this area!). The fanciful exterior of Space Mountain is one of the greatest examples of the ride designer's art because so much of it is totally unnecessary to the ride itself; it is purely and simply a statement of style that epitomises the creativity inherent in a Disney theme park. And the rides here are pretty good, too!

> **BRIT TIP**
>
> If you don't visit Space Mountain early in the day and can't get a FastPass, return in early evening to beat the worst of the queues.

**Space Mountain: Mission 2:** Completely re-themed and revamped in 2005, this breathtaking blast of a ride borrows from the Verne novel *From the Earth to the Moon* and gives it a contemporary twist. Whereas the original giant cannon Columbiad (of the Baltimore Gun Club) blasted riders to the Moon, now the over-sized gun barrel has been super-charged to send its vehicles much deeper into space, to discover the secrets of the universe! (Actually, the main ride is exactly the same, but the new theming is convincing). You queue up through the heart of the ride itself before you reach your vehicle, which is 'loaded' into Columbiad. The dry ice flows, the music rolls, the lights pulsate and then… pow! You are off at gravity-defying speed to explore outer space, dodging close encounters with meteorites and other cosmic phenomena, looping the loop, corkscrewing twice past thundering comets and evading an exploding

*Space Mountain: Mission 2*

supernova into 'a new dimension' as the unexpected climax to this 3-minute whizz. The high-tech light show alone is worth seeing and, if the description sounds disturbing, don't let it put you off. This is one of the smoothest coasters you will ride and it is a big-time thrill. It is also a FastPass ride, which is vital for peak periods as the crowds flock here from early on. Souvenir photos are also available. Restrictions: 1.32m/4ft 3in. TTTTT. (FP).

**Les Mystères du Nautilus:** As you exit Space Mountain, you encounter another *Disneyland Resort Paris* original, a clever walk-through version of Captain Nemo's famous submarine. The realism as you go down 'underground' on a circular steel staircase is all-encompassing, bringing you into the Nautilus itself and a self-guided tour of this amazing Verne creation. Take your time to peer into all the nooks and crannies and admire the intricate detail, and sit for a moment at one of the big, circular portholes. Is that a giant squid moving in, too close…? You'll have to check it out for yourself! Children under 7 must be accompanied by an adult (11.30am–5.30pm only). AAA.

**Orbitron – Machines Volantes:** Next door is this similarly eye-catching ride, which is really only a jazzed-up version of the Dumbo ride, spinning and climbing in regulation fashion as the front-seat 'pilot' takes the

*Orbitron*

*Star Tours*

controls. The clever circulation of the accompanying 'planets' really makes this ride, however, giving it the look of something more intricate, and it is another one that is fun just to watch. TTT (TTTTT for under 8s).

**Star Tours:** Behind Space Mountain is the impressive futuristic façade of Disney's wonderful collaboration with *Star Wars* director George Lucas. The queuing area alone is something of a masterpiece, as you are drawn into the make-believe world of squabbling 'droids C-3PO and R-2D2 as they prepare your Star Speeder for the light-speed trip to Endor. This is a faithful transplant of the ride in *Disneyland California* and *Disney's Hollywood Studios* in Orlando, with the one exception that the commentary provided by your robot pilot is in French. The ride itself, though, is a 24-carat thrill, as the realistic Speeders load and lift off for outer space, where all manner of mishaps lead you into a series of adventures. This was the bee's knees when it made its debut in Anaheim in 1987 and is still a magical experience for Disney newcomers (although those familiar with the ride from elsewhere may feel it is a little humdrum by now). Star Tours is also a FastPass ride, which is handy because you could spend a good 45 minutes queuing at peak periods. There is no height restriction, but those with bad backs or necks might want to give it a miss, and it is probably too intense for under 4s. TTTT. (FP).

The exit to Star Tours used to bring you into an amusing area of interactive games, L'Astroport Services Interstellaires, but sadly these have been scrapped in favour of some fairly standard (and rather dismal by comparison) video arcade fare, which you need to negotiate on your way out. Behind Star Tours is **Discoveryland Railroad Station**, but this is a good one to miss at busy times as it is second only to the Main Street station for drawing long, slow-moving queues.

## BRIT TIP

Head for Discoveryland first and you can ride either Space Mountain or Star Tours without much of a queue and then pick up a FastPass for the other. The new Space Mountain: Mission 2 draws heavy crowds throughout the main part of the day.

**Honey, I Shrunk the Audience:** Right next door to Star Tours, this 3-D film show is also a major Disney trademark attraction. Pioneered in all their American parks, it provides yet another variation on theme park thrills. Here, continuing where the two hit films left off, you enter a wacky science world of the Imagination Institute (run by the amusing Eric Idle), where they are about to honour the inventions of a certain professor Wayne Szalinski.

An entertaining 8-minute pre-show

## BRIT TIP

To prove Disney also thinks on a small scale as well as the large, check out the audio-animatronic pigeons(!) attached to the Hypérion airship at the entrance to Café Hypérion.

sets the scene for the main part of your adventure in the awards 'theatre' and then the real fun begins once you don your 3-D glasses. The inevitable on-stage mishaps are accompanied by a sequence of special effects throughout the theatre that often have the audience in hysterics (although under-5s may find it plain scary). It would be a shame to spoil it by revealing anything, so just sit back and get ready to be surprised… very surprised (and beware the sneezing dog!). This is a show that requires a full English dialogue to follow the story and headphones are provided for non-French speakers. AAAAA (plus TTT).

**Autopia:** Another attraction that you need to visit early on unless you want a long wait. Rather old-fashioned, this mock Grand Prix track – a 'futuristic Formula One circuit' – is purely for kids and sits a little awkwardly among the more sci-fi laden offerings. It is often closed for maintenance (and at off-peak times) and is notoriously slow to load, so queues can touch an hour or more and move very slowly. And, unless you are under 9, you're unlikely to get much of a thrill from

*Discoveryland*

© Disney

these tame cars that run on well-defined tracks, even if they provide the illusion of driving. Children under 1.32m/4ft 3in need to be accompanied by an adult but you are not missing much if you bypass this one. T (TTT for under 9s).

**Buzz Lightyear's Laser Blast:** This wonderful interactive family ride, which was new in 2006, appeals to all ages and is a highly worthwhile Discoveryland addition. Riders are 'recruited' into Buzz Lightyear's Space Ranger galaxy defence force and kids in particular will not want to miss this chance to join the great Toy Story character in his battle against the evil Emperor Zurg. You ride into action against Zurg's villainous robot army and shoot them with laser cannons! You can spin your car from side to side and score points as you would in an arcade game, which ensures everyone tries it again to improve their score. Watch out for a gift shop and ride photo opportunity as you exit. It is extremely popular, though, and queues are long and slow-moving, so visit early in the day. FastPasses are often all gone by early afternoon. TTT (TTTTT for under 8s). (FP).

### ⊞ BRITTIP

The Buzz Lightyear robot targets have different values, with anything moving worth a higher score. Watch out for the large robot as you enter the first room. Turn your vehicle around and aim for the target on his hand – it's worth 10,000 points. Then aim for the middle of Zurg's chest and a direct hit will score 100,000 points!

*Buzz Lightyear's Laser Blast*

© Disney

© Disney

*Legend of the Lion King*

**Legend Of The Lion King:** Sharing the impressive Café Hypérion building is the Videopolis showstage for the live entertainment offering, *Legend Of The Lion King*. A showcase of the animated film classic, with all the characters making an appearance in a mixture of clever puppetry and real-actor interaction. All the best-known songs get an airing in a celebration of the Lion King story, with Timon as the MC and his warthog sidekick Pumba adding some laughs. The 30-minute show is performed up to five times a day, alternately in French and English, and is extremely popular, so you need to plan carefully for this.

### ⊞ BRITTIP

If you miss out on a ticket for the Lion King show, grab a snack at Café Hypérion and go upstairs to where many of the tables have a view of the Videopolis stage.

Free tickets are distributed for the (limited) theatre seating twice a day at a kiosk outside the Videopolis entrance doors. You often need to queue up to half an hour before the published distribution time, then make sure you ask for the English show (as a last resort, see the French version, as the songs are still in English). To our mind, this is a slightly cock-eyed system, but it is a high-quality show and worth the extra hassle for tickets. AAAA.

© Disney

*Legend of the Lion King at Videopolis*

**BRITTIP**

Between shows, the Videopolis theatre screens classic Disney cartoons, so, if you need a rest in air-conditioned comfort or shelter from the rain, or if your kids just can't face another queue, head into Café Hypérion for a drink or snack.

As a final word on the attractions, the inevitable video games also make an appearance in the shape of **Arcades Alpha** and **Beta** on either side of the lower entrance to Videopolis. Older children and young teens who need a break from the family shackles for a while can head to either of these (or the arcade inside the exit to Star Tours) and shoot up a T-Rex or play football or air hockey. Be warned, the games are not cheap – one token costs €2 and there is a one-token minimum per game. TT.

When it comes to eating, the aforementioned **Café Hypérion** is worth investigating even if you don't visit the counter-service diner, which serves very average cheeseburgers, chicken burgers and chicken nuggets. **Pizza Planet** (easy to miss, but it's just to the right of Honey, I Shrunk the Audience) is a disappointing offering if you expect something out of the *Toy Story* film. The interior is very plain and the €7.95 (€3.90 for children) pizza served here is not dissimilar to cardboard. Try the chicken sandwich (€5.70) or pizza burger (€6.50).

The **Rocket Café** at the back of Space Mountain offers an additional few snacks and drinks that you can consume in relative peace and quiet at the tables outside Pizza Planet. There are also two main gift stores, the elaborate **Constellations** (the usual range of souvenirs but with a ceiling twinkling with a 'universe' of stars) and **Star Traders** (for all your *Star Wars*-related merchandise, other space toys and sports gear).

*Superb decorations at Constellations*

# Parades and tours

As if five 'lands' weren't enough, you have several other sources of great entertainment along the way. Chief among these is the daily parade (or parades if you are here in high season or for a special event like Halloween or Christmas). **Disney's Once Upon a Dream Parade** was new for the park's 15th Anniversary in 2007 and continues to be the daily highlight (except for the festive period from mid-November to early January when it is replaced by the **Christmas Parade** – see page 25). If you have never seen a Disney parade, this is a genuine must-see experience. Yes, the queues at many attractions do tend to shorten during the daily parade, but it is a shame to miss something as creative and dynamic as this just to take in another ride. Each parade starts in the Discovery Arcade corner of Town Square and continues up Main Street USA to the Central Plaza, where it turns right in front of the Royal Castle Stage and moves into Fantasyland before finally exiting next to 'it's a small world'.

**BRITTIP**

Be aware that people start staking out some of the best spots to view the various parades – along Main Street USA and around the Central Plaza – up to an hour in advance at peak times. There can be a bit of push-and-shove as late-comers try to squeeze in.

*Disney's Once Upon A Dream Parade*

*Disney's Fantillusion Parade*

Children are truly captivated by the scale and elaboration of the huge floats, as well as the chance to see a multitude of their favourite characters at fairly close quarters. The music is memorable, the dancing amazingly energetic (especially given the heat in summer) and the splendour of floats themed to a variety of dreams that really can come true. The eight floats feature a series of Disney characters bringing their dreams of Imagination, Fantasy, Laughter and Fun, Friendship, Power, Adventure and Romance to life, and the whole spectacle takes a good 25–30 minutes to pass by. You will take a LOT of photos – if you don't end up being sidetracked by watching children's faces around you. AAAAA.

**BRITTIP**

For the main daily parades, the route through Fantasyland is less crowded than elsewhere, while the corner of the Town Square in front of City Hall is also a good place to wait as it is often overlooked and offers some shade when it's hot.

**Disney's Fantillusion Parade** adds to the picture for the high summer and winter season evenings (usually around 10.30pm), and is equally stunning. It features an eye-popping cavalcade of Disney favourites in a high-tech setting of glittering lights and dazzling floats. The parade comes in three parts and unfolds with an

Halloween Show in Frontierland

almost balletic grace, first as Mickey himself brings the Gift of Light, then a darker section as the Disney villains threaten to take over (with some spectacular special effects as Jafar transforms into a serpent, Maleficent becomes the wicked dragon and the winged Chernabog commands fire) and finally a joyful conclusion as the glittering heroes and heroines, princes and princesses get together with Minnie to save the day.

🇬🇧 **BRITTIP**

Stake out a spot in front of the Castle. It is the only location where you can see all three stops during the Fantillusion Parade.

It features a fabulous soundtrack by Bruce Healy and a seemingly endless fairytale pageant of shimmering, twinkling lights. The overall effect is so thrilling, even by Disney standards, that it is worth keeping the kids up to see it. The whole parade stops at various points for a few well-rehearsed routines from the costumed dancers, and it can take a good 30 minutes to pass by. But, whatever you do, don't miss this one! AAAAA+.

🇬🇧 **BRITTIP**

You can watch the Fantillusion Parade from the steps of the Railroad Station on Town Square, then, once it has passed, take one of the arcades up to the Central Plaza to be ready for the fireworks while people are still watching the parade along Main Street USA!

The **Halloween Parade** adds to the daily fun throughout October (check your park map for timings) and is another visual riot of creepy costumed capers, song and dance, with various characters joining the extravaganza. Here, the Disney villains have usurped the stage for a darker (but still fun) cavalcade of ghosts, goblins and witches, with some wonderfully inventive, skeleton-inspired touches. Watch out for the Pink Witches and Pumpkin Men squabbling along the way! NB: The Halloween Parade took a hiatus in 2007 but we expect it to return in 2008. AAAA.

It is worth taking a mental step back from all the clever artistry of the floats to appreciate the non-stop energy and quality of the many dancers in the parades, who keep up their efforts for every second of every performance, day in, day out. It takes immense dedication, but they also have a lot of fun and get a real kick out of the reaction they get from their audience – especially the kids. So don't hesitate to smile and wave back, as they certainly deserve all the encouragement and appreciation you can muster.

In high season (summer and Christmas) there is also the nightly finale of the **Wishes** fireworks extravaganza, which brings down the curtain each evening. The Wishes show was pioneered at the *Magic Kingdom Park* in *Walt Disney World*,

Belle on parade

**BRITTIP**

The best place from which to watch the nightly fireworks is in front of the Castle or at the end of Main Street USA. The show is choreographed with, and symmetrically around, the château and the visual effect is stunning.

*Children love the daily parades*

and adapted for the different configuration of the *Disneyland Park*. There are fewer large-scale explosions and the vast majority of fireworks are low-level, but there is an amazing range of lighting and laser effects on the Castle and the whole show has a charm that sets it apart from the big-scale US equivalent. It is magnificently choreographed, with well-known Disney soundtracks, and features distinct bursts of films from *The Little Mermaid, Aladdin* and *Fantasia*, with additional narration by Jiminy Cricket and the Blue Fairy. It is the perfect way to conclude any Disney visit, as the company's expertise with pyrotechnic shows is legendary and well merited. Few people have the vision and capability to present fireworks in such a thrilling and well-balanced way, and the effect of seeing the many starbursts over the Sleeping Beauty Castle is breathtaking. Be warned, however, the sound and scale of the fireworks can scare young children.

One final element that was brought in for the 15th Anniversary was the **Candleabration** show, geared around the heavy birthday makeover of Sleeping Beauty Castle. The latter involves some beautiful character additions and gilding to this massive edifice, along with 15 birthday 'candles' which are lit in spectacular fashion at night. The illuminations form part of an elaborate show, with music and other lighting effects, plus a song-and-dance routine led by Mickey and friends on a central stage in the Castle plaza. The original Anniversary was geared to last only until March 2008 but proved so popular Disney extended it by a full year under the title 'The Celebration continues – big time!' Candleabration is not expected to stay after March 2009.

*Disney's Once Upon A Dream Parade*

# The Disneyland Park with children

Here is a rough guide to the rides that appeal to different age groups. Obviously, children vary enormously in their likes and dislikes but, as a general rule, you can be fairly sure the following will have most appeal to the ages concerned (also taking into account the height restrictions):

### Under 5s
Disneyland Railroad, Main Street Vehicles, Thunder Mesa Riverboats, Pocahontas Indian Village, La Plage des Pirates (Pirates' Beach) play area, La Cabane des Robinsons, The Tarzan Encounter (although check the volume isn't too loud for young ears), Winnie the Pooh and Friends, Blanche-Neige et les Sept Nains (Snow White), Pinocchio's Fantastic Journey, Le Carrousel de Lancelot, Peter Pan's Flight, Dumbo, 'it's a small world', Le Pays des Contes de Fées, Casey Jr, Alice's Curious Labyrinth, Buzz Lightyear's Laser Blast, Orbitron (not recommended for babies), Autopia, Les Mystères du Nautilus, Legend Of The Lion King, Disney's Once Upon A Dream Parade.

### 6–8s
All the above, plus Phantom Manor (with parental discretion), Fort Comstock, River Rogue Keelboats, Rustler Roundup Shootin' Gallery, Big Thunder Mountain, Adventure Isle, Pirates of the Caribbean, Le Passage Enchanté d'Aladdin, La Tanière du Dragon, Mad Hatter's Tea Cups, Star Tours, Honey, I Shrunk the Audience.

### 9–12s
Phantom Manor, Fort Comstock, Rustler Roundup Shootin' Gallery, Big Thunder Mountain, The Tarzan Encounter, Pirates of the Caribbean, Adventure Isle, Indiana Jones and the Temple of Peril, Peter Pan's Flight, Mad Hatter's Tea Cups, Alice's Curious Labyrinth, Arcades Alpha and Beta, Buzz Lightyear's Laser Blast, Orbitron, Space Mountain: Mission 2, Les Mystères du Nautilus, Honey, I Shrunk the Audience, Star Tours.

### Over 12s
Phantom Manor, Big Thunder Mountain, Rustler Roundup Shootin' Gallery, The Tarzan Encounter, Pirates of the Caribbean, Adventure Isle, Indiana Jones and the Temple of Peril, Mad Hatter's Tea Cups, Arcades Alpha and Beta, Buzz Lightyear's Laser Blast, Orbitron, Space Mountain: Mission 2, Honey, I Shrunk the Audience, Star Tours.

## There's more!

Want to learn more about the *Disneyland Park*? Sign up for a **Guided Tour** at City Hall early in the day (subject to availability; maximum 25 people) and you can take a walking tour in the company of a highly knowledgeable Cast Member who will show you what makes the theme park tick. At €15 for adults and free for under 12s, the tours last almost 2 hours and will give you a novel insight into the creation of this magnificent entertainment venue.

If you have always wanted a private tour, Disney's new **VIP Tour** offers groups of up to ten guests the chance to book a two-park tour, with time behind-the-scenes, priority seating at shows and parades and assistance with dining reservations at the restaurant of your choice. At €320 (regardless of party size) this isn't a budget option, but the chance to spend 4 hours getting tips and asking

*Autopia*

© Disney

© Disney

*Scenery on the River Rogue Keelboats*

any questions you have about the parks and attractions could prove to be a magical experience indeed!

And that, folks, is *Disneyland Park* in all its detailed splendour. Hopefully, after a day here (even when crowds are at their heaviest), you will agree with us in judging this to be a work of art in the business of having fun. Take time to acquaint yourself in advance with all that's here and you should be well prepared to get the most out of this immensely diverse range of

*Adventure Isle*

© Disney

**BRITTIP**

Unless you are particularly speedy in leaving the theme park at closing time, you might be better off taking the 15- to 20-minute walk back to the big hotels such as *Disney's Hotel Santa Fe, Disney's Cheyenne Hotel* and *Disney's Newport Bay Club,* as the crowds at the shuttle bus stop can mean another lengthy wait.

attractions. As we advise for visiting any Disney park, try to take some time along the way to slow down and appreciate all the fine, intricate detail that's involved in the park.

There is just so much packed into this theme park in particular, it would be a shame if you went home without seeing the history of Dapper Dan's barber shop, the nostalgia of the two arcades and the whimsy of restaurants like Pizzeria Bella Notte and the Blue Lagoon. It is a wonderfully complete and immersive environment that really does transport you a million miles away from everyday life, so make sure you get the most out of it.

But we can't stop here. There is a whole new park to explore yet. It's on to the *Walt Disney Studios Park…*!

## or Lights, Cameras, Action!

**While the original park is the grande dame of the *Disneyland Resort Paris*, the *Walt Disney Studios Park* is more the brash teenager – fun, lively, a bit raucous but also not yet fully polished or refined.**

It is certainly a smaller development and a completely different entity to its older sibling, something that complements the first park but doesn't attempt to copy its formula of non-stop rides and 'pixie dust' Magic. There are far fewer attractions, but what there are tend to be much bigger in scope and offer a contrasting experience. There's more emphasis on shows, plus the iconic new Twilight Zone™ Tower of Terror, while the movie theming is all-encompassing.

There is also a major difference in the geography and topography between the two, as well as the newer park being almost half the size (although with scope to grow in the coming years). It consists of just four main areas and, aside from the imposing Tower, there are no great distinguishing features once you have passed through the entrance complex known as the Front Lot. It is an easy park to negotiate, and getting from one area to another for the various shows is a lot less problematic than it can be at the older park. You can walk from one end to the other in little more than 5 minutes and it positively invites you to step outside for lunch in *Disney Village* as it's all so simple.

Another notable difference is in the sound of the two parks. In the *Disneyland Park*, the accompanying music provides a background to all the fun and rides. In the *Walt Disney Studios Park*, the music is right up front, setting the scene and providing a soundtrack almost everywhere you go, most notably in the Backlot area. This dramatic musical accompaniment underscores the film-orientated nature of the Studios and adds an important extra layer to the overall theming.

## Get with the theme

There are only 12 out-and-out main attractions, plus a daily parade, on which to concentrate. Of course, being Disney, there are always delightful extras along the way and, in the *Walt Disney Studios Park*, you

*Simon and friends*

have Streetmosphere, a series of mini-street theatres, musical acts and comedians, adding to the fun factor.

The depth and elaboration of the theming, both architecturally and in the landscaping, is not on the same scale as the *Disneyland Park* either. Some say that the Studios environment is too realistic for its own good and is lacking imagination. But, as one Cast Member explained, 'Well, our theme is a movie studio. What do you expect a movie studio to look like, apart from a collection of big, fairly bland buildings?' Of course, there is more to it than that, but it is a pertinent point.

The whole idea is to surround you with the magic of the movies and, to that end, the collection of large studio soundstages that house most of the attractions can look horribly

© Disney

*Walt Disney Studios*

functional by comparison with the neighbouring park. However, Disney's Imagineers are adding extra embellishments all the time and the internal effects are rarely short of spectacular (just wait until you see the lobby inside Twilight Zone™ Tower of Terror!).

## The Walt Disney Studios Park at a glance

| Location | Off Exit 14 of the A4 autoroute, proceed to the clearly signed car park; or turn right out of the Marne-la-Vallée RER and TGV station; or through the *Disney Village* if staying at a resort hotel |
|---|---|
| Size | 25 hectares/62 acres in four areas |
| Hours | 10am–6pm winter and spring off-peak weekdays; 10am–7pm weekends; 9 or 10am–7pm all summer |
| Admission | **Under 3** free; **3–11** €39 (1-Day Ticket), €49, €89, €111 (1-, 2- and 3-Day Park Hopper), **adults** (12+) €47 (1-Day Ticket), €57, €105, €131 (1-, 2- and 3-Day Park Hopper); **Annual Passports** (per person): Fantasy €129, Dream €179. *NB: All prices subject to increase from Easter 2008 (see **www.disneylandparis.com**)* |
| Parking | €8 |
| Pushchairs | €7.50 (Pushchair shop to left of Studio Photo, on right-hand side of entrance courtyard) |
| Wheelchairs | €7.50 (Pushchair shop) |
| Top Attractions | Twilight Zone™ Tower of Terror, Rock 'n' Roller Coaster starring Aerosmith, Moteurs… Action! Stunt Show Spectacular, Crush's Coaster, Studio Tram Tour, Cinémagique |
| Don't Miss | Disney Cinema Parade, Studio 1, Streetmosphere performers, Push, The Talking Trashcan |
| Hidden Costs | **Meals** | Burger, chips and coke €9.95; Buffet dining €20 for adults and €10 for kids (Rendez-Vous des Stars); beer €4.90 33cl; wine €4.20–4.50; Kids' meal €6 |
| | **T-shirts** | €9.90–21 |
| | **Souvenirs** | €1.90–500 |
| | **Sundries** | Face-painting €8–12 |

# WALT DISNEY STUDIOS

**Front Lot**

1 Walt Disney Studios Store
2 Studio Photo
3 Disney Studio 1
4 Les Légendes d'Hollywood
5 Restaurant en Coulisse

**Animation Courtyard**

6 Art of Disney Animation
7 Animagique
8 Flying Carpets Over Agrabah
9 The Disney Animation Gallery
10 Crush's Coaster
11 Cars Quatre Roues Rallye (Cars Race Rally)

**Production Courtyard/Hollywood Boulevard**

12 Mickey's Trailer
13 Cinémagique
14 The Studio Tram Tour
15 Catastrophe Canyon
16 Stitch Live!
17 Twilight Zone Tower of Terror
18 Rendez-Vous des Stars Restaurant
19 La Terrasse
20 Place des Stars

**The Backlot**

21 Armageddon: Special Effects
22 Rock 'n' Roller Coaster starring Aerosmith
23 Moteurs…Action! Stunt Show Spectacular
24 Le Café des Cascadeurs
25 Backlot Express Restaurant
26 Rock Around The Shop

The one possible concern for parents with younger children is there isn't as much for them to do here as next door. There are only three main kiddie rides and two shows that are primarily for them, while several attractions are definitely not for young eyes and ears (too loud, fast or scary). The daily parade, however, is a genuine source of family fun, and the Streetmosphere acts and high level of character meet-and-greets add to it all. You should certainly find it easier to meet the Disney characters here as there are several regular set-piece meeting points, plus frequent appearances throughout the park.

## Staying dry

The other clever element of the *Walt Disney Studios Park* is that nearly all of the attractions are under cover, which is vital in winter and quite welcome in the hotter months, too. With the exception of the Flying Carpets Over Agrabah and Cars Quatre Roues Rallye, the attractions provide a much longer and more involving experience. Several of the shows last half an hour or more, which means that you can spend longer doing fewer things than in the *Disneyland Park* (with less time spent queuing) but there should still be enough to keep you occupied for a full day (with the option to move between parks with the multi-day Park Hopper tickets – see page 116).

*Monsters Inc. photo opportunity*

*Café Fantasia at Disneyland Hotel*

**BRITTIP**

As with the *Disneyland Park*, you can take advantage of the Disney Shopping Service for purchases you make at the *Walt Disney Studios Park*. Instead of having to carry them around, they can be sent to *Disney Village* for you to pick up at the Disney Store from 6pm.

Another difference between the theme parks is the eating opportunities. While the *Disneyland Park* has a comprehensive mix of restaurants, cafés and snack bars, the *Walt Disney Studios Park* is limited to just four counter-service options, plus a series of snack wagons. With *Disney Village* just 5 minutes' walk from the front gates, it is easy to argue that you have plenty of choice (plus a chance to escape the hubbub), but we look forward to seeing some future development. At least one full-service restaurant is needed to provide a bit of breadth to the studio style (anyone who has eaten in the Sci Fi Dine-In Theater or the 50s Prime Time Diner at *Disney's Hollywood Studios* in Orlando will know what we mean!). However, there are also fewer shopping opportunities in this park and you don't feel quite so much a target for the big sell.

*Susan at Walt Disney Studios*

# Right on queue

One lingering concern about the new park is its ability to handle the queues, especially around its big new attractions of The Twilight Zone™ Tower of Terror (2008) and Crush's Coaster (2007). With fewer attractions but some hugely popular rides and shows, summer 2007 saw the park struggle at times to manage the crowds, especially first thing in the morning (for the initial door-opening rush) and with the capacity of its two new rides. There are only four FastPass attractions and, while they are not always needed at quieter times of the year, this can also add to the congestion at peak times as the FastPass distribution is not always predictable. What kind of strain the iconic new Twilight Zone™ Tower of Terror will cause to the park's crowd control – as it is sure to be the most popular attraction in the whole of the *Disneyland Paris Resort* – can only be imagined, but hopefully park management learned some lessons in 2007.

The main issue will be how the initial rush for The Twilight Zone™ Tower of Terror is controlled. From our observations of the summer opening of Crush's Coaster (a much smaller attraction), the mad rush to be first there in the morning was almost frightening at times and the Cast Members seemed a little overawed trying to handle the push-and-shove that developed. They had to start new opening techniques to cope with this early surge and they will almost certainly need to do something similar for the Tower, as it is likely to inspire an even more significant cavalry charge to start with!

However, there are also signs that the extra crowds pouring into the park will be more dispersed in future as the range of attractions broadens. Rides that used to draw big queues – like the Studio Tram Tour and Flying Carpets Over Agrabah – will be less pressured and the shows will continue to have the ability to soak up large numbers at one time. Queuing for the big Stunt Show Spectacular could be an ordeal pre-2007 unless you were there half an hour early, but that seems to be less noticeable these days and the big arena also helps to manage the crowd flow.

Towards the end of the day you should still be able to enjoy rides such as Rock 'n' Roller Coaster and the Flying Carpets almost unhindered (Simon's record is five goes on Rock 'n' Roller in the final hour!), even if the queues remain long at Tower of Terror and Crush's Coaster (as we expect). Many people leave the park after the daily parade and, when this is at 4 or 5pm (in high season), that can still leave a good 2 hours in which to do most of the rides.

*Character Meet 'n' Greet at Hollywood Boulevard*

## Enter, stage centre!

Okay, without any further preamble, let us introduce you to the *Walt Disney Studios Park*…

If you approach from the main car park, the Studios will be straight ahead of you as you come through the moving walkways. From *Disney Village*, bear left past the Gaumont Cinemas and, from the bus or train station, continue straight on, passing *Disney Village* on your left. The park is subdivided into four main areas, although there is little visual distinction between them, and your adventure starts as soon as you walk through the imposing gates.

The grand layout in front of you makes it clear what's in store – film adventure and lots of fun in the inimitable Mickey style. The 33m/108ft) high water tower edifice (based on the same structure at Disney's home studios in Burbank, California), topped by a large pair of mouse ears (we kid you not), is called… wait for it… the Earful Tower (!), and sets out the visual style in no uncertain terms, as well as providing a handy marker for much of the way around the park (although the completion of the 60m/199ft Twilight Zone™ Tower of Terror tends to change the perspective, putting a definitive punctuation mark on thrills and making a statement as the park's undisputed icon).

## Talking tactics

Unlike the *Disneyland Park*, this is not somewhere you need to be right on opening time (unless you are keen to try out the two new high-energy rides). With much of the entertainment centred on the big show times, such as the Stunt Show and Cinémagique, you can arrive in more leisurely style, head for the shows first and be reasonably sure you can get into most of them with only minimal queuing. With that said, if the lure of the Tower or Crush's Coaster call to you, plan to be ready for the opening rush or risk standing in enormous queues!

**BRITTIP**

Although the shows have large capacities, it is still advisable to arrive 10–15 minutes early to benefit from being the first to be seated.

If you are after the thrills, your best plan is to start by going to either The Twilight Zone™ Tower of Terror or Crush's Coaster immediately upon park opening. If you have young children with you, visit Cars Quatre Roues Rallye first, as it is slow loading and draws long queues all day. If you prefer a gentler start, make the Studio Tram Tour your first stop. Waiting times can occasionally build up to half an hour or more. If you then take in Armageddon and Rock 'n' Roller Coaster, you will have three (or four)

*Armageddon: Special Effects*

© Disney

*Walt Disney Studios decorated for Christmas*

of the biggest crowd-pullers under your belt early on. Alternatively, if you have younger children, they will certainly want to ride the Flying Carpets Over Agrabah after visiting Cars, as this is another ride where slow-moving queues can sometimes build up.

## Front Lot

Once through the turnstiles, you come into a lovely Spanish-style courtyard, that marks the entrance to the first main area, the Front Lot. This is the 'office' part of the theme park and houses the more functional elements such as pushchair and wheelchair hire, lost property, lost children centre, baby-care centre, first aid station, cash dispenser and currency exchange. You will also find the **Studio Services** here, for any queries you may have about the park (like when and where to find the characters and which Streetmosphere acts will be performing). Visitors with disabilities can also pick up a *Guide*

*for Guests with Special Needs* if they haven't done so already and the Assisted Access Card, if required, which allows guests with a disability incompatible with waiting in the regular queue to wait in an alternate area (see pages 31–32).

This area is an extremely elegant piece of design, with the central Sorcerer Mickey fountain, flanked by palm trees, providing a great photo opportunity to capture some happy memories. The left-hand side of the courtyard is taken up by the **Walt Disney Studios Store**, the theme park's biggest shop, while on the right is **Studio Photo**, for all your photographic requirements (although it is better to bring your own). In the early morning, you can meet several **Disney characters** here (usually Goofy, Pluto, Minnie, Donald, Daisy and Chip 'n' Dale), and it is worth pausing to enjoy the classic 1930s-style architecture as the theme park transports you into the world of movies, Hollywood style.

This area is also where you'll find **Toon Train: Lights… Camera… Musique!** showing five times daily. Chip 'n' Dale, dressed in mock 'gangster-wear', dance and frolic to live music against a backdrop of three mobile sets, encouraging children to participate in the fun. When Clarice, their glamorous cohort, makes her appearance, a swinging jazz-fest ensues, which is sure to get you clapping and your toes tapping.

*Concert at Studio 1*

**BRITTIP**

The Front Lot courtyard, **Place des Frères Lumières**, makes a good place to visit in early afternoon if the park is busy. Grab a drink or snack inside Disney Studio 1 and head out to enjoy the relaxing surroundings.

You really get the full effect, though, as you walk through the doors of **Disney Studio 1** (remember to pick up a park map as you enter). It is almost an attraction in its own right, even if it is in many ways just a covered version of Main Street USA in the *Disneyland Park*. It is 70m/230ft long, 35m/115ft wide and 20m/66ft high, making it the second-largest 'soundstage' in Europe (okay, it isn't actually a working facility, but the impression is pretty good). The overall effect is as if you have walked into the middle of a Hollywood film shoot, with the paraphernalia of movie-making all around.

**BRITTIP**

Visit the Studio Photo in the Front Lot courtyard and you can get your films processed in 2 hours. It's not cheap, but it is a great way to ensure that those happy snaps have come out (if not, you can go back and retake them!).

*Disney's Cinema Parade*

*Mickey's statue at Animation Courtyard*

The film 'sets' are all unfinished and provide almost a kaleidoscopic montage of scenery in each direction, with a series of façades and hoardings, which change the perspective in a multitude of ways with the aid of some brilliant lighting effects. Down the left side is **Les Légendes d'Hollywood** store, while the right flank is given over to the **Restaurant en Coulisse**.

**BRITTIP**

Restaurant en Coulisse gets pretty busy from midday–2pm but is ideal between 3 and 4pm for a late lunch or early tea.

The shop is cleverly disguised behind no less than six different façades, giving the impression of a whole movie 'street' modelled on various Hollywood stores – both real and imagined – from the 1920s to 1960s. Designs that stand out include Last Chance Gas (a mock Route 66 petrol station), The Alexandria Theater (a classic Los Angeles 'movie palace') and The Gossip Column (a news and magazine stand) and, of course, you can buy a whole range of film-related souvenirs as well as the usual Disney souvenirs. Also here is **Shutterbugs**, a fun photo studio that can put YOU in the Disney picture with various well-known characters.

© Disney

Monsters Inc. Scream Monitors

© Disney

# Toon Studio

Turn right as you exit the doors of Disney Studio 1 and you are immediately in this recently expanded area of the park (it was Animation Courtyard until Crush's Coaster and the Cars Race Rally opened in 2007), which caters mostly for younger children. As well as more chances to meet, photo and get autographs from the characters, you have two genuine kiddie rides here, the most enchanting of the park's shows and the wildly popular thrilll of Crush's Coaster.

Toon Studio

**BRITTIP**

Check the Information Board as you exit Studio 1 to find out the waiting times at the attractions and which queues to avoid.

**The Art of Disney Animation:** The first big set-piece attraction, located under the giant Sorcerer's Apprentice hat, this is a four-part adventure into the history, creation and magic of animated film. The first section concentrates on the history and is the least interesting for younger children. It is basically a pre-show area, with a series of exhibits around the room, showing how animation developed from its most basic into the art form that Walt Disney helped to pioneer. The highlight, amid several hands-on

opportunities (like a Zoetrope and a Magic Lantern), is one of only two surviving multi-plane cameras, a tool developed by Walt Disney himself in the 1930s.

**BRITTIP**

Check out the carpet in the post-show area of the Art of Disney Animation. Can you pick out a certain set of Mouse ears in the pattern…?!

As the doors close behind you, a large video screen comes to life and Walt pays tribute to the European pioneers of animation, along with former Walt Disney Company chairman Roy Disney (Walt's nephew). Annoyingly for us, it is all dubbed in French (you would have thought one of the showings would be kept in English) with English subtitles, but it sets the

The Art of Disney Animation

## Waiting for opening

If you arrive half an hour before the official opening time, you will still be admitted through the main turnstiles of the *Walt Disney Studios*. This brings you into the courtyard in the Front Lot, where you are likely to meet Goofy or Pluto as they welcome you to the park. Children can stop for a photo and an autograph, and you can then pass into Disney Studio 1 and either have a bite to eat or browse the shops. Finally, at the appointed opening hour (either 9 or 10am), the crowd starts to gather at the doors at the far end and, with a final countdown – 'Lights, Cameras, Action! – the Cast Members open all the doors simultaneously and let in the eager throng.

If you are looking for the thrills first, the new highlight of The Twilight Zone™ Tower of Terror is straight ahead of you (it's hard to miss!), and Cast Members will direct the flock of early birds into the queuing area. Turn left for the Backlot area and Rock 'n' Roller Coaster while, for Crush's Coaster, go sharp right into Toon Studio. If you have young children, you should concentrate on this area and head first for Cars Quatre Roues Rallye, which quickly builds up some long, slow-moving queues, and the Flying Carpets Over Agrabah.

stage for the 225-seat Disney Classics Theatre next. The doors underneath the screen open and you pass into the mini-cinema for 8 minutes of highlights from the Disney classics that are sure to keep everyone happy.

Stage 3 is another theatre-like auditorium, set up like an animator's office, where a part live and part film show brings Mushu from Mulan to life and explains how this dragon-character came into being (with an amusing voice-over from Eddie Murphy). The interaction between the live 'artist' and Mushu is wonderfully scripted and, although the on-stage part is in French, there are headphones to provide a full translation (watch out for the finale as the Murphy-dragon imagines himself as The Mushu of Notre Dame!).

You exit the theatre into a final room of six 'animation stations', which give you the chance to try your hand at drawing, colouring or providing a voice or sound effects for various characters. It is great fun for children of 6 upwards, and the Animation Academy with a real artist is presented in both French and English. In all, it is a fascinating and thoroughly enjoyable look at the artistry of feature animation and the queues move steadily here, so you are rarely waiting long. AAAA.

**Animagique:** Opposite the Sorcerer's Apprentice hat, this is a unique live show featuring the innovative Czech art of 'Black Light' stagecraft and Japanese 'Bunraku' puppet manipulation. If that sounds a bit dry, prepare yourself for 25 minutes of pure Disney fun in the company of Mickey, Donald Duck and the cast of *Dumbo, Pinocchio, The Jungle Book* and *The Lion King*.

### BRITTIP

Try to arrive a few minutes early for the Animagique show as the 1,100-seat theatre comes to life with a series of clever sound effects that ring and echo in delightful style around the auditorium before it begins.

The story (partly in French and Donald Duck-ese!) sees Donald stuck for inspiration at the drawing board. Ignoring Mickey's warnings, he opens the Disney vault and unwittingly lets loose a host of animated characters

*Animagique*

© Disney

© Disney

*Inside Studio 1*

who run riot on stage, with a big song-and-dance finale that will have you humming the catchy theme tune as you leave. Some excellent effects surprise you along the way (that we won't reveal) but be prepared for some extra fun, especially if you are in the first dozen or so rows. The high-tech show (involving digitally synchronised lighting, audio and machinery effects, in addition to the puppetry) is presented six to seven times a day and show times are posted both outside and on the park maps. AAAA.

### BRITTIP

If you have children, try to sit in the central section of the theatre, no more than 10–12 rows back and you will enjoy one of the best special effects of Animagique.

*Cars Road Rally*

© Disney

As you exit Animagique, watch out for the 'stars' of the latest Disney films, as they often appear in Toon Studio in the Courtyard in front of the Art of Animation and in the Plaza to the left of Crush's Coaster. In 2007, it was the Incredibles and Ratatouille.

**Cars Quatre Roues Rallye (Cars Road Rally):** This brand new attraction (in summer 2007) is opposite Animagique and borrows from the 2006 Disney-Pixar film *Cars*. It visits Radiator Springs, where Lightning McQueen is starring in a movie being filmed down in the canyon, and you're invited to co-star. But be warned: you'll be doing your own stunts and spin-outs as they are all part of the action! In all honesty, this

© Disney

*Backlot Express Restaurant*

is just another variation on the basic spinning tea cups ride and it is a fairly short experience (barely 90 seconds), but it has great kiddie appeal, so you should head here very early if your children are likely to want to do it. The ride has that swing-'em-around motion (three revolving platforms that then add an extra spin with each car) that pre-schoolers seem to love. The crowds do build up quickly here and it is a slow-loading ride, hence the queue is pretty slow moving. TT (TTTT under 7s).

**Flying Carpets Over Agrabah:** At the innermost end of Toon Studio is the second main children's ride, which is another variation on the Dumbo/ Orbitron attractions of the *Disneyland*

© Disney

*Flying Carpets over Agrabah*

*Park*. This has been transported with a slightly different theme from the ride in Orlando's *Magic Kingdom*.

**BRITTIP**

Don't head for the Flying Carpets ride just after the daily Disney Cinema Parade, as the parade finishes in Toon Studio and a large part of the crowd following it ends up in the Carpets queue.

Here you line up (in a loosely themed area like a film 'green room', where actors prepare for their next scene) to take part in a 'casting' for a role in a movie, with the Genie (from the 1992 Disney film *Aladdin*) as the director (in French and English). Once aboard your four-person 'flying carpet', there are controls in the front seats to make

it go up and down and in the rear seats to add a bit of tilt 'n' turn. In all honesty it is a fairly tame ride, but children under 10 always seem to get a thrill from it. However, the queues can build here through the middle of the day, so it is best to visit early on or wait until the last hour of the day. TT (TTTT for under 10s). (FP).

**Crush's Coaster:** Also new in 2007, this is a breathtaking, high-speed journey along the 'East Australia Current' (or EAC), riding on Crush's back as he plunges and swirls through a mock undersea world, full of inventive lighting and special effects, with a brief plunge outdoors before diving back inside again. You board your turtle shell alongside a Sydney harbour fishing village (each shell holds four riders sitting in back-to-back pairs), where guests facing forward at the start soon find themselves spinning backwards (and the back seats become the front seats), dipping and swirling through the great bubbly blue. The ride includes a slower-paced dark section where you meet Nemo and Squirt in their undersea habitat (courtesy of some high-tech visual effects) before you are bumped into the main part of the ride, a wild and twisting spin both up and down the EAC before Crush guides you back to safer waters. Dude, it's just too cool!

*Crush's Coaster*

© Disney

The attraction should appeal to most of the family, although it may be a bit too dynamic for under 6s (top speed is only 37mph/57kph, but it feels faster with all the tight twists and turns). Restriction: 107cm/3ft 5in). TTTT.

For a snack in this area, the **Studio Catering Co** has two outlets, themed like truck trailers, offering hot dogs, burgers, fish and chips, club sandwiches, popcorn, ice cream, doughnuts, muffins and cookies, as well as drinks. There is only one main shopping option, but it is a good one, **The Disney Animation Gallery** at the exit of the Art of Disney Animation (inside the giant Sorcerer's Apprentice hat), plus a smaller kiosk in the Courtyard area. The Gallery offers a rather upmarket range of souvenirs and serious collectables – figurines, statues, books and genuine Disney film cels – for those with a fascination for the true art of Disney. For a great photo opportunity, visit the Monsters Inc display between Studio 1 and Animagique – and see how loud you can be on the Scream Monitors.

*The Tower of Terror*

© Disney

# Production Courtyard/ Hollywood Boulevard

Retracing your steps brings you into the new Hollywood Boulevard, part of the Production Courtyard area (which will gradually be transformed into Hollywood Studio during the course of 2008/09). This middle section offers four main attractions.

**The Twilight Zone™ Tower of Terror:** Enter a new dimension of sight, sound and high-speed, hair-raising fear! The Hollywood Tower Hotel's glamorous heyday lies dormant beneath layers of dust and abandonment, hinting at the tragedy that befell its last 'visitors' – and now awaits you! Pass through the lobby into a dimly lit library, where Rod Serling warns of the Tower's terrible past and then invites you to step aboard a maintenance service elevator heading directly to The Twilight Zone. Sounds from the boiler room prompt you forward through grim and grimy surroundings until you finally reach the elevator and, once inside, your fate is sealed.

**BRITTIP**

The queue is so spectacular even non-riders should do it then duck out of the ride without boarding.

The remainder of the ride is a thrill-seekers dream, with astonishing special effects and moments of sensory deprivation that will leave you shaking – and eager for a second ride! And do ride again. With a drop-and-rise sequence that leaves you breathless, you may well miss some of the clever details en route, so you will need several visits to take it all in. Unmissable both visually and as an attraction, the Tower represents Disney Imagineering at its finest. Most importantly, it is also a FastPass ride, but with the ride's popularity it is quite possible that FastPasses will run out by early afternoon. Restriction: 102cm/3ft 4in. TTTTT. (FP).

# A Towering achievement

The original art deco-style Tower of Terror opened in Orlando in 1994, themed as an episode of the popular television show, *The Twilight Zone* (1959–1964). The show's host, Rod Serling, recounts that fateful night when a bolt of lightning struck the Hollywood Tower Hotel – a glamorous Hollywood Hills retreat catering to the brightest stars of the late 1930s – propelling five unsuspecting guests into the Fifth Dimension, never to be heard from again. But their ghostly figures haunt the hallways, and the door they passed through into the unknown has opened again. This time, *you* will step through it…!

California's Tower opened in 2004, based on the same storyline as Orlando. Unlike the Florida park's attraction, the façade is *pueblo*-deco and the setting is downtown Hollywood. The ride is essentially the same, but Orlando's ride vehicles utilise a continuous circular loop technology, with vehicles moving horizontally into a separate drop shaft, and guests loading and unloading in separate locations, while the versions in California, Tokyo and now Paris all feature independent drop shafts, with ride vehicles that horizontally back into the shaft before making their hair-raising journey.

The *Disneyland Resort Paris* Tower of Terror, opened in early 2008, continues the Twilight Zone theme, again in a late 1930s *pueblo*-deco style Hollywood Tower Hotel setting. Orlando's Fifth Dimension element (the appearance of ghostly apparitions before the vehicle enters the drop shaft) is replaced by a mysterious looking-glass effect, in which riders see their own reflections before their image morphs into ghostly figures.

The version in the *Disneyland TokyoSea Park* changes the storyline completely. Instead of the Hollywood Tower Hotel, this gothic-style edifice is known as Hotel Hightower and the setting is New York City in the late 1890s. The hotel's owner, Harrison Hightower III, collector of rare artefacts, has unwittingly transported Shiriki Utundy, protector spirit of the tribal Mtundu village, into the hotel, where the idol takes its revenge, plunging Harrison to his death inside an elevator. But his body has never been found. Years later, in an effort to save the abandoned hotel, guided tours are being offered, but the curse – and the mystery – persist.

The Tower of Terror is arguably Disney's most recognisable ride worldwide. The artistry that went into creating a totally convincing environment, from Rod Serling's seamless delivery (Serling himself died in 1975, at the age of 50, and his 'presentation' was achieved by the laborious process of splicing together segments from the TV show, then adding a voice-over where needed) to the placement of props from famous episodes, the Tower's eerie silence, broken only by screams coming from the elevator shaft, will convince you to…Fear Every Drop!

**Cinémagique:** One of the park's undoubted highlights and a real *tour de force* of imagination, this half-hour film show, exclusive to *Disneyland Resort Paris*, starts out superficially as a tribute to the history of both European and American cinema, but soon takes an unexpected dramatic turn. It ends up as a hilarious series of scenes featuring comedian Martin Short as a hapless 'time traveller' moving through a whole range of cinematic genres linked together by a wonderful love-interest storyline.

The show includes numerous funny scene shifts (the 'cowboy shoot-out' scenario is truly inspired) and a couple of eye-popping special effects, which we won't reveal but that add hugely to the fun (hint: an umbrella might be a good idea!). French actress

*Lights across the Studios*

© Disney

Julie Delpy is the co-star and the show takes place inside a beautiful 1,100-seat theatre with an art deco theme harking back to classic 1930s' Hollywood movie palaces.

**BRITTIP**

Waiting in the holding pens for Cinémagique is fairly dull, but the large capacity of the theatre ensures everyone usually gets in, while you can often wait until the last minute and still find a seat. There are up to six shows a day in high season, and it is perfectly possible to see this twice in one day.

It probably won't hold the attention of younger children (say, under 4s) for the full 30 minutes, but there is enough amusing on-screen action to keep older children entertained. Adults will enjoy the clever interweaving of scenes, with Short popping up in all manner of unlikely but well-known film scenarios. AAAAA.

As you exit, children will probably want to head straight for **Mickey's Trailer** next door (NB: this may move back to the Toon Studio area in 2008, as it was originally next to the Flying Carpets ride before Crush's Coaster was built). This usually draws a queue as the 'star' needs a break from time to time, so it can take a while. But it is a well-organised line (unlike a few of the scrimmages that can develop around the characters in some places) and children are usually well behaved when they can see the famous Mouse at the end!

*Studio Tram Tour*

© Disney

*Streetmosphere*

**BRITTIP**

Disney changes the live Streetmosphere shows at regular intervals, so look out for something new in 2008.

Just outside the Cinémagique theatre, the Place des Stars stage is home to more live entertainment in the form of **Lilo & Stitch's Catch The Wave Party** featuring Minnie, Goofy and Pluto as well as the mischievous alien and his owner. The 25-minute production features a variety of song and dance numbers as Lilo & Stitch celebrate the Hawaiian family tradition of 'Ohana, with guests invited to dance the hula! AAA.

**Studio Tram Tour:** This large-scale, 15-minute ride has been adapted from *Disney's Hollywood Studios* in Orlando and enhanced with several new elements, making it a must-see attraction. Cleverly arranged with an English-French soundtrack, it is a tour of mind-boggling proportions.

The tram takes you on a behind-the-scenes look at a movie studio, learning some tricks of the film trade, such as location sets, props, costumes and special effects. Each tram has a video screen with a full commentary (the English version supplied by a wonderfully laconic Jeremy Irons) that points out the key areas along the way. You pass a whole array of film props and scenery (notably the imposing Waterfall City façade from

© Disney

*Narnia Meet ' n' Greet on the Backlot*

the *Dinotopia* mini-series) before entering the tour highlight, **Catastrophe Canyon**.

## BRIT TIP

Young children may be scared by all the loud and dramatic special effects in the Studio Tram Tour. Explain to them what's going to happen and reassure them it is all quite safe and just another film trick. The left-hand side of the tram may also get a little wet.

Here, you are supposed to get a dry-run version of an elaborate special effects set-up but the 'director' mistakes the tram for his film 'extras' and starts the action sequence with you in the middle! Before you know it, the tram has been hit by earthquake, fire and flood, and the culmination, when 265,000 litres/58,300 gallons of water are dumped on the flaming set, is quite breathtaking.

Having 'survived' the canyon, you continue on past some more film props (look out for some planes from *Pearl Harbor*) and the costume studio, before passing the **Star Cars** garage exhibit of well-known movie vehicles (like Cruella de Vil's car from *101 Dalmatians*, the Humvee from *The Rock* and the sports car from *Runaway Bride*). Finally, you enter the smoking ruins of London, circa 2022 (or at least a remarkable film set facsimile). Here, for anyone familiar with the summer 2002 blockbuster film *Reign of Fire*, you get a close encounter with one of its 'stars'. Well, not actually one of the dragons, but a fairly 'hot' close-up of its fiery breath, which blasts out twice on the right side of the tram. The shock effect, the noise of the fire and the feel of the heat will definitely scare young children (and some adults!), so think carefully before taking your youngster on this tour. However, the encounter is over pretty quickly and the rest of the set is something to marvel at. Avoid this just after a Stunt Show has finished in the Backlot area, as many of that 3,000-strong crowd head straight here (and there's not much to see while waiting). AAA/TTTT. (FP).

**Stitch Live:** Opening early in 2008, this is your chance to interact with the mischievous blue alien when Disney Studios send a satellite beam directly into outer space for a live audio and visual connection between

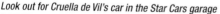

*Look out for Cruella de Vil's car in the Star Cars garage*

© Disney

Stitch and the studio audience. Children can ask questions and Stitch responds directly to each child – and may even ask a few questions of his own! Each encounter is personalised, unpredictable, hilarious and filled with the sort of gentle irreverence that makes Stitch a family favourite.

The 20-minute theatre-style show located inside the former Walt Disney Television Studios runs up to three times per hour, with shows alternating in French and English (check the times schedule posted outside the attraction). Although the attraction is geared toward youngsters, the technology is so convincing (if you have seen Turtle Talk With Crush at the *Epcot* park in *Walt Disney World*, you will have some idea of what to expect), even older children and adults will be enchanted. AAAA.

When it comes to grabbing a bite to eat, the Production Courtyard has the best of the theme park's dining in the shape of the **Rendez-Vous des Stars Restaurant**, a 300-seat café-type diner in full art deco style, which now offers a set-price buffet meal. The speciality is a meat carvery but the range of food is extremely broad (similar to the Plaza Gardens Restaurant in the *Disneyland Park*), from baked fish to penne pasta bolognese, roast chicken, vegetable lasagne and a wide variety of salads (€20 for adults, €10 3–11s). The walls display a fine array of authentic Hollywood photos and film memorabilia.

© Disney

*Rendez-Vous des Stars*

### BRITTIP

For that extra special occasion, you can order a birthday cake at the Rendez-Vous des Stars at the beginning of your meal. It costs €22 and serves 4–8. But be warned: don't come here when the Stunt Show has just finished and 3,000 people are in the vicinity!

## The Backlot

The Backlot area is past the Rendez-Vous des Stars and features some more action-packed offerings, with three contrasting top-drawer thrill elements.

**Armageddon: Special Effects:** This unique, elaborate show that puts YOU at the heart of the action (although it's not one for young children) is the first of the thrills. You enter a pre-show area, full of models, exhibits and diagrams from the blockbuster film starring Bruce Willis (there are two

*Armageddon: Special Effects*

© Disney

**BRITTIP**

The props on display in the pre-show area of Armageddon: Special Effects include the spacesuit worn by actor Ben Affleck in the film.

studios for this purpose, 7A and 7B, and the array of models does vary), where a Cast Member greets you and acts as the show's 'director'.

With the help of your director and a video that explains the eye-popping scenario of the film, your role as 'extras' in a special effects scene is explained in amusing detail (in English and French). The screen is then turned over to a tribute to Frenchman Georges Méliès, who is credited with inventing film special effects. It shows how the movie world has taken his ideas and developed them with astonishing creativity in the last 100 years.

The video continues with the explosive arrival of Michael Clarke Duncan, another of the *Armageddon* stars, who explains how the film's technical wizardry was carried out. You are then invited to see for real how it is done and walk through, under 'directorial' guidance, into an amazing mock-up of the movie's Russian space station – just as it comes under threat from a meteor shower! The ensuing chaos, as the station almost literally blows up all around you, is brilliantly scripted and the array of effects incredibly realistic, with smoke, sparks, bursting pipes, buckling doors and a huge central fireball that adds some real heat to proceedings.

In our opinion, the sights and sounds (it is pretty loud) are much too intense for under 7s, but there are no real warnings of this outside. However, the space station itself is a work of art and the hectic action is suitably breathtaking. They could do with adding a bit of interest to the plain waiting area outside, though. TTTT.

**BRITTIP**

It is a good idea for an adult to experience an attraction first to check on its suitability, if you are worried that certain elements might be too scary for your children.

*The Backlot*

© Disney

© Disney

*Rock 'n' Roller Coaster*

**Rock 'n' Roller Coaster starring Aerosmith:** This next attraction is a real blast of a ride that rockets you from 0–100kph/62mph in just 2.8 seconds! It is a slightly revised version of the ride of the same name at *Disney's Hollywood Studios* in Orlando, making it a different experience.

**BRITTIP**

Listen out for Aerosmith lead singer, Steve Tyler, completing a clever 'sound check' as you board the Rock 'n' Roller Coaster – it adds considerably to the fun.

Here, you enter the rock 'n' roll world of the American supergroup Aerosmith, as they discuss the creation of this unique rockin' ride, described as a 'revolutionary musical experience' produced by Tour De Force Records. As the record company's VIP guests, Aerosmith invite you to enter the 'research and

*Rock 'n' Roller Coaster*

© Disney

development' area to try it out at first hand and you pass into the launch area, complete with 'sound engineers' and computer models of the ride systems, which feature 'Soundtracker' cars. These are fitted with five state-of-the-art speakers per seat so you literally 'ride the music'.

Once you are firmly harnessed into your seat, the countdown begins and you blast off into a topsy-turvy 'rock video' that features two loops and a corkscrew as well as some eye-popping lighting effects on the way round. There are five music tracks that accompany the ride, hence five variations on the ride experience. Aerosmith have even re-recorded a couple of their tracks, so see if you can notice the new lyrics (hint: the 'adapted' songs are 'Love In An Elevator' and 'What Kind of Love Are You On?'). Waiting time can hit an hour at peak periods but there is rarely much of a queue for the first couple of hours or in late afternoon. It is not recommended for anyone with back or neck problems or for pregnant women. Restriction: 1.2m/3ft 9in. TTTTT. (FP).

**BRITTIP**

The queue for the Rock 'n' Roller Coaster drops off during a performance of the Stunt Show next door but it should be avoided just after the show finishes as many people make a beeline for it.

**Moteurs...Action! Stunt Show Spectacular:** Next door to the Rock 'n' Roller Coaster, this is one of Disney's most remarkable shows. Full of genuine high-risk stunts and hugely skilful car and motorbike action, it will have you shaking your head in amazement for quite a while afterwards.

> **BRITTIP**
>
> People start queuing for the Stunt Show a good half-hour before a performance at peak times (three–four a day) and the middle shows of the day are always packed. It is better to head for the first one or stay until the last to minimise your wait.

Seating starts a good 20 minutes prior to show-time, and there is some amusing pre-show chat (in English and French) and freestyle show-boating by one of the bike riders to keep people amused before the serious stuff starts. An audience member is also recruited to help in one of the scenes and a roving cameraman picks out people from the crowd to highlight on the big video screen in the centre of the 'square'. The huge set is based on a typical Mediterranean village and is magnificently crafted to have an 'aged' appearance.

Once the preliminaries are completed, you are treated to a 45-minute extravaganza of daredevil stunts, with a Car Ballet sequence, a Motorbike Chase and a Grand Finale that features some surprise pyrotechnics to complete a truly awesome presentation (keep your eyes on the windows below the video screen at the end). Each scene – featuring a secret agent 'goody' and various black-car 'baddies' – is set up and fully explained by a movie 'director' (and the need for bilingual commentary is handled skilfully). The results of each 'shoot' are then played back on the video screen to show how each effect was created and how it is all spliced together to create the desired end product.

> **BRITTIP**
>
> Be aware there is some loud mock gunfire during the Stunt Show, which can upset young children, while the motorbike scene includes a rider catching fire, which can be quite frightening for them.

*Moteurs ... Action!*

© Disney

All the cars were specially created for the show by Vauxhall and there are some extra tricks (including an amusing appearance by Herbie from *The Love Bug* film) in between the main scenes. The whole thing was designed by Frenchman Rémy Julienne, the doyen of cinematic car stunt sequences, who has worked on the James Bond films *Goldeneye* and *Licence to Kill* and other epics such as *The Rock, Ronin, Gone in 60 Seconds* and *Enemy of the State.*

It all adds up to a breathtaking show, and kids are sure to want to come back, another good reason to see it early on. There is nothing like it in any other theme park in the world (except from the copycat that opened in *Disney's Hollywood Studios* in Orlando in 2005), and the fact so much of it involves genuine, live co-ordination makes it truly thrilling.

However, the exit is quite a scrum as 3,000 people have to leave through two fairly narrow thoroughfares and it can take 10–15 minutes to get clear of the auditorium. So, if you can sit towards the front either on the right or left of the grandstand, you will be out quicker. TTTTT.

One last new element (in summer 2007) is **High School Musical On Tour**, a roving stage show that is a big hit with teenagers. Join the students from East High in a high-energy pep rally, Wildcat style! All the biggest hits from the popular Disney Channel TV movie send an unstoppable beat through the Backlot as it moves into Hollywood Boulevard and into Place des Stars, before exiting alongside Studio 1, up to five times daily. The excitement is contagious when East High's cheerleaders, athletes and students coax park guests into the action, and fans of the film won't want to miss the action-packed 11-minute performance. AAA. Look out also for the periodic Chronicles of Narnia photo meet-and-greet in The Backlot.

When you need to stop for something to eat in the Backlot, **Le Café des Cascadeurs** is an imaginative little diner (themed as an art deco studio café for the stuntmen and women) around the corner from Armageddon, serving a fairly simple selection of salads, sandwiches, hot dogs and crisps, but the train carriage setting is good fun. The **Backlot Express Restaurant** is a counter-service café with another highly themed interior – like a studio's art department, full of props, tools, light fittings, furniture and other film accoutrements – that makes dining fun. The food is fairly ordinary – Mickey pizza (€3.90), toasted sandwiches, baguettes and salads – ranging from €4.90–6.50, but it holds up to 500 inside, plus there is outdoor seating in summer.

*Backlot Express Restaurant*

# Walt Disney Studios Park with children

Here is a rough guide to the attractions in this park that are most likely to appeal to the different age groups (taking into account any height restrictions):

### Under 5s
The Art of Disney Animation, Animagique, Flying Carpets Over Agrabah, Meet Mickey, Cars Quatre Roues Rallye, Studio Tram Tour (with parental discretion), Stitch Live, Moteurs…Action! Stunt Show Spectacular (also with parental discretion), Disney Cinema Parade, Lilo & Stitch Catch The Wave Party

### 6–8s
All the above, plus Crush's Coaster, High School Musical On Tour, Disney Studio 1, Cinémagique, Armageddon (with parental discretion), Streetmosphere

### 9–12s
All the above (except Cars Race Rally), plus Rock 'n' Roller Coaster starring Aerosmith and The Twilight Zone™ Tower of Terror

### Over 12s
Crush's Coaster, Disney Studio 1, Art of Disney Animation, Animagique, Studio Tram Tour, Cinémagique, Armageddon, Rock 'n' Roller Coaster starring Aerosmith, The Twilight Zone™ Tower of Terror, Moteurs…Action!, Streetmosphere

---

## BRITTIP

In Le Café des Cascadeurs, help yourself to a selection or two on the classic 1950s-style jukebox.

The only shop around here is **Rock Around The Shop**, at the exit to the Rock 'n' Roller Coaster, offering a range of Aerosmith and rock-related goods, plus the chance to buy your ride photo (€10–20).

## Here comes the parade

In best Disney park fashion, no visit is complete without the daily procession and here it is, the **Disney Cinema Parade**, at either 1.30pm or 5pm according to the season. Starting between the Backlot Express Restaurant and the Rock 'n' Roller Coaster and winding down into Animation Courtyard, it is a positive extravaganza of kids' favourites, from *Mary Poppins* to *Toy Story* and *Pinocchio*. The series of elaborate floats – starting with Tinker Bell, then Minnie and ending with Mickey Mouse – also includes *The Lion King, Peter Pan* and *101 Dalmatians*, and a host of characters on foot, while a handful of guests are also chosen to ride aboard with Mickey. The whole thing takes about 25 minutes to pass as it stops at regular intervals for the cast to interact with onlookers (especially children) along the route, backed by another wonderfully infectious theme song. It is an easy parade to catch and watch in relative comfort as it doesn't usually draw the huge crowds of the *Disneyland Park*. Wait in the Hollywood Boulevard area and you should get a great view. AAAA.

*Disney's Cinema Parade*

© Disney

Summer 2008 may also see a new parade here, as **Disney's Stars and Motor Cars Parade** is being wrapped up at the *Disney's Hollywood Studios* park in Orlando and there are strong rumours it will be moved here. This is themed on a 1930s Hollywood film premiere, with a series of genuine vintage cars and clever replicas being used to mount a cavalcade of Disney showbiz favourites. It provides the likes of *Aladdin, Mary Poppins, Mulan,* the *Muppets* and *Monsters Inc.* with a chance to show off in larger-than-life fashion. Watch out for the *Star Wars*™ 'Land Speeder' with a radio-controlled R-2D2, while the lead car also features any special guests at the Studios that day – or a visiting family instead.

**Streetmosphere:** The park's additional fun is provided by various alternating performing acts, like Ciné Folies in Studio 1, who pop up here and there to give impromptu shows that have a central theme but include some improvisation, too. Special acts perform at Halloween and Christmas (including an *a capella* carol group), which vary from day to day, so you never know who's going to appear. Look out in particular for **Push, The Talking Trashcan**, a remarkable interactive 'performing rubbish bin' that moves, rattles and even talks to visitors!

*Art of Animation*

© Disney

© Disney

*Chicken Little meet 'n' greet in Toon Studio*

For those keen to learn more about the park, there is a 1-hour **Guided Tour** (€10 for adults; children 11 and under free), which gives an in-depth view of the park's history and architecture. Book at Studio Services when you first arrive (subject to availability).

As with the *Disneyland Park*, the *Walt Disney Studios Park* looks even better in early evening, when all the clever (and hidden) lighting effects come into play. There is definitely room for improvement, but the high quality of the attractions here (Twilight Zone™ Tower of Terror, Cinémagique and Moteurs…Action! are true works of art) still provides a rich and rewarding experience. You will also leave with an improved knowledge of the movie business and a heightened respect for those who work in it. The essence of a theme park is that it envelops you with its sense of design and purpose and we feel the *Walt Disney Studios Park* does this, ensuring you believe you have truly had a movie-world adventure.

Right, that should be your fill of the theme parks for now. But the fun doesn't stop here. Oh no! There is still plenty to do and see when we visit the *Disney Village*, Val d'Europe and more. It's time to go beyond the theme parks…

# 8 Beyond the Theme Parks

## or Let's shop till we drop and other fun pursuits

**H**aving led you, quite literally, up the theme park path, it is now time we took you beyond those confines and explored some more of what makes this resort – and this whole area of the Ile de France region – so enticing.

To backtrack slightly and put things in context, the Ile de France is the central region of France, the 'island' around which lie the other great regions of Normandy, Picardie, Champagne-Ardennes and Burgundy. The Ile itself is made up of eight *départements*, namely **Yvelines**, **Essonne**, **Seine-et-Marne** and **Val d'Oise** (that form a large outer ring) and then **Hauts-de-Seine** (immediately to the west of the city), **Seine-St-Denis** (to the north-east), **Val-de-Marne** (to the south-east) and Paris itself. The *département* of Val-de-Marne should not be confused with Marne-la-Vallée, where *Disneyland Resort Paris* is situated, in the *département* of Seine-et-Marne.

Prior to 1989, when construction began, there was little here apart from sugar beet fields, but the development since has been swift and dramatic. There is, in fact, no real town or village of Marne-la-Vallée, it is a made-up name given to the RER/TGV station here, which acts as the terminus for the RER's Line A. The nearest sizeable village is Chessy,

hence the RER station is properly known as Marne-la-Vallée Chessy. However, to all intents and purposes, Marne-la-Vallée IS the site of *Disneyland Resort Paris*, hence this is how the majority refer to it.

Marne-la-Vallée is also (highly confusingly) a sub-district of the Seine-et-Marne *département* closer to Paris (between the towns of Noisy-le-Grand and Lognes). When driving, therefore, you should always aim for 'Les Parcs Disneyland'.

*Circus performers at Disney Village*

© Disney

# More to see and do

When it comes to the associated attractions 'beyond the theme parks', there are five distinct topics to cover. First and most obvious is all the fun, fine shopping and dining of **Disney Village**. Second, Disney has also developed its own sporting connections – at **Disneyland Golf**, plus the novel challenge of **Davy Crockett's Adventure** nearby. Next, the neighbouring development of **Val d'Europe** offers another scintillating array of great shops and restaurants, including the Auchan hypermarket and the outlet shopping village of La Vallée. Finally, the highly family-friendly **Sea Life** aquarium centre is situated inside the Val d'Europe shopping centre and is another excellent reason to go beyond the theme parks. Sadly, Disney's in-resort collaboration with the **Manchester United Soccer School** was only a short-lived one; starting in spring 2004, it lasted until November 2005 before it was closed down, with no sign of it being revived.

The golfing opportunity is obviously primarily for devotees of the sport but the other four should all be on your must-see list if you are here for 4 days or more (or if you are on a repeat visit). The new **Panoramagique** balloon flights over *Disney Village* are quite breathtaking and especially worthy of note here.

*Entrance to Disney Village*

As this is primarily a new-town area (the great Disney trail-blazing has given rise to a flurry of modern suburban development all around), there are not many other out-and-out tourist attractions here, but it does make a great base from which to explore Paris and some of the more genuinely historic points of interest in the region (notably the towns of Provins and Meaux, see Chapter 9).

## Disney Village

Starting at the top, it is almost impossible to miss this hugely colourful and imaginative entertainment centre situated between Disney's hotels and the theme parks. This impressive complex was designed by American architect Frank Gehry, who was also responsible for the Guggenheim museum in Bilbao, Spain, and it

*Panoramagique*

# Disney Village

## DISNEY VILLAGE

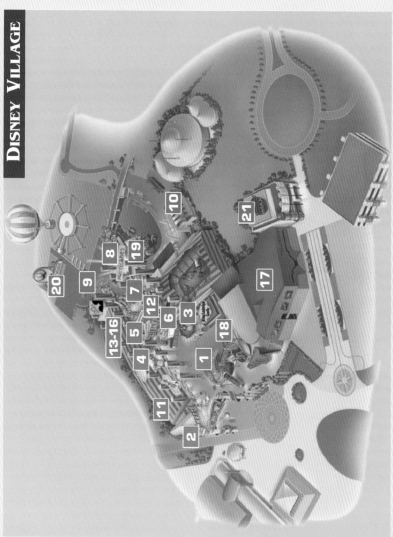

1. Planet Hollywood
2. Annette's Diner
3. King Ludwig's Castle
4. Sports Bar
5. New York Style Sandwiches
6. Billy Bob's Country & Western Saloon
7. The Steakhouse
8. Rainforest Café
9. Café Mickey
10. McDonald's
11. The Disney Store
12. Buffalo Trading Co
13. The Disney Gallery
14. Disney Fashion
15. Hollywood Pictures
16. World of Toys
17. Gaumont Cinema
18. Buffalo Bill's Wild West Show
19. Hurricanes
20. Marina Del Ray/ Panoramagique
21. IMAX Cinema/NEX Fantasy Leisure Zone

originally featured a host of complex, almost abstract ideas designed to link the Village to the railway station. However, some of these were removed in 2005/06 (notably a series of large towers), giving the Village a more open look.

If you come straight in by car or train, you just might not notice *Disney Village* on your left as you scamper headlong for the *Disneyland Park*, but otherwise it is fairly obvious. From one end (nearest the theme parks), it is dominated by a massive gateway topped by a huge red banner with 'Disney Village' emblazoned across it. From the hotels end, you enter via the Lake Disney entrance, with a spread of restaurants – Café Mickey, Rainforest Café and McDonald's – before you.

In a way, it is easy to see the Village as just one big merchandising opportunity. There are a dozen different ways to spend money here – from the shops to video games – and even some of the restaurants have their own gift store. But, ultimately, this has the hallmark of the Imagineers once again (even if the Rainforest Café, Planet Hollywood and McDonald's all have their own internationally recognisable stamp). It has a wonderful outdoor café style, especially in the evening, and the brilliant lighting is well worth stopping to see. Famously, Cast Members tell of the family who were into their second day in the resort

*Inside the Sports Bar*

*Christmas windows in Disney Village*

when they stopped a shop manager to ask where all the rides were – they hadn't yet made it out of *Disney Village*!

The main concourse provides periodical live entertainment (weather permitting) and there are other stalls, vendors and games from time to time, which all help to create a carnival atmosphere (as well as set-piece seasonal events, such as St Patrick's Day in March and the Christmas festivities). When you add in the entertainment possibilities of Buffalo Bill's dinner show, the cinema complex, the live music of Billy Bob's and the late-night disco, Hurricanes, you have a serious array of choice as to how to spend you time. The one thing, perhaps surprisingly, they don't have here is a good coffee bar.

## What's there

Roughly speaking, you can divide the offerings of *Disney Village* into the **Restaurants and bars**, the **Shops** and the **Entertainment**. But, to get maximum enjoyment, you need to be aware of a couple of things. Firstly, the restaurants normally start to fill up from 6–7pm. In high summer, when the theme parks are open until late, the peak period for the restaurants and shops is more likely to be 9pm. Unless you've made a booking (and only four of the restaurants actually accept reservations), you are likely to find queues of up to half an hour for places such as The Steakhouse, Planet Hollywood and even Annette's Diner.

## The rumour mill

The basic form of *Disney Village* has changed little since the early days of the resort, with King Ludwig's (2003) the only substantial addition in recent years, apart from the cosmetic changes of 2005/06. However, if the rumour mill is to be believed, there is a LOT of new development in store.

The main thrust of the suggestions is that, with the closing of the old open-air car park and the provision of a multi-storey version, a new area of the Village will be developed at the lower end, creating a whole new 'street' behind the existing one. Certainly, there is plenty of room for expansion, from the new IMAX cinema (behind the main Gaumont multiplex) all the way back to the old car park area (behind McDonald's on the lake side of the Village).

The most likely of the proposed scenarios is for this new area to consist of the **ESPN Sports Club** (like that in The Boardwalk Resort in *Walt Disney World* in Florida), the **NEX Fantasy Leisure Zone** (a new gaming, billiard table and 10-pin bowling complex underneath the IMAX cinema), a themed **Chinese restaurant**, a giant **World of Disney** store and a brand new nightclub (that may mean a change of character for the existing Hurricanes). The arrival of the ESPN Club would mean a change for the current Sports Bar, with an **Italian restaurant** being a possible replacement there.

These plans first surfaced in 2006 but had not been followed up on by late 2007. However, they remain on the drawing board and a possible timescale for all this dramatic development would be from 2009–2012, with a new **RER station** entrance also included in the design.

**BRITTIP**

The restaurants at the theme parks end of *Disney Village* fill up the quickest, with Planet Hollywood being the most popular venue.

The other factor is the weather. On a fine evening, it will be easier to get a table; while if it is wet, everywhere fills up extremely quickly, so you need to anticipate the rain to avoid being left out in it! It is also worth pointing out that the Village is relatively quiet during the day, so it is the ideal spot for a more relaxed lunch away from the parks and some leisurely afternoon shopping. You have free pick of all the restaurants (apart from Billy Bob's, where the buffet is available evenings only) and it is particularly convenient if you are in the *Walt Disney Studios Park*, where there is no table-service dining. If you just need a quick snack, there are plenty of fast-food carts dotted throughout the Village.

*Imax Gaumont*

© Disney

# Restaurants and bars

**Planet Hollywood:** Taking *Disney Village* from the theme parks end, as soon as you come through the gateway you face the immediately recognisable two-storey edifice of this popular international chain. Planet Hollywood is a huge draw from early evening until late, and reservations can be made in early evening only, which takes care of most of the queues. But, if there is a line, there is a great bar area and some snazzy bar staff to make the wait more fun. An unhurried lunch is also available from 11.30am–3pm. If the queue can be seen outside, you'll be looking at a good 30-minute wait for a table.

### BRITTIP

When the *Disneyland Park* is open until 11pm, head to Planet Hollywood for dinner at about 6pm and you should have your pick of their best tables.

The huge variety of movie models, costumes, portraits and other memorabilia in this 500-seat restaurant are subdivided into differently themed areas, each with its own video screen that shows well-known film clips, music videos and (worth looking out for) special trailers for forthcoming movies. The memorabilia, which will certainly get film buffs wandering around to study it, varies from James Cagney to Wesley Snipes, Arnold Schwarzenegger and Sylvester Stallone. The upstairs section includes a sci-fi dining area and an adventure area, as well as the lively bar, while downstairs there is a *Raiders of the Lost Ark* section and the Zebra Room (for obvious, stripy reasons). In the inevitable gift store, also downstairs, you will probably find the Planet Hollywood merchandise a bit cheaper here than in London.

Curiously, different nationalities seem to dine at different times of the day. The Brits tend to eat earlier, hence there will be a UK predominance in the restaurants from 5–7pm, while the Spanish are almost invariably the last ones out! The menu has also been adapted for the more European mix of customer, so several dishes have been tweaked (spinach dip replaces the more usual nachos, and their lasagne is a house speciality). Several regional specialities have been added (such as the typically French Croque Monsieur, a ham and cheese toastie).

*Planet Hollywood*

© Disney

*Night-time at Planet Hollywood*

**BRITTIP**

Can't decide what to pick at Planet Hollywood? Look for the VIP Platter for starters, which compiles four of their best offerings, and the Dessert Sampler, which features a taste of several of their best menu items.

The full range offers salads (€14.50–14.90), sandwiches and burgers (€14–14.90), steak, chicken, ribs, salmon, boeuf bourguignon and fajitas (€18.50–22), pasta dishes (€14.50–15.50); while desserts include chocolate brownie, banana frosted cheesecake, strawberry shortcake, ice cream and an excellent white chocolate bread pudding (€6.50–€10.50). Of all the Planet Hollywood restaurants we have visited, the food here is consistently the best, which we ascribe to that extra bit of French flair. They also freshen the menu from time to time (new dishes in 2007 included a bruschetta starter, a chicken and ranch wedge salad and an excellent coconut shrimp main course) and have some tempting cocktails, including an exclusive Summer Specials menu. TVs in the bar show all the major sports events and the latest football results are usually available.

**BRITTIP**

If you have visited the cinema, save money at Planet Hollywood by showing your cinema ticket stub for a €5 discount.

If you haven't been to a Planet Hollywood before, you will probably be wowed by their lively entertainment mix (even their soundtrack is carefully balanced so you can talk at the table without having to shout), so you should make a beeline for this one. If you are already familiar with their style, head here anyway and try their LA Lasagne (a layered pasta that is rolled, cut in half, deep fried and then smothered in their tomato sauce), which will make your taste buds quiver with delight and your waistline shudder!

We will admit to being slightly biased in our liking for the brash cinema-style motif of Planet Hollywood, but we reckon it is one of the most fun dining experiences in the whole resort – and it stays open until the last person leaves!

**Annette's Diner:** Opposite PH stands this classic 1950s' rock 'n' roll-style restaurant. Straight out of *Grease* and *Happy Days*, the bright, vivid decor provides a suitably fun, family atmosphere, with waiters and waitresses who dance on the bar top at various moments. The large icons are all typical Americana from this period, and the menu is equally in keeping with the theme, with a line-up of burgers, hot dogs, chilli, fajitas, salads and sandwiches. The restaurant has two (rather noisy!) levels, the mezzanine floor offering the best views of the restaurant, which also features a classic Cadillac and Corvette photo opportunity at the entrance.

*Annette's Diner*

© Disney

Open from 10am for their American-style breakfast (until 2pm, at €12.90), there is also a featured set Kids' Meal for lunch/dinner (for under 12s) at €12.25, while the burgers range from €12.50–18.95 (for the humongous 'Big One' – finish it all and qualify for a free milkshake!). The desserts are possibly their best feature, with a range of ice creams, sundaes and shakes to appeal strongly to those with a sweet tooth. When the queues get long (as they often do), there is a handy take-away window at the side of the restaurant. Annette's is open 10am–midnight Sun–Thur and 10am–1am Fri and Sat.

## BRITTIP

To book any of the restaurants in *Disney Village*, up to 2 months in advance, call (from the UK) 00 33 1 60 30 40 50 or make a reservation through the concierge at your hotel.

**King Ludwig's Castle:** Continuing along the main *Disney Village* thoroughfare brings you next to this hugely elaborate establishment, which opened in June 2003. Inspired by Neuschwanstein Castle in Bavaria (built by 'mad' King Ludwig II), King Ludwig's has been designed primarily for German visitors but will, we think, appeal to anyone who enjoys good beer, Bavarian food and castles in general. With 297 seats on two floors, the interior of the restaurant is redolent with castle theming, including wooden panelling, flags and ornate carvings.

*Inside King Ludwig's Castle*

© Disney

© Disney

*King Ludwig's Castle*

The menu (updated in summer 2007) is designed to appeal to international tastes, with starters (€6.90–8.50) such as *weisswurst* (sausages with mustard), traditional leek and potato soup and morteau sausage and potato salad; and main courses (€16.90–26.50) such as Oktoberfest chicken, *wiener schnitzel*, beer-braised veal with rosti potato and mushrooms and Royal Sauerkraut (smoked pork loin, bacon, sausage and potato on a dome of sauerkraut); while desserts (€7.50–13.50) include various strudels and a delicious chocolate cake. There are also more straightforward salads and pastas, plus burgers and a tandoori chicken dish, as well as a simple kids' menu (€11.50), but the feature dishes are all well worth trying.

This can all be washed down with a good choice of beer and schnapps, plus a generous Happy Hour from 7–10pm with various beer specials. There is also a set menu at €24.90 (a starter and main course, or main course and dessert, including a 1-litre beer). A magnificent design inside and out, the Castle has a fantasy-orientated and whimsical touch rather than the usual more formal approach. The set lunch menu (main course, dessert and drink) is €15–23 (11.30am–4.30pm), and their gift shop sells branded merchandise – glass, porcelain and the inevitable swords – under the mark of Prince Luipold of Bavaria (a direct descendant of King Ludwig II and the owner of the

© Disney

*Sports Bar*

Kaltenberg brewery). Open from 11.30am–11pm (Sun–Fri) and 11.30am–midnight (Fri and Sat).

**Sports Bar:** Standing diagonally opposite the Castle, this regular haunt for many Brits is the nearest the Village gets to a proper pub. With an outdoor terrace, indoor seating and a cinema-style video screen at one end (plus a dozen TV screens sprinkled through the bar), this is the place to come for a British-style beer, a quick snack and, more importantly, the footy on telly at weekends and midweek! They show a great variety of European action and keep all the latest scores and tables on big blackboards behind the bar.

**BRITTIP**

For smokers, the Sports Bar has a tobacco kiosk at the front that is open 4–11.30pm daily.

Popular with Disney Cast Members, the Sports Bar can be a lively place most evenings, but especially at weekends when the locals come out to play. The draught beers are Kronenbourg 1664, Fosters, Beamish (stout) and Carlsberg, while there is a good choice of bottled beers, including Heineken, Guinness, Budweiser, and Strongbow. Open 2pm–1am Mon–Fri, midday–2am Sat and midday–1am Sun (with food until 11pm), it serves hot dogs, pizza, nachos and chicken nuggets; chips and crisps are also available (with a set meal of a hot dog and fries, or chicken nuggets, plus a brownie and a soft drink for €11, or a beer instead of a soft drink for €12). It is usually packed for the big European football games and can be a bit rowdy, so it is not an ideal atmosphere for children, although they are always welcome.

**New York Style Sandwiches:** Immediately next door to the Sports Bar (and sharing the same outdoor terrace), this rather nondescript deli-style, diner/take-away offers baguettes, hot and cold sandwiches, soups, salads and paninis, plus ice cream, hot dogs, crisps and drinks. The set children's menu (choice of cheese sandwich, hot dog or chicken

*Wild West antics in Disney Village*

© Disney

nuggets and chips, plus a yoghurt and a drink) costs €7, while main menu items run from €4–9. The deli is open from 9am–midnight (Mon–Thur), 9am–1am (Fri and Sat) or 8am–midnight (Sun).

**Billy Bob's Country & Western Saloon:** Just down from King Ludwig's Castle, you come to this wonderful mock cowboy saloon, with a large bar and a stage for live music every evening. There are periodic guest performers, while excellent house band Big Joe and the Space Cowboys are usually on stage Sun–Thur at 9.30 and 11pm. The three-storey Grand Opry-style building (copied from an original in Austin, Texas) is superbly designed inside (anyone who has been in the old Cheyenne Saloon in Orlando will know the idea), with tiered balconies all providing a good view of the stage. You can learn to line-dance here (8pm on Thursdays), take in some rock 'n' roll (every Wednesday), try their salsa classes (one Friday every month) or just sit back with a drink and enjoy the Space Cowboys, who are genuine American exponents of the Country & Western genre (even if it's not your usual cup of tea, their live style is worth checking out).

*Billy Bob's*

### BRITTIP

If the other restaurants are heaving in the evening, try Billy Bob's Buffet upstairs in La Grange Restaurant. Not many people actually notice it and it is usually possible to get a table without much of a wait.

Bar snacks include chicken wings, spare ribs and nachos, or try out the excellent **Billy Bob's Buffet**, which is at the top of the bar at the back (go up the stairs to your left and keep going!). The **La Grange Restaurant** buffet is available from 6–10.30pm, and it offers a great value meal (€27/adult and €12/child) featuring salads, roast pork and beef, fajitas,

*La Grange*

© Disney

*The Steakhouse*

chilli con carne, rice, pasta and vegetables, chicken wings, spare ribs, cheese tray and a huge choice of desserts. Billy Bob's can be booked in advance through your hotel concierge. It is open from 4pm–1am (Sun–Thur) 4pm–2am (Fri and Sat), with snacks (€6.50–13) served from 6–10.30pm. Early evening usually sees a kids' dance session, when the saloon is given over to a more youthful, energetic vibe, ideal for the 8–14 brigade. To book before you go, call 00 33 1 60 30 40 50 from the UK.

**The Steakhouse:** Right next door, this offers the real fine-dining opportunity in *Disney Village*. In fact, only the California Grill in the *Disneyland Hotel* and Hunter's Grill in *Disney's Sequoia Lodge* can rival this for quality. It is a spectacular venue, with a Chicago-style warehouse interior in three sections – the main warehouse, the smart bar and the conservatory-like annexe. It is all decorated in 1930s' Americana, with lots of dark woods, rich upholstery, wood panelling and elaborate candelabra lighting effects. The bar area is straight out of the TV programme *Cheers*, but it is also extremely elegant for such a large restaurant and provides a great backdrop for a special occasion meal (although it is also popular with families early in the evening and you will find a lot of children here).

The mouth-watering menu is pretty broad-based, too, although the obvious speciality is steak (fillet, entrecôte, rump steak, sirloin, Brazilian strip, rib-eye and steak tartare) along with spare ribs, a couple of excellent fish dishes (try the grilled bass fillet), a chicken curry and a vegetarian lasagne. The à la carte prices are not too outrageous (the steaks are €16.50–40, while the starters are €7.90–10.50) and there is a set menu for €32 that offers a choice of four starters, main courses and desserts.

For children, the Scrooge McDuck Menu (€11.90) is also a cut above the usual kiddie fare (although they can still get the ubiquitous chicken nuggets). Reservations are highly recommended at most times and the restaurant is open daily midday–midnight. This is also the place to come for a superb **Sunday Brunch** with Disney characters, midday–3pm. It's a tad pricey at €32/adult and €12/child, but it does make a memorable meal and is rarely crowded, so the kids have plenty of time with the characters. Call 00 33 1 60 30 40 50 (from the UK) to book.

**Rainforest Café:** This unmistakable, international chain restaurant, providing a larger-than-life jungle adventure and whose decor owes a lot to the artistry of the Imagineers, is next up on the grand Village restaurant tour. Here you will find tropical aquaria, waterfalls, streams

*The back of the Rainforest Café*

© Disney

and a host of (animatronic) animals to accompany your meal, all in a realistic rainforest setting punctuated by thunderstorms and rainfall. You don't just go to eat here you go 'on expedition' and it is as much the decor and atmosphere as the food that creates the experience.

In truth, the food is fairly regular diner fare given a bit of a twist and a few fancy names (Rasta Pasta is penne pasta with chicken, broccoli, peppers and spinach tossed in a cream sauce, while Mojo Bones is BBQ ribs with coleslaw and chips), but the portions are huge and usually work out good value for money. Salads, pasta, burgers and grills (try the Steak and Shrimp skewer or Siva's Curry – chicken and shrimp with pineapple in a mild, creamy curry sauce) range from €15.90–25.90, while the starters are €6.00–18.50. Cocktails and desserts are both specialities of the house, and the Giant Brownie Volcano alone is worth coming in for (along with the delicious Gorilla In The Mist Cheesecake and Bambas Pancake).

Children in particular love the rainforest style and pick up on the many environmental messages, while the kids' menu (€14.90) is one of the best. The Café doesn't accept reservations, so you just have to turn

*Inside the Rainforest Café*

up and wait, but there is a huge gift shop to inspect before you eat and plenty of audio-animatronics to keep the kids happy (the big 'alligator' outside seems to provide an almost endless source of amusement). The Rainforest Café is open 11.30am–midnight every day, with the gift shop open from 9.30am.

**Café Mickey:** This is another really fun and lively venue that stages character meals throughout the day. Once again, the decor is both bright without being garish and amusing without being obvious. The upstairs dining area has a magnificent view over Lake Disney from the terrace. TV screens showing classic Disney cartoons help to keep children happy if the food doesn't (and the food is way above average), but it is more likely to be the excellent character visits that make their day. A big breakfast buffet runs 7.30–10.30am (with separate seatings at 8 and 9.30am), while lunch is available noon–5pm and dinner 5–11pm (Sun–Fri) or 5pm–midnight (Sat). The dinner menu is basically just an extended version of the lunch fare.

*Café Mickey*

### BRITTIP

Tigger, Pluto and Co appear in front of Café Mickey (weather permitting) in early evening to strut their funky cartoon stuff and amuse the younger crowd. This is also one of the best character dining experiences in the whole resort.

*McDonald's*

You can perhaps see the European influence at work here most, with a wide-ranging choice and a highly thoughtful and appetising selection (from pizza and pasta standards to seafood, vegetarian dishes and salads), way above usual diner fare. Try the Fantasia Mushrooms starter (garlic mushrooms beautifully roasted with pesto and parmesan), then progress to Pinocchio Pasta (creamy wok-cooked penne pasta with chicken and broccoli) or King Triton's Favourite (pan-sautéed fish medley), or give their wood-fired oven pizzas a try. Then follow up with a wonderfully tempting array of desserts (of which Dopey & Grumpy's Chocolate Delight is quite dreamy!). The three-course set meal is €34 for adults. Children (under 12) get their own menu (€15) and a special Mickey surprise at the end. The characters circulate fairly constantly to keep everyone happy and the smart decor ensures adult sensibilities are not forgotten either. Booking is highly advisable (with the possible exception of lunchtime). In France, you can call 01 60 30 40 50.

**BRITTIP**

If *Disney Village* is too crowded for your tastes or you can't get a table for dinner, try going to *Disney's Hotel New York* (see page 80) for their Parkside Diner, where you can usually get a table at any time, or the upmarket Hunter's Grill at *Disney's Sequoia Lodge* (see pages 83–85). Both have great bars, too.

**McDonald's:** Completing the impressive spread of restaurants throughout the Village is the inevitable McDonald's, albeit quite a smart, almost high-tech version of the ubiquitous American burger chain. Open from 8am–midnight (8am–1am on Fri and Sat), it is a major draw in the evenings as it is obviously one of the cheaper options, but it also has a high capacity with an outdoor terrace, providing a pleasant place to sit in the right weather. The original architecture is based on Italian theatre and the split-level arrangement also offers a games area for the kids.

**Hand-carts:** Finally, if you're after a late-night snack, there are various hand-carts throughout the Village where you can grab a hot dog, popcorn, crêpes or toffee apples to send you on your way, plus a new **Ice Cream Kiosk** beyond McDonald's overlooking the lake.

## Shopping

Okay, if that sums up your eating opportunities in the Village, the retail therapy offerings aren't quite so wide ranging, as you will find much of the merchandise recurring in different shops. However, there is still an imaginative array of interior styling and it is worth wandering through the likes of The Disney Store and the Rainforest Café shop just to have a look at the splendid decor.

*Rainforest Café*

**The Disney Store:** This is first on your left when you enter *Disney Village* from the theme parks end. It's the biggest in the resort and underwent a major external makeover in 2007 to make it look more, well, Disney. (Anyone who has seen the massive *World of Disney* stores in either Orlando or *Disneyland California* will know what we mean – these huge character emporiums are veritable Aladdin's caves of merchandise, with a seemingly infinite variety of souvenir goods and brilliant ways of displaying them.) It sells the widest selection of character and souvenir wares of any of the stores, from books and cuddly toys, to DVDs, watches and jewellery, plus an extensive clothing selection and, nearer the festive season, an array of Christmas decorations, too. Kids will love browsing here (if they can be prevented from trying to buy everything in sight!), while above them are a host of wonderful things to watch – large-scale moving models, mobiles and Mickey Mouse flying a spaceship.

**Planet Hollywood:** This gift store is almost opposite, for restaurant souvenirs and other movie memorabilia. You can also check out the movie and TV star hand prints on the wall outside.

**King Ludwig's Castle:** Next door, this fun restaurant also has a specialist shop, with various Bavarian souvenirs as well as a selection of toys and the all-important swords and shields for kids to re-stage the Battle of Waterloo!

**Buffalo Trading Co:** Continuing down the right of the main thoroughfare brings you to the Buffalo Trading Co, which offers a wide variety of Disney-branded merchandise, all with a Wild West theme (plus some smart Western gear, like overcoats, leather jackets and waistcoats). You may be hard pressed to extricate your offspring without buying them some kind of cowboy paraphernalia to take home. (This becomes the Halloween Store during September and October, with some suitably spooky special effects and lighting.)

**Disney Gallery:** This is opposite the Buffalo Trading Co, offering a more upmarket selection of gift items for cinema and art fans. Disney collectors will want to make a beeline here to check out the range of limited series lithographs and original animated film cels. There are some great books (here's where you might still get a copy of Didier Ghez's superb book *Disneyland – From Sketch to Reality*) and photographs, and it also has the latest collections of china figurines and snow globes, plus novelties like a Mickey telephone (every home should have one!).

*The smart exterior of The Disney Store*

© Disney

*World of Toys*

**Disney Fashion, Hollywood Pictures and World of Toys:** Immediately next door, you enter these three interconnected shops (handy in the rain) and, while you will probably have seen some of the merchandise already, there is more novel stuff, too. Disney Fashion (formerly the fun Team Mickey) is a rather ordinary clothing store (everything from hats to shoes), Hollywood Pictures offers an array of film-themed clothing, photo albums and gifts (and the inevitable cuddly toys), and World of Toys is almost a reprise of The Disney Store, with yet more kids' playthings (beware the pirate paraphernalia and swords!), costumes and a big sweet counter. You will also find a Pin-Trading Super Station here.

**Rainforest Café:** Finally, inside the main entrance to this café lurks an animal-themed gift shop just waiting to ensnare the unwary with another line-up of soft toys, games, clothing and environmentally aware souvenirs. Their audio-animatronics make it fun for children and should keep the kids amused while the grown-ups browse the merchandise.

**Other shops:** Essential services are provided by a **currency exchange** next to The Disney Store, two regular **cash dispensers**, an **Information & Ticket** kiosk in front of Hurricanes nightclub and **Baby Change** facilities (between The Disney Store and Sports Bar), while there is also a big **tourist information office** just outside the

*Disney Village* gates in front of the train station. There used to be a **post office** in the Village but that is now just inside the RER station, facing the tourist office.

## Village entertainment

If all that isn't enough to keep you occupied, then Disney has a third array of opportunities to entertain and amuse. Foremost of these is **Buffalo Bill's show**, plus **Hurricanes** nightclub, but there is also live music and other street performer type entertainment throughout the Village (weather permitting, once again). When you consider the big seasonal events, like Christmas, St Patrick's Day and Halloween, which are all either based or have a significant presence here, this can be an exceptionally lively scene at times.

One of the most eye-catching features of the theme parks end of the Village, however, is the fully modern 15-screen **Gaumont Cinema** complex, which is largely a French-language operation, and the neighbouring **IMAX Cinema**. However, Monday night is Original Language night (usually at 7.45 and 10.30pm) and there is always one major current-release film shown in English without the drawback of French subtitles or dubbing. The IMAX (which opened in 2005) can offer both the signature giant-screen films and 3-D movies, as well as DMR productions – digitally re-mastered versions of normal-

*Rainforest Café*

© Disney

screen films (like the Spiderman series), which can be shown in clear, sharp pictures on the IMAX screen. The plush interior was designed by French design guru Christian Lacroix and features some of the most comfortable cinema seats anywhere, plus the kind of sound system to make audio fans salivate. Underneath the IMAX is the new (in 2006) **NEX Fun Bowling & Games**, a mix of games arcade (including a unique car and motorbike racing area), billiards/pool hall and scaled down 10-pin bowling alley, complete with the latest video games, ride simulators and high-tech bowling lanes.

## Buffalo Bill's Wild West Show

Next door to the Gaumont – and arguably the most prominent feature of the village – is **Buffalo Bill's Wild West Show**, a near 2-hour sit-down dinner spectacular that relives the myths and legends of America's cowboy country. The huge indoor arena, some eye-catching stunts and the full Western style ensure this is a hit with all the family (but especially children in the 4–12 age range).

© Disney

*The entrance to Buffalo Bill's*

### BRITTIP

Buffalo Bill's is not advisable for anyone who suffers from asthma or other respiratory complaints as the animals kick up a fair bit of dust in the indoor arena.

The food is unremarkable, but there is always plenty of it – chilli con carne, chicken, ribs, sausage, vegetables and potatoes, plus apple cobbler, ice cream and either tea or coffee – and there is a separate children's platter (roast leg of chicken, sausage, potatoes and chocolate mousse, plus a soft drink or mineral water), which

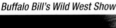

*Buffalo Bill's Wild West Show*

© Disney

*Buffalo Trading Company*

always seems to go down well. There is also a constant supply of either beer or Coca-Cola (with the meal only – you pay for your drinks in the pre-show Colonel Cody's Saloon) as part of the entrance price. Everyone gets a straw cowboy hat to wear, and you sit in one of four colour-coded sections corresponding to the different cowboys in the show, who go through a series of games and competitions to decide the 'numero uno' for the evening.

### BRITTIP

In summer, watch out for Wild Bill's Show Parade in the *Disney Village* at 6pm as a prelude to the first show of the day (weather permitting).

You need to be in best audience participation and hat-waving mood as you cheer and clap for your cowboy and hiss and boo the others, and it all adds up to good fun, raucous stuff. Annie Oakley, the 'Queen of the Winchester', puts in an appearance and literally shoots the lights out (there are some magnificent horse-riding tricks and skills, too), and much of the narration is carried out in English as the 60 performers are nearly all American. A Native American element also features and, at one point, the curtain at one end of the auditorium rises to reveal a majestic rocky outcrop, which complements the superb lighting and sound effects. There are wagon trains and cattle drives, cavalry charges and

rodeo games, along with a big finale with the inevitable stagecoach – and it is all performed with great gusto and zest by the large cast.

### BRITTIP

A vegetarian or pork-free menu is available upon request at Buffalo Bill's. You can also order wine or champagne (at additional cost).

The degree of authenticity is remarkable, with the Native Americans from a variety of tribes (including Blackfeet, Sioux and Cherokees), the buffalo from Canada and longhorn cattle from Texas, while the horses are all original Pintos and Appaloosas (for the Native Americans) or quarterhorses (for the cowboys). It is staged twice a night – at 6.30 and 9.30pm. Guests can arrive up to 45 minutes before and enjoy the saloon bar atmosphere and live music and, at €59/adult and €39/child (3–11), it provides an excellent mix of entertainment, spectacle and fun.

You can book your tickets in advance by calling (from the UK) 00 33 1 60 45 71 00, but it is usually possible to book when you arrive, either at your hotel or at the ticket office in *Disney Village*.

*Annie Oakley at Buffalo Bill's*

# Hurricanes

If the Wild West is not your scene, then Caribbean-themed dance club **Hurricanes** may be (especially if you can arrange child-minding or babysitting for the evening through your hotel concierge). Here, upstairs and to one side of the Rainforest Café, the late-night crowd can really expend some energy as Hurricanes only gets going at 11pm and keeps bopping until 4am (Mon–Sat). The weekdays are usually quieter (especially out of season), but Fridays and Saturdays can be extremely lively when the locals flood in. The dance floor is large, the sound system excellent and, if the bar service is a little slow when busy, that is only a minor quibble.

Hurricanes offers free entry for all Disney hotel guests (with hotel ID) and Annual Passport holders, otherwise it costs €15/person. The evening line-up varies from week to week, but there are regular special events and themed nights, like their Foam Parties (Sundays in summer) and 1980s Night.

Of course, you can also check out the live music (and dance) at **Billy Bob's Country & Western Saloon** (see page 194), with two or three sessions a night (highly recommended if Big Joe and The Space Cowboys are playing) or the soccer on the big TV screens in the **Sports Bar** (page 193).

*Sports Bar*

*Billy Bob's*

# Fun, games – and Panoramagique

*Disney Village* is sprinkled with various types of fun games (all of which require a few extra euros), such as mechanical bull-riding and Ring the Bell (the typical fairground attraction). There are also – strictly for kids – three variations on the remote-control driving games, with boats and trucks. The more energetic might also like to try their hand (and feet) on the bungee trampolines at either end of the Village, plus a new rock-climbing wall, which adds another – extra cost – element to the entertainment line-up.

> **BRITTIP**
>
> The Village's main toilets are located between the Sports Bar and The Disney Store. However, their cleanliness often leaves something to be desired, so a dash across the plaza to The Steakhouse is usually better.

Then, from **La Marina** on Lake Disney, you can hire pedaloes, junior jet-skis (VERY slow moving) and *bateaux electrique* (not much faster!) from 1.30pm every day until early evening (again, weather permitting). They cost from €7–14 for 20 minutes and you need to wear a life jacket at all times but, on a summer evening, it is a great way to while away some Disney time. Or you can stick to dry land and hire **Surrey bikes** (or Rosalies, as they call them here),

*Imax cinema*

which make a very gentle and fun pedal around the whole of Lake Disney. Two-seater bikes cost €8.90 for 20 minutes, four-seaters are €12.90.

At peak times and for seasonal events, the Village comes alive with a series of **street performers** such as jugglers, stilt-walkers and diabolo throwers, which all helps to enhance the carnival nature and intent of this long entertainment thoroughfare. There is also a summer season **Village Circus**, with a clown, juggler and acrobat performing along the main street. It is definitely a lively, and occasionally even raucous, affair (not a big hit with seniors usually), although the atmosphere is decidedly different in the cold and/or wet.

The newest addition here (in 2005) is easily the most dramatic. **Panoramagique** is a magnificent tethered balloon that takes flight over Lake Disney up to six times an hour, soaring to 100m/328ft (dependent on the wind) over the Village, with a truly superb view in all directions. The flights last around 6 minutes and can carry up to 30 passengers at a time. It is one of the largest balloons of its kind in the world, taking off and landing from its own purpose-built platform on the water, and is styled in best Jules Verne Victorian fashion. It can fly in most weathers (although you wouldn't want to go up when visibility isn't good) but winds of more than 35kph/22mph will see the

balloon grounded for a while. It costs €12/adult and €6/child (3–11) and, on a clear day, it is possible to see all the way to Paris and the Eiffel Tower.

However, the real fascination is getting a true perspective on *Disneyland Resort Paris* itself, seeing how all the elements fit together, including the hotels of Val de France, getting a bird's eye view of the parks and looking at all the areas of future development. It is truly amazing just how much you can take in and its smooth take-off, ascent and landing – plus the huge size of the cage-like metal basket – mean you feel totally safe. We would certainly rate it a must-do attraction for the resort. However, it is probably not the ride for you if you have a fear of heights or suffer from vertigo at all.

### BRITTIP

Susan – not the happiest of people with heights – found she could ride Panoramagique quite comfortably as long as she looked out to the sides and not down the middle at the balloon's cable system!

If you are staying at a Disney hotel or even if you are at a hotel nearby, you are very conveniently placed for *Disney Village*, and the new multi-storey Vinci car park, which brings you out by the new IMAX cinema. Once on site, everything is within a short walking distance and it is so easy just to wander around, sample a

*Panoramagique*

variety of different establishments and then wend your way 'home' again in this safe, well-organised and thoroughly entertaining environment.

Of course, for those without a car or a Disney hotel booking, the usefulness of the **RER station** is paramount. Here, you can enjoy the convenience of a public transport system that runs on schedule 99 times out of 100 and keeps working until a little after midnight each day, ensuring you can get back to the great number of hotels linked to the Line A (and within walking distance of the stations along the way). It may not be America (for those who think in such terms), but it is still efficient, user-friendly and good value. Miss out on a night in *Disney Village* at your peril!

*Disney Village at night*

### BRITTIP

The new Vinci car park, which costs €2/hour, is free to Disney hotel guests. Just take your ticket and show your hotel ID to the office on the ground floor when you are ready to leave.

## Disneyland Golf

Golf aficionados will certainly be keen to indulge in their favourite sport at the **Disneyland Golf Course** in the neighbouring village of Magny-le-Hongre, which is barely 10 minutes' drive from the resort itself. Although quite a modern set-up, it has all the characteristics of something a lot

*Disneyland Golf*

more mature and its three nine-hole courses should provide a good test for all standards of golfer, as well as offering what amounts to three different 18-hole rounds. All three courses start and finish right in front of the clubhouse so they can easily be combined.

Open year-round, 7 days a week, the facilities are second to none in the Paris area (there is another good course at nearby Bussy-St-Georges, but the variety and challenge at **Disneyland Golf** are far superior).

A driving range and practice green (complete with a well-known Mouse head silhouette!) are situated to either side of the clubhouse, which has an extremely pleasant bar and restaurant, and an outdoor terrace where you can enjoy the best of the summer weather.

From the striking circular restaurant building, the view over the green of what is, effectively, the 18th hole, the driving range and the practice green is superb and highly conducive to a satisfying lunch. There is also a well-equipped pro shop that hires electric and manual carts, full sets of clubs and golf shoes, as well as offering the usual range of equipment and clothing to buy. A TV lounge, changing rooms and showers complete the clubhouse set-up and there is a large car park.

Green fees start at €30 for a winter weekday 18-hole round and go up to

*Everyone will enjoy Davy Crockett's Adventure*

*Davy Crockett's Adventure*

€60 for a summer round on a weekend or bank holiday. For a nine-hole round, prices are €25–42, with reduced rates for under 18s. Club hire is €5 per club or €25 for a full tailor-made set, while hand-carts are €6 and electric ones €25 for an 18-hole round. A bucket of 30 balls for the driving range costs €4, five buckets is €14 and 11 buckets €30. Tuition is available from one of the two fully qualified instructors from €25 for a half-hour lesson to €75 for an accompanied round. For more details about playing there, visit the website **www.disneylandparis.co.uk** and click on the 'Golf' section.

## Davy Crockett's Adventure

Thrill-seekers with a love for the natural will surely enjoy this unique forest adventure next to *Disney's Davy Crockett Ranch*. The **Davy Crockett Adventure** comprises five trails with more than 80 activities in five levels of difficulty, from green – the easiest, accessible to children at least 1.10m/3ft 7in tall – to black, for real daredevils. The activities are linked by platforms and ropes that blend in with the environment. Each course features suspended stations (Tyrolean traverses, monkey bridges and swings) linked by platforms and cables, and adventurers move from tree to tree using special harnesses, tethers, karabiners and pulleys. The course includes creeper-swinging,

suspended bridges, wobbly tree trunks and monkey bridges, as well as a dizzying 200m/656ft suspended footbridge and their trademark 16m/52ft Tarzan leap.

Davy Crockett's Adventure covers 5 hectares/12 acres of the Grains national forest full of 100-year-old oak trees. The entrance is just to the right of *Disney's Davy Crockett Ranch* (see pages 88–90), just after the reception (off Exit 13 of the A4). Access, parking and reception are all located at the Ranch (and you will have to drive here as no transport is laid on). There is a 30-minute initiation on the equipment and safety rules, but then participants are on their own to tackle the course progressively, under the close watch of the course supervisors. It should provide around 3 hours of physical challenges in the great outdoors and costs €25 for those over 1.40m/4ft 7in tall and €15 for those shorter (or €3 just to watch). It is open from 9am in high season (first departure at 10am, last departure at 4pm) and from 1pm in low season (last departure at 3pm). However, you MUST book in advance, either on 0825 150 280 (in France) or online at **www.aventure-aventure.com**.

© Disney

# Val d'Europe

It is finally time to leave the immediate environs of *Disneyland Resort Paris* behind and venture a little further afield (although not very far!). If you are staying at *Disney's Newport Bay Club* (or you peer over the back walls of the *Walt Disney Studios Park*), you will be able to see, across the fields in front of the hotel, the huge, sprawling structure (still surrounded by cranes and other building construction) that is the **Val d'Europe** shopping, leisure and business complex. Opened in October 2000, it has an RER station and has given rise to a new-town development. Covering some 24.5 hectares/60 acres, the central portion is basically a glorified (but highly attractive) mall, with two additional elements (the Sea Life Centre and a big health and fitness centre called Moving), plus the associated development of **La Vallée Village** (outlet shopping) in an outdoor pedestrianised area at one end.

**BRITTIP**

If you are finding it too expensive to feed your brood at *Disney Village*, head for Val d'Europe where prices are much lower and you can stock up on snacks etc., at the Auchan hypermarket.

*Val d'Europe*

*Val d'Europe centre*

As well as the mall and associated development, the main street through the town (right outside the RER station) also boasts a number of pleasant restaurants, cafés and hotels, notably the pub/brasserie of **L'Agape Café**, the **Asian Wok** and the **Pizza Di Roma**.

**BRITTIP**

Need petrol? The Shell service station in the Val d'Europe car park is rated the cheapest in the Ile de France, so it is the ideal place to fill up for the journey home. However, you CANNOT use the ground-level petrol pumps (they accept only French credit cards), so you must use the services in the underground car park.

For anyone who enjoys retail therapy, this should definitely be high on their list of priorities. The two-level mall has a huge number of high-quality shops (around 130 stores, restaurants and cafés), many of which are internationally recognisable (Sephora, Etam, Quiksilver, Esprit, Levi's, Naf Naf, Gap, Zara, Benetton, Swatch, Swarovski and H&M) or uniquely French and wonderfully chic. Choose from the likes of L'Occitane en Provence (candles, perfumes and cosmetics, made with plants and flowers from southern France), Yves Rocher (make-up and beauty products with the accent on health), Carnet de Vol and Brice (men's fashion and sportswear), Carré

*There's a range of shops at Val d'Europe*

Blanc (household items such as towels and carpets, all with that essential French style), Côté Maison (chic crockery and other household effects), Maisons du Monde (some fabulous interior decor items from around the world), Petit Bateau (the must-have women's T-shirts), Armand Thierry (men's and women's fashions), Le Tanneur (leather handbags, luggage and wallets) and – women take note – Orcanta lingerie.

> **BRITTIP**
>
> July usually means *Sales!* in French shops, so don't forget to check out the mall and La Vallée for some real bargains if you're here in the summer.

There are five shoe shops (check out Taneo and San Marina for the latest fashions), nine jewellery outlets (including Claire's and Swatch), four children's clothing shops (with Sergent Major offering a whole range from 1 month to 14 years) and three sports stores, plus one of our favourites, the Belgian chocolates and ice cream of Jeff de Bruges. There is even a high-quality Paris souvenir shop, Articles de Paris, where you can get that essential mini Eiffel Tower; and another Disney store, Rendez-vous Disney, which is worth checking out for periodic sales.

## Services

The clean, airy, uncluttered confines of the mall, some wonderful architecture (inspired by the great Parisian styles of the late 19th century) and the user-friendly way of doing things all add up to a true 21st-century shopping experience, enhanced by an array of tempting cafés and rest areas (around 250 armchairs are dotted throughout the mall). If you avoid the weekend, you will also find it free of crowds and easy to negotiate – no queues here!

There are five 'welcome points' (including two in the huge car park) to assist with finding what you need, along with baby-care centres for nursing mothers where hostesses can even provide jars of baby food. Four free play areas are available for children, with a variety of slides and climbs (excellent for 3–8s). Other services include valet parking, shoe repairs, photo printing, hairdressers (three) and opticians (three).

Tired of walking? Take the new **Le Petit Train** that goes from one end of the mall to the other and back again at regular intervals (for a small fee). It also stops at each of the main four entrances to the mall.

> **BRITTIP**
>
> Need a chemist? There are two pharmacies in Val d'Europe, located between the RER stations and the shopping mall.

*Val d'Europe*

## Hypermarket

Also here, and on both levels, is the **Auchan hypermarket**. If you have brought the car, this is where you can fill up with essentials such as wine, beer, spirits and a host of other items. The lower level features all the food (a huge choice in serious quantities, with a magnificent wine selection at *very* reasonable prices!) while the upper (ground floor) level stocks a massive range of domestic goods, clothes, books, CDs, toys, Disney merchandise and even furniture. The two levels are linked by a sloping moving walkway, which means you can take your trolley around the whole store with ease.

### BRITTIP

If you regularly take the car to Calais to stock up at the many hypermarkets, Val d'Europe offers a much more civilised and user-friendly way to do that much-needed shopping.

The Auchan chain is well known all over France and offers considerable savings on comparable goods in the UK, so it is worth having a good look round. The whole store covers some 21,000sq m/more than 5 acres! and is open 8.30am–10pm, independent of the rest of the mall. Look up more on **www.auchan.fr**.

*Auchan hypermarket at Val d'Europe*

## Les Terrasses

The Val d'Europe RER station is only 5 minutes from Marne-la-Vallée, and the mall is only a couple of minutes' walk from the station (turn right as you exit and it is straight in front of you). Walk right through the mall and you come to the main café area, **Les Terrasses**, a monumental conservatory-style annexe, with luxurious vegetation filling the iron and glass construction. Here, your choice of dining options is both wide and mouth-watering – from a fine tea-house and crêperie (just called Paul) to a proper Italian pizzeria, a fine seafood restaurant (the boat-themed La Criée), an elegant Chinese (Le Dragon d'Europe, with set menus at €10, €13, €15 and €22, plus a kids' menu at €9), a wonderfully fresh

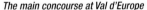
*The main concourse at Val d'Europe*

*Sea Life Centre*

and inviting cafeteria, Casino, the eclectic Hippopotamus (beef, lamb, steaks and kebabs) and the inevitable McDonald's (although even that has a much smarter appearance than usual). Other highlights include Le Paradis du Fruit restaurant for natural drinks, salads and desserts, the new Kyoto Japanese restaurant and the Lebanese cuisine of Noura, with sandwiches, salads and meze. You will also find live entertainment, with shows for the children and music in the evenings for an older audience.

The shopping part of the mall is open 10am–9pm from Mon–Sat (closed Sun) but Les Terrasses is open 9am–midnight every day. Visit **www.valeurope.fr** (then click on English version and 'Vos magasins') for more information.

**BRITTIP**

For an excellent cup of tea and the chance to sample some exquisite crêpes, give yourself a break at **Paul** and just sit and admire the wonderful architecture of Les Terrasses.

# Sea Life Centre

On the lower level of Les Terrasses (down the escalators) is the Moving health and leisure centre and the excellent **Sea Life Centre**. If you have children aged between 2 and 12, this interactive aquarium (belonging to the UK-based Merlin Entertainments Group, which has six similar Sea Life Centres in Britain and another 23 in Europe and beyond) will keep them amused for a good couple of hours, and provides a welcome diversion from all the hectic theme-parking.

Many hotels offer a free daily shuttle to Val d'Europe, so you can usually come straight here or you can just get a bus to the Marne-la-Vallée RER station and take the 5-minute train ride. Seasonal special offers for Sea Life – such as 'free child entry with every full-paying adult' – are worth looking out for.

Opened in April 2001, this 'aquatic park' offers a marine journey through 50 contrasting displays, exhibits and shows that trace an underwater journey from the source of the Seine river out into the Atlantic and on to the Caribbean. From tiny shrimps to menacing sharks and moray eels, from small tanks to the gigantic main aquarium holding 600,000 litres/ 132,000 gallons of water, there is plenty to amuse, entertain and educate young minds.

The journey starts with a theatre experience (in French but with English subtitles), which offers a strong environmental message about

*Simon at the Sea Life Centre*

sea life conservation. The 5-minute film introduces you to the aquarium and all it contains, including the hands-on stuff for kids. Children can pick up a scratch card at the entrance, which invites them to visit the ten question panels throughout the centre and choose the right answer on their card. Get more than eight correct and they win a prize! All the explanations are bilingual and staff can give talks and answer questions in English.

## BRITTIP

The Sea Life Centre is a good alternative when the weather turns cold and wet. It is also worth a visit when the temperature outside goes sky high, as it is air-conditioned and blissfully cool on hot days.

*Sea Life Centre walkway*

Each fish tank and aquarium is presented in a different way. The highlights are the walk-through underwater tunnel (a 360-degree experience with sharks, rays and other fish swimming all around you), the Lost City of Atlantis exhibit, the Stingray Pool (where children can actually touch these fascinating creatures if they are patient and gentle), a film presentation on the Atlantic Ocean (and how deep-sea exploration developed) and the Coral Reef tank.

The interactive theming, with different walkways, passageways and alcoves, invites you to explore every nook and cranny – and learn quite a bit along the way. Talks and demonstrations with the sharks, stingrays and touch-pool are given at regular intervals, while various feeding times add still further to the experience. At the end, there is a handy little seating area, with vending machines, where parents can grab a drink and sit while they unleash their offspring in the play area, which has a ball pool, climbing structure, nets and slides – a very thoughtful addition.

They have a new feature every two years and, in 2007, it was 'Pirates – The Legend of Blackbeard', a challenge to find the treasure of the infamous pirate. Sea Life is open every day (not Christmas Day and 1 January) from 10am–5.30pm and costs €13.90/adult and €9.90/child 3–11 (under 3s free; children under 14 must be with an adult). For more details, call 00 33 1 60 42 33 66 (from the UK) or visit **www.sealifeeurope.com**.

## BRITTIP

You can come and go as you please once you have bought your Sea Life Centre admission. That means you can go shopping and come back later in the day if there is a particular show or demonstration you want to see. The Sea Life Centre is also fully accessible to the disabled.

*La Vallée*

# La Vallée Village

Now, step through the doors of Les Terrasses and you enter **La Vallée Village**, right outside the Val d'Europe complex. This outlet shopping village will appeal most to dedicated shoppers as it means major bargains on big-name brands. All prices are guaranteed to be reduced by at least 33% on high street stores and you can save much more in many instances.

The 85 shops vary from homeware, luggage, shoes and accessories to high fashion, but most are clothing stores, with the accent on designer names and famous labels. Luxury goods feature strongly, too, but, at prices like these, they are more akin to regular high street offerings. There is a **Starbucks** coffee shop and a (much better, to our mind) French café called **Bert's** when you need a drink or a bite to eat. A major expansion in 2007 saw an extra 'wing' added to the Village, bringing in new brands such as **Paul Smith**, **Guess**, **Marlboro Classics**, **M Missoni** (part of the Valentino fashion group), top French linens, bedding and soft furnishings name **Descamps**, the French fashions of **Sandro** and the Italian women's style of **Pinko**.

## BRITTIP

Unlike Val D'Europe, which closes on Sundays, La Vallée is open 7 days a week.

The Village design, with its winding streets, encourages you to stroll the length of the complex and all the shops are unfailingly inviting, with courteous staff seeming light years away from the usual high street surliness and disdain you encounter. There is a useful **Welcome Centre** to get you started, a well-designed children's play area and clean, well-maintained toilets and baby-changing facilities. Start by visiting the Welcome Centre for the latest news and store promotions, and you can also use their pushchairs and umbrellas, if necessary.

For decoration and homeware you have the choice of Bodum, Villeroy & Boch (a famous glass and china store), Anne de Solène (household linens), Lagostina (top-quality Italian kitchenware) and Lalique (one of the leading French brands), while the Samsonite store, the French Lancel and Lamarthe and the Italian Furla and Mandarina Duck offer a wide range of luggage, handbags and accessories.

For outlet children's wear, you have Tartine et Chocolat and Miniman (both famous French brands). Teenagers can choose from well-known names such as Miss Sixty/Energie, Guess and Cerruti Jeans. If you are hunting for designer shoes, check out Charles Jourdan, Robert Clergerie, Heschung (all French), Fornarina (Italian), Camper (Spanish) or Manfield-Bowen (international).

*La Vallée*

Women's high fashion is represented by Anne Fontaine, Arayal, Batiste, Blanc Bleu, Façonnable, Kenzo, Gerard Darel, Cachemire Crème, Celine, MaxMara, Versace, Christian Lacroix, Givenchy, Furla, Zadig & Voltaire, Nitya and Ventilo, plus the Lingerie Shop, Chantal Thomass, Wolford, Calvin Klein and Chantelle for lingerie; while the men can choose from Café Coton, Porsche design, Charles Tyrwhitt, Mexx, Feraud Homme, Kenzo and the Spanish casualwear brand Gerry.

### ✚ BRITTIP

Stop at **Bert's** for a truly delicious lunch. Bert's specialises in a health-conscious range of salads, sandwiches and quiches, plus some delicious pastries, fresh fruit yoghurt and muffins.

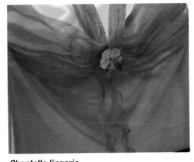

Chantelle lingerie

International brands positively abound and you will find tempting outlet stores for all of the following: Longchamp, Diesel, Polo Ralph Lauren, Salvatore Ferragamo, RiverWoods, Barbour, Molton Brown and Tommy Hilfiger, plus other well-known names such as Reebok, Puma, Timberland, Dunhill and Burberry. And there is plenty more besides.

For serious shoppers it is a veritable Aladdin's cave of desirable items, all with some major mark-downs, which makes you wonder why we ever

Armani at La Vallée

bother paying the usual high street rip-off prices (you can tell we enjoy shopping here!). There is so much packed in, you can't fail to come away with a major bargain or three.

La Vallée is open 362 days a year (closed on Christmas Day, New Year's Day and 1 May) 10am–8pm Mon–Sat (to 7pm 1 October–30 April) and 11am–7pm Sun. A useful daily shuttle bus service operates from the Disney and Val de France hotels. Check with your hotel concierge for details and visit **www.lavalleevillage.com** for all the latest news, as they are still adding shops to their line-up.

And that sums up all the various alternative fun and entertainment on offer away from the theme parks. A meal in Les Terrasses is highly recommended at any time, while the general opportunity to travel easily thanks to the great convenience of the RER line (and the good road system) comes as a major bonus for those who like to explore a little.

But let's not stop here. There is much more to be seen in the city itself – and beyond – so we'll conclude with a closer look at the main attractions of Paris and the Ile de France…

# 9

# The Attractions of Paris

## or Getting an Eiffel of the city

**O**kay, we will admit to a certain bias here but Paris is a wonderful city and we reckon you'd be crazy to spend several days just 32km/20mls away and not consider paying a visit. Even with children to keep amused, there is a huge amount of family-friendly fare on offer, while the Eiffel Tower itself remains one of the greatest sources of child fascination and wonderment in the world.

Given that it is so easy to get into the city centre from Marne-la-Vallée on the RER (and even easier from some of the off-site hotels in the vicinity of Line A), visiting some of the great monuments, parks and museums of Paris is a natural adjunct to all the theme park frolics. Public transport in the city is plentiful and reliable, and is far and away the best, cheapest and most hassle-free way to see the sights (driving – with the eternal bugbear of parking – is not recommended, even if you are comfortable with using your own car in France).

It takes just 35–40 minutes to go from Marne-la-Vallée into the city centre, which means you can have almost a full day in one of the Disney parks and then head off for an evening in Montmartre, the Latin Quarter or for a stroll along the Champs-Elysées. Paris is chock-full of evening entertainment of all kinds, from humble bars to fabulous restaurants and full-blown dinner cabarets such as the **Moulin Rouge** and the **Lido de Paris**. For couples, it is hard to imagine a better city and a more tempting array of possibilities, especially for a meal out.

It is not our intention here to give a detailed description of all Paris has to offer, but we can't let the chance pass without providing a look at what makes the city so special – highlighting the real must-see and must-do opportunities – and also pointing out those the whole family will enjoy. The city is fairly easy to get to grips with and you should be able to get a decent perspective in just a day or

*Moulin Rouge*

### BRIT TIP

Arguably the best ticket in town is the *Paris Visite*, a travel card enabling you to use all the public transport services. The all-day, go-anywhere pass covers the RER, Métro and bus systems, and a 1-day pass costs around €17.05 (see pages 214–215).

two (and the organised bus tours are a great way to start here, even if the heavy traffic sometimes makes it seem like one of the most chaotic places on earth.

## Introducing the city

Paris is laid out like an architect's dream in 20 districts or *arrondissements* all running out in a spiral from the centre (and all locations in the city are referenced according to their *arrondissement*, hence the Louvre is in the first, the Arc de Triomphe in the eighth, etc.).

The architectural core of the city dates back to Baron Haussman in the 19th century, whose urban development programme from 1852 essentially created the outline plan we see today, with its grand boulevards, wide streets and geometrically elegant squares. It is city design on an epic scale (although constrained within relatively modest confines – the whole of Paris covers just 106sq km/41sq mls – less than *Walt Disney World Resort* in Florida), punctuated at key points by monuments like the Arc de Triomphe (Napoleon's 'Triumphal Arch' commissioned in 1806 and finally finished long after his death in 1836), the Place de la Concorde (dating back to 1755), the monumental Ecole Militaire (the army school and museum of the 18th century) and the

*Notre Dame*

Louvre (arguably the greatest art gallery in the world and home to the *Venus de Milo* and the *Mona Lisa*), the oldest part of which dates back to the 12th century.

### BRITTIP

You can pick up a Paris Visite card at the Eurostar ticket offices in St Pancras and Ashford.

Effectively, Paris is also split in two by the River Seine: the **Left Bank**, or southern half; and the **Right Bank**, or northern sector of the city. The most famous landmark though, is 'only' 119 years old and the brainchild of Gustave Eiffel. Built for the International Exposition of 1889, La Tour Eiffel offers three stages up its 324m/1,063ft height, with a view from the topmost of up to 80km/50mls. More modern developments have seen the construction of the *périphérique* ring road (1973), the modernist Pompidou Centre (1977) and the Louvre Pyramid (1989).

## Getting around

Thanks to the comprehensive and truly integrated public transport system, involving the trains (RER, or Réseau Express Régional), underground (the Métro) and buses, getting to the sights is a doddle. Signposting is usually clear, the modern buses each have a route map and a board indicating each stop, and reliability is outstanding. The Métro system will get you to every tourist site in the city with only the minimum of walking and it runs until around 1am every day, while the last RER service back to Marne-la-Vallée is around midnight (check **www.ratp.fr** for public transport details – in English as well as French).

The **Paris Visite** card is almost an essential adjunct to sightseeing and can be purchased at any Métro ticket office, RER and SNCF railway station, bus terminal counter, airports and Paris tourist offices. The card provides

*Arc de Triomphe*

unlimited travel on the whole Paris public transport system, including the SNCF (suburban) trains and the Montmartre funicular. The system is divided into eight regional zones and *Disneyland Resort Paris* is situated in zone 5. An adult 1-day Paris Visite card is €17.05 for zones 1–5, a 2-day card is €27.15 and a 3-day card €38.10 (€8.50, €13.55 and €19.05 for 4–11s; under 4s free).

### BRITTIP

The Paris Visite card also comes with an array of discount deals and special offers with a host of tourism partners in the city, including the Cité des Sciences (the excellent Museum of Science), Bateaux Parisiens river cruises, the Wine Museum and Crazy Horse dinner show.

## Do it all with Disney

With all these possibilities virtually on the doorstep, it stands to reason Disney would see a way to give guests even more value and purpose to staying on-site. So they have teamed up with **Cityrama bus tours**, offering a daily sightseeing excursion into and around the city on one of their big, modern double-decker coaches. They run daily at 9.45am from *Disney's Hotel New York* and have proved immensely popular, so it is advisable to book early – with your tour operator in advance or at the hotel concierge desk when you check in.

The tour returns at about 6pm, so you still have some park time left at the end of the day. The Cityrama buses are very comfortable and well equipped, with air-conditioning, toilets, drinks service and an audio commentary on multi-lingual headphones.

The basic route takes you into the heart of the city to start with and provides a well-narrated overview of the geography, architecture, art, history and culture. The history is graphically illustrated with sites such as **La Bastille** (one of the city's oldest districts, now transformed into a more upmarket and happening area, with nightclubs, restaurants, piano bars and cafés) and **Le Marais** district, a mini-city in its own right, full of little streets, markets and several substantial mansions, now occupied by chic art galleries, cafés, health food shops and piano bars.

### BRITTIP

The key word to look for in shop window displays is 'Soldes'. This means 'Sales' for all keen bargain hunters!

At the heart of Paris is the **Ile de la Cité**, the original settlement site, dating back to the 3rd century BC. The tour continues through the **Quartier Latin** (Latin Quarter), the famous Left Bank district that has been the centre of the city's university life for more than 700 years, and offers a cheaper selection of cafés and

*Jardin des Tuileries*

shops for more student-like budgets. You then pass the magnificent **Palais du Luxembourg**, with its 20-hectare/ 50-acre gardens, and travel along **Rue Bonaparte**, Paris' version of Bond Street, for exclusive shopping.

## The Louvre

Across the **Pont Neuf**, one of the 12 main bridges that link the two halves of the city, you drive past the **Louvre**, the massive repository of just about every example of artwork known to mankind. Its principal claims to fame are the exhibits of the *Venus de Milo*, *Mona Lisa* and Van Gogh's *Sunflowers*, but you can easily spend a day or more investigating the wealth of art on display. It is divided into seven departments – Oriental Antiquities (including Islamic Art); Egyptian Antiquities; Greek, Etruscan and Roman Antiquities; and, for the modern period, Paintings, Sculptures, Art items, Prints and Drawings. Open 9am–6pm daily except Tue (with late opening on Wed and Fri to 10pm), entry is €9 (or €6 from 6pm–9.45pm). For more details, visit **www.louvre.fr**.

Continuing your coach tour, you head back along the Left Bank and through the St Germain area, passing the **Musée d'Orsay**, another of the great repositories of French artwork. A conversion of the Orsay Railway Station inaugurated in 1900, it houses an art gallery of the finest order, featuring works from 1848–1914. Open from 9.30am–6pm Tue–Sat, 9am–6pm Sun (with late opening

*The Louvre*

*Place de la Concorde*

until 9.45pm on Thur), entry is €7.50 (€5.50 on Sun; €5.50 for 18–25s; under 18s free; closed Mon). Visit **www.musee-orsay.fr**.

### BRITTIP

Many Paris museums are free on the first Sunday of the month (though queues will be longer). The museums owned by the Ville de Paris (except the Catacombs) are free every Sunday from 10am–1pm; visit **www.parisinfo.com/museum_monuments** for details.

## Champs-Elysées

A drive around the vast octagonal expanse of the **Place de la Concorde** reveals more of Baron Haussmann's outstanding design, especially as you continue along the **Champs-Elysées** and into the **Place Charles de Gaulle** (aka Etoile), at the centre of which stands Napoleon's magnificent **Arc de Triomphe**.

Along Avenue Kleber you can marvel at some more monumental architecture, especially as you enter **Place du Trocadéro et du 11 Novembre**, where a statue of the First

### BRITTIP

If you are going into central Paris on public transport the main Métro stops to look out for are Concorde, Charles de Gaulle–Etoile, Trocadéro, Palais Royal–Musée du Louvre and Cité.

# Les Bateaux Mouches

Paris is famous for its river tours along the Seine, providing both a great view of many well-known monuments as well as a relaxing and highly enjoyable form of transport. The collective name for the half a dozen or so companies that run these tourist boats is Les Bateaux Mouches. They ply their trade along the central section, from the Eiffel Tower to the Ile de la Cité and back, with plenty of history during the day and a generous helping of romance in the evening, when you can choose just an alternative view of Paris by night or a more elaborate dinner cruise.

In low season (October–March) they run every hour from 10am–10pm (some half-hour departures; no departure at 1.30pm) and every hour 10am–11pm in high season (April–September; no departure at 1.30pm). They cost around €10 for adults and €5 for under 12s (under 3s free). Dinner cruises (8–11pm) are from €95–140, but must be booked in advance. Call 00 33 1 46 99 43 13 (from the UK) or visit **www.bateauxparisiens.com**.

World War military leader Marshall Foch stands in front of a grand vista representing three centuries of architecture. The view across the Seine to the Eiffel Tower is breathtaking and on a par with the great landmarks of the world such as the Sydney Opera House, the Acropolis and the Statue of Liberty.

The **Hôtel des Invalides** is another significant 17th-century landmark and its Musée de l'Armée showcases 2,000 years of military history, from antiquity to the end of the Second World War, in an opulent setting. The Dôme within contains the tomb of Napoleon Bonaparte and is open from 10am–5pm October–March, and 10am–6pm April–Sept, €8 for adults, 18 and under free.

## River trips

After all this coach-bound sightseeing, it is time to step on to a different mode of transport (all part of the Cityrama tour) and view the city from the River Seine on the **Bateaux Parisiens**. Here, either under a glass roof or out on deck soaking up the sun, the English commentary (on a hand-held audio device) continues to cover just about every angle of the city, ensuring you get a well-rounded experience and an in-depth view of the history and accomplishments of Paris and its people (or just a fabulous view if you choose to put your feet up and watch the vistas as you sail by).

## Notre Dame

Your boat drops you off back in the Ile de la Cité for lunch – and an opportunity to visit the stunning cathedral of **Notre Dame** (open 8am–6.45pm daily). This masterpiece of

*Notre Dame*

Gothic architecture was built from 1163–1345, and is free to enter to view the awe-inspiring serenity of its vast interior. There are some serious queues here at most times of the day (you'll be used to that at Disney!), but they move steadily. There is a small fee to visit the belfry and you may have to wait 30 minutes or so for your turn. You have a good 90-minute break here, so you can divide your time between the cathedral and lunch.

### 🇬🇧 BRITTIP

There are two handy, quiet restaurants on the Quai de Montebello, on the south bank of the river flanking Notre Dame. Stroll to the rear of the cathedral, turn right across the bridge and the crowds quickly disappear.

## Up the Eiffel Tower

You get back on the boat at the Ile de la Cité pier and continue your hour's cruise, finally returning to the marina at the Port de la Bourdonnais in front of the **Eiffel Tower**. Your city tour then finishes in style with an organised visit to the tower itself. Your tour guide will lead you up the steps and across the Quai Branly to one of the lifts and a trip to the first floor (the second and third floors are extra, but you usually have time if you wish to go the extra distance yourself). This 324m/1,063ft), 10,100-ton steel edifice is a breath-taking sight close up, and the trip up by lift or stairs is a rewarding one, both for the view and the story of the tower told along the way.

*View from the Eiffel Tower*

*The Eiffel Tower*

The perspective on the city is quite startling (especially from the glass-sided lifts between the first and second floors!) and totally unequalled. There is even a high-quality restaurant on the second floor – the Jules Verne – that you can book separately. If the price tag (in excess of €100) puts you off, try the first floor Altitude 95, with its 1930s' airship decor (book from the UK on 00 33 1 45 55 66 62 for Altitude 95 and 00 33 1 45 55 61 44 for Jules Verne).

### 🇬🇧 BRITTIP

At peak times in summer (midday to around 5pm), the Eiffel Tower often stops selling tickets for the top deck, and the second floor becomes extremely crowded, too.

The Eiffel Tower has three lifts (at the north, east and west legs) and three staircases (south, east and west), and ticket office queues reach up to an hour in high summer. However, if you are travelling independently, arrive early and you will enjoy this amazing attraction at its very best, while the evening sees it in truly sparkling mode, with a magical lighting

*Hotel des Invalides*

presentation. From dusk to 2am (1am in winter), the Tower's 20,000 special light bulbs (requiring 40km/25mls of electrical cord and 120kw of power) come to life in a glittering display each hour on the hour for 10 minutes. Once you have been up this modern marvel, you can walk the gardens of Le Champ de Mars for the full ground-level perspective.

### BRITTIP

The Eiffel Tower draws some sizeable crowds during the day, attracting the inevitable vendors (selling bottled water and trinkets) who are a constant nuisance. Take extra care with your belongings.

At the north leg you can check out the memorial to Gustave Eiffel, while ticket-holders have access to the clever lift machinery that he designed under the east and west pillars. A bureau de change can be found in the concourse under the Tower, plus a Paris Tourist Office (not to be confused with the ticket office) and souvenir shops (as well as those on the Tower itself), plus a cafeteria-style snack bar.

For those coming independently, the nearest RER station is Champ de Mars/Tour Eiffel (on Line C or Métro Line 6; from Marne-la-Vallée, the best route is to change at Charles de Gaulle Etoile and go five stops south on the Métro Line 6), while you can also use the Métro at Ecole Militaire

or Trocadéro. The Eiffel Tower is open every day, 9.30am–11.45pm for the lift and 9.30am–6.30pm for the stairs (1 January–14 June, and 2 September–31 December); and 9am–12.45am (15 June–1 September), final admittance 30 minutes prior to closing. To take the lift to the first floor costs €4.50/adult and €2.30/under 12s (under 3s free); to the second floor is €7.80 and €4.30; and to the top is €11.50 and €6.30; the stairs (up to the second floor) are a single rate of €4 (25 and older, €3.10 under 25s). For more info, **visit www.tour-eiffel.fr**.

All in all, the Cityrama day tour provides a pretty comprehensive beginner's guide to the city and the perfect way to get an overall appreciation of all the main sites in just a few hours. For Disney resort guests it costs £44/adults and £23/child 3–11 (lunch not included). Tickets can be purchased at any of the Disney hotels or those in the Val de France area.

## Paris By night

If that is the story by day, Cityrama's **Illuminations** tour (1 October–3 April), also organised by Disney, is the city by night. Paris fully deserves its alternative title of 'The City of Light' and the tour portrays this to the full. The English commentary, via individual earphones, is especially adapted to the ambience of Paris by night, bringing its history to life with a series of amusing stories, accompanied by background music

*Beneath the Eiffel Tower*

and French songs that celebrate the city. The Cityrama coach departs every Tue, Thur, Fri and Sat at 9pm from the front of *Disney's Hotel New York* and returns to each Disney hotel at around midnight (depending on traffic). It costs £31/adult and £10/child (the tours are sometimes not available on a few dates in June and July). If you are staying at *Disney's Davy Crockett Ranch* you must arrange your own transportation back to your resort.

## L'Open Bus Tour

If you prefer the DIY approach, head into central Paris under your own steam and pick up the official sightseeing trip. **L'Open Bus Tour** features four routes around the city on open-topped double-decker buses, which you can hop on and hop off at any point on their routes. They offer both 1- and 2-day passes, and the routes cover just about every major sight around Paris. The green route is the main *Paris Grand Tour*, (including the Louvre, Notre Dame, Musée D'Orsay, the Champs-Elysées and the Eiffel Tower; 9.30am–6pm November–March, 9.20am–8pm April–October); the orange route covers *Saint-Germain-Montparnasse* (including Jardin de Luxembourg, Observatoire, Invalides and Catacombes; 9.30am–6.40pm year-round); the yellow route covers *Montmartre et Grands Boulevards* (including L'Opéra, Montmartre and the Sacre-Coeur, Gare de l'Est and

*Pompidou Centre*

*Place du Tertre*

Gare du Nord; 9.35–6.10pm November–March, 9.25am–6.30pm April–October); and the blue route covers *Bercy-Bastille* (including the Bastille, Saint Paul, Gare de Lyon and Parc de Bercy; 9.30am–7.15pm year-round). There is commentary in both French and English (via headphones – keep them with you when you leave the bus) and they operate 7 days a week. It costs €26/adult and €13/child 4–11 (save €4 with a Paris Visite card) for a 1-day pass and €29 and €13 for the 2-day. For more info, call (from the UK) 00 33 1 42 66 56 56 or visit **www.paris-opentour.com**. Tickets can be purchased directly on any bus and at most RATP and Paris Tourist offices, and buses run every 15–25 minutes.

## And there's more

Of course, the bus tours are only a snapshot (albeit a fairly wide angle one) of the city and there is plenty more in store for the keen sightseer. A great number of attractions are geared for families, which are worth highlighting here.

**Montmartre:** One of the must-sees of Paris, this district was a separate village up until the 19th century and became the intellectuals' and artists' quarter. Its two main focal points are the **Place du Tertre** (peaceful and serene during the day, humming with activity in the evening) and the breathtaking church of the **Sacre Coeur** (Métro Anvers), set on a hill with fabulous views of the city. Entry to the church is free, but to visit the Dome and the Crypt costs €5. You can also enjoy the highly child-friendly funicular ride up to the Sacre Coeur (included in the Paris Visite card, see pages 214–215).

**BRITTIP**

Lunch in the vicinity of the Sacre Coeur is a must. There is a huge range of cafés and restaurants in the rather touristy Place du Tertre nearby but there are better and cheaper places to eat if you wander a few streets further away.

**Pompidou Centre:** (Métro Hôtel de Ville) This will appeal to all lovers of modern and contemporary art as it has one of the world's finest collections. The collection dates from 1905 to the present, featuring Miró, Giacometti, Dubuffet, Picasso, Matisse, Léger, Chagall, Warhol and many more. The ultra-modern design of the building is not to everyone's taste, but it is a fitting showcase for its contents. Open every day (except Tue) from 11am–9pm, €10/adult and free for under 18s (**www.centrepompidou.fr**).

**Parc de la Villette:** Perhaps right at the forefront of the great new family opportunities is the futuristic complex of this science park. Set in the 19th *arrondissement* in the north-east corner of the city (just inside the *périphérique*, Métro Porte de la Villette), it provides a comprehensive, 52-hectare/128-acre panorama of science and technology in an extremely entertaining, hands-on fashion. It includes the science museum itself (**Cité des Sciences et de l'Industrie**), with a wealth of exhibitions, shows, models, lectures and interactive games, in addition to the Planetarium, the Mediterranean aquarium, Louis Lumière cinema (films in 3-D) and multimedia library.

In the park, there is also the Argonaute – a real submarine – La Géode, a giant sci-fi IMAX cinema with a 1,000-sq m/10,764-sq ft hemispherical screen and Cinaxe, a large-scale simulator ride. Open from 10am–6pm Tue–Sat (10am–7pm Sun), it costs €7.50 for a Cité Pass (€5.50 under 25s, under 7s free), €6 for the Cité des Enfants, €7–11.50 adult and €6.75 under 25s for La Géode, €3 for the Planetarium, €3 for the Argonaute and €5.50 for Cinaxe. The aquarium is free. For more info, call 00 33 1 40 05 70 00 from the UK, or visit **www.cite-sciences.fr**.

**BRITTIP**

At the Parc de la Villette, children (3–12) will enjoy a junior version of the science village at La Cité des Enfants, which has an adventure playground, Electricity (5–12s) and Techno Cité (11 and up) and lots of hands-on experiments.

*Sacre Coeur*

**Bois de Boulogne:** Out in west Paris (Métro Porte Maillot) this 846-hectare/2,090-acre park is ideal family territory, providing a multitude of walks and pleasant spots. Special attractions for children include the 24-lane **Bowling de Paris** and the **Musée en Herbe** in the **Jardin d'Acclimatation**, a dedicated children's museum set in an imaginative play garden with a carousel, train ride, hall of mirrors, go-karts and mini-menagerie (€2.70 for entry to the gardens with extra tickets for rides and attractions – a book of 14 tickets costs €27). It is open from 10am–7pm daily, 10am–6pm October to May. In fine weather, people flock to the banks of the two lakes, where you can go rowing or just watch the model yachts at play. Look up **http://www.jardindacclimatation.fr**.

## BRITTIP

In the Bois de Boulogne, bikes can be hired opposite the main entrance of the Jardin d'Acclimatation daily mid-October to mid-April and Wednesdays, weekends and public holidays mid-October to mid-April. There are 35km/22mls of cycle routes to explore.

Shakespeare plays are put on in the Jardin Shakespeare at the **Théâtre de Verdure**, by the Pré Catalan park in the centre of the Bois de Boulogne woods.

*Champ du Mars*

*Parc Zoologique de Paris*

**Parc Zoologique de Paris:** (Métro Porte Dorée) For animal lovers (and most kids!), this excellent zoo is another ideal place for children to visit, extending over 15 hectares/37 acres in the middle of the Bois de Vincennes in the south-east corner of the city. It houses some 1,200 species – from lions, elephants and giraffes to the little microcebe from Madagascar – in a series of naturalistic settings (no tiny cages here). Open 9am–6pm in summer, 9am–5pm in winter, €8/adult and €5/child (4–16).

**Aquaboulevard:** Paris can even offer the more up-to-date children's fun of an indoor water park, out on the southerly outskirts (by the Balard Métro station). The wonderful tropical theming is divided into three sections – The West Indies (especially for young 'uns), Réunion Island and Polynesia – with a whole series of giant slides, wave machines, water cannons and waterfalls set around a large central lagoon. Year-round warm weather is guaranteed and there is even an outdoor beach when the summer is in full swing. Open 9am–11pm (Mon–Thur), 9am–midnight (Fri), 8am–midnight (Sat) and 8am–11pm (Sun), €20/adult and €10 for under 12s.

**Parisian gardens:** When it comes to the more small-scale delights, take a stroll in the thoroughly British **Champs-Elysées gardens** (Métro Champs Elysées-Clémenceau), where you might discover a puppet show (hourly on Wednesday afternoons and weekends) or the **Jardin des Tuileries**, adjacent to the Louvre (Métro Concorde), with its child-friendly pony rides, trampolines and fun fair from the end of June to the end of August. Both are open year-round (except for public holidays) free of charge.

**Versailles:** The final must-see Paris attraction is a trip to the magnificent château at Versailles (actually a 30-minute ride on the RER Line C to the south-west of the city centre). Another of the world's most famous heritage monuments, it was commissioned by the Sun King, Louis XIV, in 1668.

**BRITTIP**

The immediate environs of the Château de Versailles are also worth exploring, with a series of narrow streets and quaint shops – plus several mouth-watering crêperies!

The buildings trace the architectural styles of the 17th and 18th centuries and include the Royal Apartments, the Hall of Mirrors, the Chapel, the Royal Opera and the Museum of the History of France. The park, designed by André Le Nôtre, is tastefully adorned with statues, flower beds, ponds and fountains, with several further buildings, the Grand and Petit Trianon, the Temple de l'Amour and the tiny hamlet of Queen Marie-Antoinette.

The Château is open 9am–6.30pm from 3 April–31 October (last admission 6pm) and 9.30am–5.30pm from 1 November–2 April (last admission 5pm). Admission is arranged into different categories: €20 weekday Pass from 3 April–31 October (under 18 free); €25 including access to Grandes Eaux Musicale on weekends from 3 April–30 September and public holidays (except 1 May); €16 from 1 November–2 April. Rates include audio-guide for over 18s (audio-guides €6 for 18 and under); Palace Ticket €13.50, €10 from 4pm April–October, €10 from 3pm November–April; and Marie-Antoinette's Estate Ticket €9 (€5 from 5pm) April–October, €5 November–April. For more info, call 00 33 1 30 83 78 00 or visit **www.chateauversailles.fr**.

A recent addition to the line-up here is the Palace's **Academy of Equestrian Arts**, a specialised teaching college open to the public year-round (it was recommissioned in 2003), with daily performances of horsemanship. The two different shows are the 1-hour dressage of *Les Matinales des Ecuyers* (€9.50/adult, €6.50/5–18s; at 10.30am and 11.15am Sat and Sun, also from Tue–Sun during school holidays), which also includes a guided tour of the stables and the 75-minute *La Reprise Musicale*, which illustrates the work of the apprentice riders with musical accompaniment, and a visit to the stables (€21/adult, €13/5–18s; Sat 8.30pm, Sun 3pm). For more info, call 00 33 8 92 68 18 91 or visit **www.acadequestre.fr**.

*Château de Versailles*

# Lido de Paris

Having geared the majority of the chapter towards family activities and sightseeing, here's one that is definitely for adults only and is highly recommended as one of the most entertaining – and surprising – shows in the city. The Lido de Paris is one of several internationally renowned cabarets but is, in our view, the most sophisticated and eye-catching. It is also extremely popular with both couples and singles right across the age spectrum (although the majority tend to be couples in the 45–55 age group). It is a touch risqué, with topless dancers at various points, but it is all extremely tasteful and glamorous. You can opt for the dinner-dance and full 90-minute show or just the show itself.

For dinner, there is a choice of four separate menus, all of which have been designed by top French chef Philippe Lacroix and which include a half-bottle of champagne. Within the four options (Soirée Plaisir, Panache, Bonheur and Premier respectively €140, €160, €190 and €250), there is a choice of two starters, main courses and dessert, and even the Soirée Plaisir menu is barely less than spectacular, meaning the Premier lives up to the highest standards of cuisine (including duck foie gras, poached lobster and fillet of beef Charolais). The meal takes a leisurely

*Lido de Paris*

2 hours to serve and clear away, and there is live music throughout.

**BRITTIP**

The Lido dinner show is totally fabulous but beware the drinks' prices – a half bottle of champagne will set you back around €55.

*Revue Bonheur* then follows for the next hour and a half, with a remarkable mix of spectacularly choreographed dancing, live music, ice-skating, acrobatics and magic, all cleverly interwoven into themed sections. The staging is quite breath-taking, with some stunning special effects, and the high quality and originality of the acrobats and magicians lend an air of grand pageantry to the show (and, if the acrobats don't leave you with your jaw

*Revue Bonheur* at the Lido de Paris

*The Arc de Triomphe*

on the floor, you need to check your pulse!). The majestic finale, when the whole stage seems to unfold before your eyes, provides a fitting conclusion to what can only be described as superb entertainment.

## BRITTIP

Getting to the Lido from *Disneyland Resort Paris* couldn't be easier. You simply take the RER from Marne-la-Vallée to Charles de Gaulle– Etoile station (about 45 minutes), then change to the Métro for one stop to George V, and the Lido is right outside the station. If you go for the first show, you exit just after 11.30pm and there is an RER service back to Marne-la-Vallée from Charles de Gaulle– Etoile at 12.02am.

Admittedly, it is not a cheap option (the show on its own is €100), but we feel it is terrific value for money and you are unlikely to be disappointed. There are two shows a night, the first at 9.30pm preceded by the 2-hour dinner-dance, and the second (a show only) at 11.30pm. For more information, call 00 33 1 40 76 56 10 (from the UK), or visit **www.lido.fr**. There are also a handful of Sunday lunch matinees at 1pm, plus a special children's show several times a month, with an array of aerial ballet, giant fountains, ice-skating and song and dance to positively mesmerise youngsters.

## Paris information

Of course, there are dozens of museums, churches, monuments, gardens, memorials and parks, not to mention the shops, restaurants and nightclubs and other modern city paraphernalia that make Paris such a deliciously heady place. For all the essential information, contact **Maison de la France**: 178 Piccadilly, London W1J 9AL; France Information Line: 09068 244123 (60p per minute), email: **info.uk@franceguide.com** or visit **http://uk.franceguide.com**.

**Ile de France Tourist Office:** Tel 00 33 1 73 00 77 00 (from the UK), or **http://english.pidf.com**.

**Paris Tourist Office:** Tel 08 92 68 30 00 (in France), or log on to **www.paris info.com**.

## BRITTIP

The *Paris Museum Pass* costs just €35 for a 2-Day pass, €40 for a 4-Day and €60 for a 6-Day. It gives no queuing, no-limit access to 70 museums and monuments in Paris. It is on sale at the tourist office, FNAC shops and online at **www.parismuseumpass.com**.

*The Lido puts on a spectacular show*

# Further afield

If you would prefer to escape from the hubbub for a while, the **Seine-et-Marne** region can offer some more down-to-earth but equally enchanting sources of fascination. With a car, there are some wonderful possibilities a little more than an hour's drive from the resort, where you can get a feel for rural France, untouched by the hectic rush and modernity of the city.

**BRITTIP**

The Seine-et-Marne region has an excellent tourist office in Fontainebleau – tel 00 33 1 60 39 60 39 (from the UK), **www.tourisme77.net**. They also have a tourist office next to the Marne-la-Vallée RER station open 9am–8.45pm every day.

Barely half an hour from the Disney resort is the magnificent 17th-century masterpiece of **Vaux-le-Vicomte**, a historic château and gardens some 24km/15mls to the south down the D471. In the rich land of Brie, this pinnacle of period architecture – created by some of France's greatest artists, including Le Vau, Le Brun and André Le Nôtre – was the inspiration for Versailles. Here you will discover the full splendour of Vaux-le-Vicomte, from the kitchens to the magnificently decorated reception rooms (that have featured in many films).

**BRITTIP**

If you can visit Vaux-le-Vicomte on a Saturday from May to October or Fridays in July and August, you can enjoy the amazing Festival of Light, when some 2,000 candles are lit throughout the château and gardens.

Your visit should include a full tour of the château (complete with audio-guide), the extensive French gardens, designed by Le Nôtre, who was also responsible for the Jardins des Tuileries in Paris, plus the Carriage Museum and the Le Nôtre exhibition in the cellars. Every second and last Saturday from April–October, you can see the eye-catching Fountain Show from 3–6pm. The château is open every day from mid-March to mid-November, 10am–6pm (closed weekdays from 1–2pm), and costs €12.50/adult and €9.90/child (6–16), or €15.50 and €13.40 for the Festival of Light (8pm– midnight). For more details, call 00 33 1 64 14 41 90 from the UK or visit **www.vaux-le-vicomte.com**

**BRITTIP**

A perfect complement to any visit to Vaux-le-Vicomte is dinner at the L'Ecureuil gourmet restaurant, which is open 10am–6pm (12am on Festival of Light evenings).

*Château Vaux-le-Vicomte*

*Place St Jean, Melun*

The nearby city of **Melun** is also worth exploring. The ancient capital of the Capétiens kings offers some interesting walks, an artistic museum and the listed building of St Aspais Church – plus its speciality, the Brie de Melun, often regarded as the ancestor of all Brie cheeses. Just outside the city, August 2006 marked a significant event, with the re-opening of the fortified **Château de Blandy-les-Tours**, a superb example of 16th-century military architecture and a little-known gem of the Ile de France.

Bohemian **Barbizon**, 'The Painters Village', is about 70km/44mls away to the south (down the N104, A5B, N105 to Melun, N372 and the N37). Here, against a backdrop that an array of famous landscape painters have made utterly timeless, you can discover the Auberge Ganne, a museum-home of the 19th century and a tribute to an era of artists who influenced the world's landscape and colourist painters (closed Tuesdays – 00 33 1 60 66 22 27).

Take a slight detour to the south-east and you come to **Fontainebleau** and its 16th-century château, home to the kings of France from the Middle Ages (closed Tuesdays). Another major architectural and artistic gem in the panoply of French monuments, its extensive gardens and Napoleonic Museum of Military Art and History offer a fascinating glimpse into another world (**www.musee-chateau-fontainebleau.fr**).

Travel still further (about another 10km/6mls south-east again and you come to **Moret-sur-Loing**, a medieval city curled up between the banks of the Seine and Loing rivers. Wander the town and see why it was the inspiration for some of the Impressionist painters such as Monet, Renoir and especially Sisley.

Further south still you come to Souppes-sur-Loing and the stunning **Château Landon**, perched on a rocky outcrop overlooking the verdant valleys of the Fusain. The medieval city boasts a host of memorable monuments, including the Notre Dame church, the St Severin abbey, the St Thugal tower and St Andrew priory, plus the beautiful Parc de la Tabarderie.

## Closer to home

Nearer to Marne-la-Vallée (just off the A4 at Ferrières-en-Brie), you have the **Château de Ferrières**, a sumptuous pastiche of Renaissance architecture, embellished with one of the most extraordinary English parks in France. The town of **Champs-sur-Marne** just to the west (on N34) boasts another stately home emblematic of the bourgeoisie in the Chateau de Champs-sur-Marne, the residence of Madame de Pompadour in 1757, with stately gardens, flower beds and ornamental lakes.

*Château de Ferrières*

Then travel east for 20km/12mls on the N34 to **Coulommiers**, another medieval town whose commander's residence was built by the Knights Templar in fortress style in the 12th century. Make sure you visit the St-Anne Chapel and the round dovecote, plus the stunning Capucins Park. You can also enjoy some picturesque river trips from Coulommiers on the Grand Morin.

A short drive to the north-east is another destination full of Middle Ages character, that of the Episcopal city of **Meaux**. The impressive St-Etienne Cathedral is well worth a visit, along with the Episcopal Palace (which now houses the Bossuet Museum) and the Jardin Bossuet. On certain weekends in June–September you can also enjoy the stunning *Meaux Grand Spectacle Historique*, an epic event featuring 500 actors, dancers and equestrians, re-enacting the saga of the city.

**BRITTIP**

Don't leave Meaux until you have tried the local culinary speciality – Brie and mustard.

In between Meaux and Coulommiers you will find the **Abbaye de Jouarre**, the region's most outstanding sacred site, with 12th-century crypts displaying some astonishing sarcophagi from the early Merovingian era. Food lovers will be interested in the Musée Briard, which

*Meaux*

*Provins city walls*

traces the history of Brie's cheese-making traditions.

## Provins

The jewel in the region's crown is the World Heritage Site and medieval city of **Provins**, some 60km/37mls down the D231 to the south-east. Pass the 12th-century ramparts and you are truly transported back to the Middle Ages, with narrow streets, half-timbered houses, monuments and dungeons! Here you can try various medieval crafts, such as calligraphy and stained glass making, design coats of arms and watch the free-flying birds of prey. Provins provides the perfect setting for various period events (**www.provins.net**) organised every summer and, if you happen to be in the area during the last week of August, definitely stop by to experience some of the week-long **Carnival**, which is one of the highlights of the Seine-et-Marne region. There are also three large-scale medieval shows, including a spectacular jousting competition.

## Auvers-sur-Oise

Art lovers may well be lured away to the north-west to spend a half-day or so in the utterly charming village of **Auvers-sur-Oise**, the burial place of painter Vincent Van Gogh. Although the great artist lived here for only 3 months before his untimely death, his stay produced some of his most startling work, and its inspiring influence is still present today (not surprisingly, as Cezanne, Pissarro, Daubigny and others also painted here). The village also hosts an annual International Musical Festival (late May–June), which attracts some high-quality performers.

Start by visiting the Office de Tourisme on Rue de la Sansonne to see the 15-minute audio-visual presentation on the village and Van Gogh, then wander out and drink in the wonderful scenery, quaint farms and cafés that inspired so many great painters. To reach Auvers-sur-Oise, take the A15 out of Paris to Exit 7 (Mery-sur-Oise), then pick up N184 alongside the River Oise into the village (**www.auvers-sur-oise.com**).

## Now it's up to you!

And that, folks, is that. You now have the essential wherewithal to not only plan and prepare for your holiday in *Disneyland Resort Paris*, but also to get the most out of it when you are there. As you can see from the last two chapters, there is a lot more to a holiday here than just theme park frolics (although, if you choose to do just that, you will still have a pretty good time!).

It is a world of almost infinite charm and substance, a combination of Imagineering pixie dust and ages-old culture and allure. The Walt Disney Company wasn't that crazy when it brought its major slice of Americana to Europe and, while it was not an instantly comfortable fit, the Franco-European influences now sit comfortably and enjoyably alongside the transatlantic ones.

Most of all, however, we hope you have taken on board how much artistry is involved in providing such obvious entertainment, whether it be on the rides, shows, restaurants or hotels. The resort is the product of 50 years of imagination, perspiration and inspiration, with some pretty amazing architecture and engineering thrown in along the way (not to mention the vast backdrop of Paris and its environs).

After countless visits to Disney theme parks (we lost count many years ago!), we still find them absorbing, fascinating and downright fun. There is so much involved, we would hate for anyone to pay their hard-earned money and then miss some of the essential 'Magic'.

So, we challenge you to keep this book with you at all times, read and inwardly digest the contents before you go and then get out there and have FUN!

*Bonnes vacances…*

*Above all, have fun!*

# 10

# Your Holiday Planner

Here is a way to help you decide what you can do given three or four days in *Disneyland Resort Paris*. This planner is simply designed to give you an idea (from our own practical experience) of what a typical family might be able to achieve in the time allotted. Obviously, you are free to make up your own schedule (on the blank form at the end), but be aware of the different requirements of the theme parks and associated attractions. The two examples are designed around a visit in high season (the summer), and are for different modes of transport and different durations (reflecting two of the most popular packages being booked in 2007). Have fun with your planning!

## Example 1: 2-night/3-day trip with Eurostar

| Day and time | Schedule | Notes |
|---|---|---|
| **Day One** | | |
| 8.53am | Depart London St Pancras | |
| 12.27pm | Arrive Marne-la-Vallée | Check bags in with *Disney Express* at station |
| | Have lunch in *Disney Village* | Nice and quiet in Planet Hollywood! |
| 2.15pm | Head to *Disneyland Park* | Closing time 11pm |
| | Visit Discoveryland | Get FastPass for Buzz Lightyear |
| 4pm | Disney's Once Upon A Dream Parade | |
| 5.15pm | The Tarzan Encounter | |
| 7.15pm | Winnie the Pooh and Friends, Too | |
| 7.45pm | Stop for dinner | Great pizza in Pizzeria Bella Notte! |
| 9pm | Leave the park and walk back to *Disney's Hotel New York* to check in | Our bags are already here! |
| **Day Two** | | |
| 9am | Head for buffet breakfast in Parkside Diner | Bit of a late start! Book Billy Bob's Buffet for dinner tonight |
| 10am | Off to *Walt Disney Studios Park* and start with the Twilight Zone Tower of Terror (for the big thrills) or Studio Tram Tour | |

| Day and time | Schedule | Notes |
|---|---|---|
| 11am | Moteurs…Action! Stunt Show | |
| 11.45am | Get in the queue for Armageddon | |
| 12.15pm | Cinémagique showing | Watch some of Lilo & Stitch show from queuing area |
| 1pm | Lunch at Backlot Express | |
| Afternoon | Do all the attractions of Toon Studio | Did Animagique twice! |
| 5pm | Catch the parade | |
| | Stop for refreshment in En Coulisse Restaurant | Watch the Ciné Folies |
| 5.30pm | Rock 'n' Roller Coaster | Should be no wait by now! |
| 7.15pm | Have dinner at Billy Bob's | |
| 8.15pm | Then it's on to the *Disneyland Park* | |
| 8.45pm | Spend time in Fantasyland | |
| 10.15pm | Find a spot for the Fantillusion parade | Head back to Town Square for the best view! |
| 10.45pm | Time to take tired but happy children back to the hotel | |
| **Day Three** | | |
| 9.30am | Another slow start – not up until 9.30am! | Check bags in at hotel with *Disney Express* system. We'll see them later! Book late lunch at Blue Lagoon |
| 10.30am | Off back to the *Disneyland Park* | |
| Morning | Frontierland | Get FastPass for Peter Pan. Do Big Thunder Moutain Railroad (with FastPass) and Phantom Manor |
| 2.15pm | Time for lunch in our favourite restaurant | Blue Lagoon |
| 4pm | Adventure Isle | Chance for kids to play after lunch as many people are watching the parade |
| Afternoon | Do Pirates of the Caribbean and last main rides | |
| 5.30pm | Stop at Fort Comstock in Frontierland on our way out for play and pictures | |
| 6pm | Head back to the station | |
| 7.25pm | Return on Eurostar to London | |
| 9.13pm | Arrive at St Pancras | Children asleep – tricky final journey home! |

# Example 2: 4-night/5-day coach trip with Leger Holidays

| Day and time | Schedule | Notes |
|---|---|---|
| **Day One** | | |
| Noon | Pick-up from home bus station at midday | |
| 1.30pm | Arrive Dover | |
| 2.15pm | P&O ferry to Calais | Stock up with drinks and snacks on the ferry for the 4-hour coach journey to *Disneyland Resort Paris* |
| 4.30pm | Arrive Calais; brief stop at hypermarket | Don't forget the 1-hour time difference! |
| Evening | Long, rather dull drive through northern France | |
| 9.30pm | Arrive at *Disney's Hotel Santa Fe* | Check in and go straight to room |
| **Day Two** | | |
| 8am | Up for hotel breakfast | Book character lunch at Lucky Nugget Saloon at hotel front desk |
| 9am | Off to the *Disneyland Park* for the day | Get FastPass for Peter Pan |
| Morning | *Disneyland Park* | |
| 1pm | Stop for lunch at Lucky Nugget Saloon | Have fun with Chip 'n' Dale, Goofy and Pluto! |
| Afternoon | *Disneyland Park* | |
| 4pm | Catch the afternoon parade | |
| 5.15pm | Winnie the Pooh show | |
| 6.30pm | Leave park and head for *Disney Village* | |
| 7pm | Dinner at Planet Hollywood | Only 10-minute wait for table |
| 8.30pm | Slow wander back to hotel via *Disney Village* | |
| **Day Three** | | |
| 9am | Slow start this morning! | Book character breakfast for tomorrow at Café Mickey in *Disney Village* |
| 10am | Head for *Walt Disney Studios Park* | |
| 11am | Queue up for Tower of Terror | Watch High School Musical |
| Noon | Meet Stitch at the Stitch Live attraction, then head to Cinémagique | Just missed midday Cinémagique – go on to Art of Animation instead |

| Day and time | Schedule | Notes |
|---|---|---|
| 1.30pm | Stop for lunch at Restaurant En Coulisse | Live fun from Ciné Folies while we eat |
| 2pm | Stop at concierge desk in Disney Studio 1 | Book dinner at Silver Spur Steakhouse |
| 2.10pm | Queue for 20 minutes to get in to 2.30pm Moteurs…Action! Stunt Show | |
| 3.30pm | Catch Armageddon attraction | |
| 4pm | Stop for a drink at Studio Catering Co outside after show | |
| 5pm | Time for the Disney Cinema Parade | |
| 5.30–6.30pm | Enjoy another hour at park | No queues for Magic Carpets ride and Rock 'n' Roller Coaster |
| 7pm | Head next door and have dinner at Silver Spur Steakhouse | |
| 8pm | Head back to Fantasyland for kids' favourite rides | |
| 10pm | Bag a prime spot to watch evening Fantillusion parade on Main Street USA | Dad goes off to get drinks! Still long queues at most of the counter-service cafes |
| | Straight back to the hotel on the bus after parade | |
| **Day Four** | | |
| 8am | Manage to get everyone up and out to make breakfast in *Disneyland Park* | |
| 8.45am | Stop at City Hall to book evening meal at Blue Lagoon | |
| 9am | Enjoy Fantasyland! | In the first hour, we do Peter Pan, Snow White, Pinocchio (twice!) and the Carousel before the crowds arrive |
| 11am | Leave park for RER Station | |
| 11.15am | Catch train to Val d'Europe | 5-minute journey |
| 11.30am | Visit Sea Life Centre | Spend 2 hours looking round all the exhibits, and children finish up in the soft-play area! |
| 1.30pm | Have great lunch at pizza restaurant in Les Terrasses | |
| 2.30pm | On to La Vallée outlet shopping village | Kids get to play in playground while parents enjoy a coffee! |

| Day and time | Schedule | Notes |
|---|---|---|
| 4pm | Quick tour of Auchan hypermarket before catching RER train back to Disney | |
| 5pm | Catch Animagique show at *Walt Disney Studios Park* | |
| 5.30pm | Quick refreshment stop at Studio Catering Co | |
| 5.45pm | One last Flying Carpets ride | |
| 6pm | Time to leave for *Disneyland Park* | |
| 8pm | Dinner at Blue Lagoon | |
| 8.30pm | Just time for another trip to Fantasyland! | |
| 9.30pm | Back to *Disney's Hotel Santa Fe* on shuttle bus | Pack cases for coach tomorrow |
| **Day Five** | | |
| 8am | Up early and straight off to breakfast | |
| 10am | Coach departs for Calais hypermarket; then on to ferry | |
| 3pm | Ferry leaves Calais | 2pm UK time |
| 4.30pm | Arrive back at home bus station | Mission accomplished! |

# Your holiday – have fun now!

| Day and time | Schedule | Notes |
|---|---|---|
| | | |
| | | |
| | | |
| | | |
| | | |
| | | |
| | | |
| | | |
| | | |
| | | |
| | | |
| | | |
| | | |
| | | |
| | | |
| | | |
| | | |
| | | |
| | | |
| | | |

# Further reading

*Disneyland Paris – From Sketch to Reality*, by Alain Littaye and Didier Ghez (Nouveau Millenaire Editions; $176.44, out of print and now collectable, on www.amazon.com). A truly sumptuous book, in full colour and with a wealth of brilliant photography, it charts the building of the *Disneyland Park, Disney Village* and the hotels. It also provides a magnificent insight into the creativity of the Imagineers.

*Walt Disney Imagineering – by The Imagineers* (Hyperion, £21.99). Another lavish 200-page volume providing a riveting look at how Disney's creative force thinks and works, with a fascinating series of original concept illustrations from their attractions worldwide.

*Disney – The First 100 Years* (David Smith and Steven Clark; Hyperion £17.99). For true fans of all things Disney, this 203-page epic charts the story of Walt and all his creations, from his humble beginnings to the 100th year after his birth, looking at the annual landmarks of the man and his company.

# Acknowledgements

The authors wish to acknowledge the help of the following in the production of this book:

The Walt Disney Company, Maison de la France (French Government Tourist Office, London), Eurostar, Leger Holidays, P&O Ferries, SpeedFerries, Thomas Cook, Port of Dover, MyTravel, Thomson Holidays, Aéroports de Paris, Cityrama, Newmarket Group, Inter Continental Hotels, La Vallée Outlet Shopping Village, Planet Hollywood, Sea Life Paris, Seaview.

In person: Nikki Palmas, Claire Fine, Alix Vonk (Walt Disney London), Eugenio Raez (Maison de la France), Marco Mori (Leger Holidays), Gareth Headon, Tom Parker (Eurostar), Lynn Houghton (Thomson), Sarah Anderson (Thomas Cook), Phil O'Sullivan (Newmarket), Sebastien Farris (Aéroports de Paris), Andy Brannan, Gualtiero Raimondi Cominesi (Planet Hollywood), Nick Stevens (Norfolk Line), Natalie Hardy (P&O Ferries), Deborah Cameron (SpeedFerries), Chantal Villeneuve (Sea Life), Sebastien L'Hôte (La Vallée).

Special thanks also go to Andy De Maertelaere, our principal research assistant, and to David Simpson (Seaview).

# Photographic Acknowledgements

t = top of page; b = bottom of page

Walt Disney Company 6, 8, 10t, 11, 14, 15, 16, 18, 19t, 21, 22, 23, 24t, 25, 26, 27t, 28, 29, 30t, 31, 32b, 33, 34, 35, 36, 38, 40, 42, 44, 46, 54t, 55t, 60t, 61t, 62b, 63t, 64, 65b, 67b, 68, 69, 70, 72b, 73, 75, 77, 78, 79b, 80, 82, 83, 84, 85, 86, 87, 88, 89, 90, 94t, 98t, 103, 109, 110b, 111, 112, 113, 114b, 117t, 119b, 121, 122, 123, 126b, 128t, 130, 131, 132b, 133b, 136, 137, 138t, 139, 142b, 144t, 145t, 146t, 148, 149, 150t, 154t, 155, 156, 157, 158, 159, 160t, 161, 164t, 165, 166,167, 168, 169b, 171, 172 centre, 173t, 174, 175, 176, 177, 178b, 179, 180t, 181, 182, 183, 184, 185, 186, 188, 189, 190, 191t, 192t, 193b, 194b, 195b, 196, 197, 200b, 201, 202, 203, 204, 205, 229

Best Western Abbay du Golf 102t; Best Western Marne-la-Vallée 101t; Brittany Ferries 52; CDT Seine-et-Marne 104b; Chanteloup Hotel 100t; Château de Versailles 223; Eurostar 17, 56, 57; Melissa Hobson 4, 10b, 12, 19b, 24b, 30b, 32t, 74b, 79t, 115, 116, 119t, 120b, 126t, 128b, 129, 132t, 134b, 135t, 138b, 140b, 141t, 142t, 143, 144b, 145b, 146b, 147b, 150b, 151, 152, 153, 154b, 160b, 162, 170b, 178t, 180b, 192b, 194t, 195t, 199b, 200t; Wendy Hobson 47, 48b, 60b, 71, 72t, 214, 201, 216b, 217, 219, 220, 221; Holiday Inn 97b, 98b; Hotel Kyriad 106; Hotel l'Elysée 93b; Hotel Moulin de Paris 91; Hotel Saphir 102b; Leger Holidays 65t, 66, 67t, 94b, 95, 96, 97t, 99, 100b; Lido de Paris 13, 118t, 224, 225b; Marriott's Vacation Club 105; David Monniaux 61b; Moulin Rouge 213; Navette 63b; Novotel Collégien 101b; P&O Ferries 48t, 49; Parc de la Colline 104t; Parc Zoologique de Paris (Jonas) 222t; Radisson SAS Hotel 93t; Sea France 50; Sea Life Centre 209, 210; Sofitel 108; Kaihsu Tai 59; Val d'Europe 206; La Vallée 9, 211; Simon and Susan Veness 5, 7, 20, 27b, 37, 58, 74t, 76, 110t, 114t, 118b, 120t, 127, 133t, 134t, 135b, 140t, 141b, 147t, 164b, 169t, 170t, 172t andb, 173b, 191b, 193t, 198, 199t, 216t, 218, 220, 222b, 225t; www. offrench.net (Olivier Ffrench) 228t; www.all-free-photos.com 226; www.answers.com 41; www.calais-port.com 51, 53; www.cdef.com 227; www.channels.nl 107t; www.classictravelling.com 52; www.cnu.org 207; www.dlp.info 207, 208; www.eurotunnel.com 55b; www.great4hotels.com 107b; www.hotels.fr 108; www.lavalleevillage.com; www.lavoixeco.com (Jean-Pierre Brunet) 54b; www.meaux.com (Yann Mathias) 228b; www.rotarymelun.org 227; www.trainweb.org 62t; www.whereisjennifer.com 117b.

# Index

Page references in *italics* refer to maps or tables; those in **bold** refer to major references. (D)= Dinner show (R)= Restaurant (S)= Show (T)= Tour operator